Beyond the Synagogue Gallery

Beyond the Synagogue Gallery

Finding a Place for Women in American Judaism

KARLA GOLDMAN

HARVARD UNIVERSITY PRESS

Cambridge, Massachusetts, and London, England   2000

Publication of this book has been aided by an award from the Myer and Rosaline Feinstein Center for American Jewish History at Temple University, a prize made possible by a gift from Mr. and Mrs. Edward L. Snitzer.

Library of Congress Cataloging-in-Publication Data

Goldman, Karla, 1960–
   Beyond the synagogue gallery : finding a place for women in American Judaism / Karla Goldman.
      p.   cm.
   Includes bibliographical references and index.
   ISBN 0-674-00221-0 (cloth : alk. paper)
   1. Women in Judaism—United States—History—19th century.
   2. Judaism—United States—History—19th century.
   3. Jewish women—United States—History—19th century.
   I. Title.
   BM729.W6 G65 2000
   296'.082'0973—dc21   00-021149

To my parents,
Merle and Marshall
Goldman,
in love and hope

Contents

Acknowledgments

I was assisted in the writing of the dissertation upon which this book is based by the generous support of the Congregational History Project, overseen by James P. Wind and James W. Lewis, and by the Frances Grabow Goldman Fellowship at Hebrew Union College–Jewish Institute of Religion. My further work on the book manuscript was supported by a Faculty Fellowship from the Yale-Pew Program in Religion and American History. Finally, I am grateful to have received a dissertation prize from the Myer and Rosaline Feinstein Center for American Jewish History with its provision of a financial subvention toward the publication of this book.

My first visit to the American Jewish Archives as a Levi A. Olan Fellow, then the chance to return to conduct dissertation research, and finally the opportunity to teach at the Hebrew Union College–Jewish Institute of Religion in Cincinnati has brought me to an unparalleled setting for the study of American Jewish history. During my first four years in Cincinnati, I was able to learn from Jacob Rader Marcus what a great privilege it can be to engage in that study. Dr. Marcus's vision, of a bountiful archival institution where researchers are made to feel at home, lives on in the Center which now bears his name. The staff of the Jacob Rader Marcus Center of the American Jewish Archives, now under the leadership of Gary Zola, has been unfailingly helpful and supportive. I thank Fanny Zelcer, Abraham Peck, Eleanor Lawhorn, Camille Servizzi, Elise Nienaber, Dorothy Smith, Kathy Spray, Tammy Topper, and Ruth Kreimer for all their work on my behalf. Kevin Proffitt, chief archivist, has brought me much more than documents. His constant encouragement and the countless ways in which he has contributed to this book have left me greatly in his debt. I would also like to acknowledge the assistance of Judith Leifer of the Center for Judaic Studies at the University of Pennsylvania, Stephen Frank of the National Museum of American Jewish History, Phyllis Sichel of the Reform Congregation Keneseth Israel in Philadelphia, and the staff of the American Jewish Historical Society in Waltham, Massachusetts. The faculty, staff, and administration at HUC-JIR have supported my research in many ways. The staff of the Klau Library has been particularly helpful. Marilyn Krider and Jason Neely, especially, have responded graciously to my usually urgent requests for microfilm. I also thank Gail Mermelstein for her assistance on this project. I am especially grateful to Michael Meyer who, many years ago, helped me to frame the subject of this book. In the years since, as both mentor and colleague, he has been a valued source of knowledge, encouragement, and scholarly engagement. Like so many others in our field, I have come to rely upon Jonathan Sarna's citations, advice, and enthusiasm. I also remain grateful to Stephan Thernstrom, my dissertation adviser at Harvard, for his steady support and counsel.

The many new colleagues and friends who have come my way via the Marcus Center have also contributed a great deal to this project. I am particularly beholden to Tobias Brinkmann, Lane Fenrich, Eric Goldstein, Leah Hagedorn, Andrew Heinze, Bobbie Malone, Joan Nathan, Connie Östreich, Ira Robinson, and Cornelia Wilhelm.

Jacquie Giere and Katherina Gerstenberger deserve special mention for the many hours they spent with me going over translations of dense German texts. Miriam Tsevat used her training as a German schoolgirl during the 1920s to help me decipher the handwritten script of ladies' society secretaries from Fort Wayne, Indiana, and Quincy, Illinois. I also thank Dale Fulcher for his valuable assistance with translations.

Over the years many people have generously devoted their attention to various versions of the words finally inscribed on these pages. Julie Pavlon, Mark Peterson, Gail Diamond, Sarah Queen, Seth Korelitz, Dianne Ashton, Susan Zeiger, Pleun Bouricius, Wendy Gamber, Susan Einbinder, Lori Ginzberg, and Laura Levitt all offered critical readings that left an impact on me and on the text. Recently,

Caroline Light has often seemed to be around whenever I was struggling with a new idea or approach—I thank her for her indulgence. Similarly, Mark Bauman, on his recent visits to Cincinnati, has challenged me to think carefully about the contributions of southern Jewish women. Maura O'Connor, Katherina Gerstenberger, Victoria Thompson, Geoffrey Plank, Sigrun Haude, and Catherine Raissiguier, as part of a work-in-progress group, also brought valuable perspectives and insights to this work. Thanks also to Hannelore Künzl for sharing some of her vast knowledge of synagogue architecture with me. Beth Wenger read critically, responded encouragingly, and very generously lent me materials that came out of her own research. My thanks to M. B. Baader for many stimulating discussions and for reminding me how little we know about Jewish women's religious lives. Joanne Meyerowitz's calm guidance and clear vision have often soothed and reassured me, even as her suggestions have strengthened my prose and analysis. Annie Rose responded quickly and generously to my dissertation, and Bob Liberles read through my evolving manuscript many times, always offering some praise and appropriate criticism. Joyce Antler's encouragement has been invaluable. Lee Simmons, as copyeditor for Harvard University Press, made this a much better book.

My brothers and sister, Ethan, Avra, and Seth, have defined me and together with Julie, Steve, Julie, Jessica, Todd, Jacob, Sam, Jonah, David, Elie, Nathan, Lauren, and, Isaac, have sustained me with love through this and all endeavors. Nancy Klein, Sue Oren, Chris Cuomo, Miriam and Matitahu Tsevat, Daveen Litwin, Lycette Nelson, Catherine Raissiguier, Jonathan Cohen, and Gene Tensing have all helped make a home for me in Cincinnati. Kathi Kern shared much of the book-making process with me, encouraging and entertaining me all the way. Judy Goldberg inspired me at critical moments over the life of this project. In so many ways, David Kaufman's questions, insights, enthusiasm, and friendship have enriched both my scholarship and my life. Ursula Roma has waited a long time, sometimes patiently. She continues to teach me the beauty of a loving heart.

My parents have also long anticipated the completion of this project. I dedicate this book to them, in gratitude for so many gifts of sustenance, heart, spirit, and mind. I thank my father for his encouragement and for his dedicated commitment to the things in which he believes. Time and again, my mother turned from her own writing to bring the gift of her care and attention to almost every line of mine. Of the many people who have given me so much in the process of completing this book, nobody has been more constant, helpful, or appreciated.

Throughout my work on this project, I have been mindful of a number of Jewish women whose stories I have not told here, but who taught me that there is much more to this world than the limited horizon of our own moment. Anya Barsella, Dottie Resnick, and Faith Cummins lived with a sense of history, as do Libby Elan and Ruth Fein. They taught me that we need to value our own place in the larger stories of which we are a part.

When I submitted the dissertation that led to this book, I went straight from Cambridge to New York so that I could present a copy to my grandmother Rose. I won't be able to give her this book. I miss her eloquence, her strength, and her laugh, but her faith remains with me. It is fitting that just when I was ready, I was able to turn to my grandmother for the inspiration I needed to understand how the story should end.

Introduction:
Women and the Synagogue

In 1855 the editor of the Jewish weekly *Asmonean* considered the
plight of traditional Jewish congregations in the United States. "How
are our Synagogues now attended?" he asked. Despondently, he answered his own question: "The empty benches send forth a sad reply.
Apart from the female attendance, we have a few old men, and boys
(forced to go by their parents) who cease to attend as soon as they
become men."[1] An 1854 correspondent to Cincinnati's new Jewish
weekly, the *Israelite*, had voiced similar misgivings about synagogues that had turned to innovation in an effort to increase their attractiveness: "They have reared synagogues, magnificent and splendid, have trained skillful choirs, and bought powerful organs; but for
whom? Surely not for themselves, for they do not come to be edified;
women, children, and strangers, curious people must fill the deserted
temples."[2]

Buried within these woeful midcentury accounts of "empty" synagogues lies a startling bit of news. Despite the emphasis of their reports, both observers make clear that, in fact, the benches were not all
empty. In both the traditional and reforming synagogues, there were
Jews; they just did not happen to be men. Testimony to the imbalance
of male and female worshipers in American synagogues during the
second half of the nineteenth century leaves little question about the
widespread nature of this trend. As one early-twentieth-century rabbi

would later observe, "the synagogues are abandoned to women, our men have largely abdicated."[3]

Women's substantial presence in the American synagogue, together with declining attendance by men, pointed to radical transformations in male and female religiosity and in the meaning of public worship within American Judaism. The female-dominated pattern of attendance in the nineteenth-century American synagogue had no precedent in the Jewish past. Historically, the synagogue had chiefly been a province for the expression of male religiosity. Women may have attended public worship, but their regular attendance was not, like men's, a prescribed religious duty nor a centerpiece of their religious identity. In the United States this pattern shifted, signaling a fundamental realignment in the shape of Judaism.

As the Jewish community Americanized, synagogue attendance became a central expression of Jewishness for many women, and male Jewish leaders learned that they needed to find ways to validate this particular expression of female religiosity. These developments emerged in an environment in which, as Ann Braude has noted, "the numerical dominance of women . . . constitutes one of the most consistent features of American religion." The predominant presence of women in the synagogue sanctuary was thus consistent with an American Christian context that identified religious piety as a feminine trait, a context in which women consistently outnumbered men in church attendance, activity, and membership.[4]

If, as seems likely, the growth of female synagogue attendance among Americanizing Jews was influenced by prevailing models of American female religious behavior, it is important to note that women's role in the synagogue remained limited to filling their seats in the sanctuary. For the most part, nineteenth-century American Jewish congregations, like traditional synagogues, continued to deprive women of any official status within the community. Women were consistently excluded from lay and religious leadership, and even from membership. The scope of female activity within the synagogue appears particularly limited when compared with American Christian experience, which suggests that the religious practices of even the most Americanized Jews should not be understood as simply imitation of American models. As American Jews worked to discern and emulate the behaviors and style associated with respectable American religiosity, they needed to address the tensions that arose between these perceived requirements and the often conflicting demands of Jewish tradition. All the choices about the roles and place of women in the synagogue confronted these tensions as they helped to define the evolving boundaries of American Judaism.

Bringing the era of the almost exclusively male synagogue to an end inevitably involved much more than the personal decisions made by thousands of individual women to attend worship services on a regular basis. The adjustments necessary to accommodate women in the physical space of the American synagogue also signaled a conceptual shift among American Jews. If women were to fill synagogues on a regular basis, prevailing notions of women as religious actors and of synagogues as sacred spaces had to be redefined. Once women began to find a place in the synagogue, their presence became an implicit and persistent challenge to the structure and essence of the institution.

The challenge inherent in redefining women's proper place in the synagogue arose from the inevitable clash between New World conceptions of gender and religiosity and those associated with traditional Judaism. Although European Jewish experience never yielded any one static model of Jewish life, the avenues to religious identity for most European Jewish women were found in activities conducted outside the formal institutional space of worship. Men's principal religious expression, on the other hand, centered in the synagogue and study hall.

In America, where a powerful middle-class ideology prescribed a church-centered expression of female religiosity, this particular delineation of gender difference proved unworkable. Colleen McDannell has pointed out that antebellum Protestant thinkers, led by Horace Bushnell, made a strong association between women's religiosity and the home.[5] Still, middle-class American Protestants also expected to see female piety expressed in regular church attendance. This expectation obscured the centrality of the domestic religious responsibilities assigned to women in traditional Judaism. Nineteenth-century America's powerful middle-class gender ideology prevented non-Jews from being able to recognize the potential importance of a female-centered, home-based Jewish religiosity. To many Protestant observers, women's marginality in the synagogue was proof of their marginality within Judaism.

As Jews sought acceptance and validation in the American mainstream, the status of women in the synagogue came to seem increasingly at odds with prevailing bourgeois notions of female religiosity. A public ritual that segregated women's bodies and silenced their voices seemed to contradict claims by Jewish leaders that their own tradition had always embraced the ideals that defined nineteenth-century American versions of female piety and excellence. Inevitably, the Jewish community's aspirations to respectable religious, ethnic, race, and class identities in American life necessitated a restructuring in the position assigned to women in Jewish religious practice.

Jewish women's presence in America's synagogues challenged male congregational leaders to accommodate their voices and their needs. The redefinition of women's religious place accompanied or led to other adjustments involving synagogal sacred space, education, membership, music, and liturgy, as well as congregational participation, attendance, and leadership. As female religiosity was reconstituted in the American setting, so too were the American synagogue and American Judaism.

Synagogues without Women

The story of women's emerging presence in the American synagogue is highlighted by the contrast with Jewish historical experience, in which religious life was sharply divided into male and female realms. Within traditional Jewish practice, as Paula Hyman has pointed out, public prayer and study constituted "the heart and soul of traditional Judaism . . . and [they] were the pursuits almost exclusively of men."[6] In many locales married women might be present in the synagogue's women's section on Sabbath mornings, on High Holidays, and on other festivals. Some of the more educated among them might take on the often honored role of *vorsangerin* (also transliterated as *firzogerin, zugerin,* or *zugerke*), monitoring the service as it was conducted by the men and serving as a prompter and guide through the liturgy for the other women present in the *ezrat nashim* (women's section). Thus, many women took a great interest in the synagogue and its doings and may certainly have experienced religious fulfillment and a sense of community among themselves, but women remained essentially peripheral to the institution's purpose and practices.[7]

The same traditional prayer experience that limited women to passive participation drew male worshipers into active engagement. The typical public prayer of Europe's Jewish men was loudly participatory and individualistic in its communality, as each worshiper sought his own rhythm of prayer recital and movement. Orchestrating the pivotal event of the religious service, the reading of the Torah, demanded extensive congregational involvement. In fact, the honors associated with the Torah reading were considered among the prime religious rights, privileges, and duties of a male member of a Jewish religious community. Even those men who did not actively participate in the service could prove indispensable to making the ritual possible as a member of the quorum (minyan) of ten men required for public worship. The presence of each male worshiper was integral, and as a maker of the minyan, potentially crucial, to the worship of the community.

At the same time that the traditional synagogue prized male religious participation, its structure discounted the significance of female prayer. Because of the expectation that women might at any moment be distracted by the demands of child rearing and housekeeping, women were freed from most of the time-bound commandments incumbent upon men. Thus, unlike men, they were not obligated by Jewish religious law (halakhah) to pray three times a day at particular times, nor was their presence required to enable public worship. As a result, although women's prayers were encouraged, they were not accorded the ritual and communal importance given to men's worship. Because women were not required to participate in public prayer, they were excluded from religious leadership. Someone who was not obligated to participate in prayer could not presume to serve as a leader for those who were so obligated.[8]

Limits on women's participation in public worship extended well beyond questions of obligation and leadership. Traditional proscriptions against reciting the Shema, a central prayer in the liturgy, when in the potentially distracting presence of a woman's voice, led to prohibitions against women's voices in prayer assemblies. Women's marginalization in public worship found physical expression through their segregation in closed-off sections of the synagogue. Proscriptions against the mixing of men and women in public worship were derived from Talmudic descriptions of a women's section in the ancient Temple in Jerusalem. All eighteenth- and early-nineteenth-century synagogues replicated this segregation. Only in a few cases, such as the requirement to read or hear the Book of Esther on the holiday of Purim, was a woman's presence ritually required, and then her role was usually as auditor rather than participant. Most of the requirements incumbent upon women were best performed outside the synagogue.[9]

Evidence from contemporary Orthodox practice reinforces the perception of women's historical marginality in the synagogue. A recent study updates the observation that, though present, women are "not legitimate participants" within the traditional sphere of prayer, study, and community. Anthropologist Samuel Heilman observes that in the Orthodox congregation of his ethnographic study, "plainly and simply, the shul [synagogue] is for men; and prayer as practiced in shul is for men, too."[10] For many, the denigration of women's experience within Judaism is all too conveniently summarized in the daily prayer enjoined upon Jewish men, as part of their morning ritual, that praises the creator "for having not made me a woman."[11]

Engendering the Jewish Past

Not surprisingly, most accounts of Jewish history have reflected this dominance of men in Jewish cultural and religious experience. Female experience, whether in or out of the synagogue, has generally received little attention. Recently, however, students of Jewish history, like those in most fields of historical inquiry, have begun to redress the traditional exclusion of women from accounts of the past. They have argued that any legitimate portrayal of Judaism as a traditional culture must attend to women's lives. To incorporate the experience of women into an integrated understanding of Jewish religious life, scholars have begun to look beyond the categories, places, and institutions most readily associated with conventional histories of Judaism.

This approach has been both prompted and reinforced by a general expansion of historical interest into areas beyond institutions and politics. Historians who seek to excavate the historical outlines of popular religion insist that the categories used to describe religion must encompass the actual religious lives of its adherents. They suggest that the elite-driven institutions that historians have traditionally studied may ultimately have little to do with the actual religious lives of most of the practitioners of a particular faith.[12]

Historical observers focusing on women's experience within Jewish culture have also emphasized the importance of ordinary, undocumented lives that were, nevertheless, religiously vital and crucial to communal identity. Such experience has often been dismissed as peripheral because it fell outside the normative categories of institutional Judaism. Historians who approach Judaism as an evolving way of life, however, refuse to dismiss the importance of female contributions to sustaining Jewish communal and religious life on the basis of their irrelevance to the synagogue and study hall. This perspective has expanded and enriched contemporary visions of the Jewish past.[13]

One consequence, however, of this important effort to address the gender imbalance of Jewish historiography has been the tendency of feminist historians to overlook the public sphere of religion as a potentially useful site of inquiry.[14] The synagogue's history as an institution designed for male religious expression has prompted those interested in women to exclude it as a subject of interest. For the same reason, students of the synagogue have rarely considered the institution's changing gender dynamics to be an important part of their story.

Although a number of historians have recognized that America provided a transformative setting for Jewish women, students of American Jewish women have been reluctant to emphasize the formal institutions of Judaism. Most studies on American Jewish women have focused primarily on the compelling twentieth-century experiences of eastern European immigrants, uncovering a world in which women were powerfully engaged in a wide range of economic, political, and social settings. Studies that have taken more in-depth looks at Jewish women in the nineteenth century have generally not given extended attention to the changes in female religious identity that were centered in the synagogue.[15]

The general scholarly neglect of the synagogue as an arena relevant to women's religious experience is particularly apparent in existing analysis of posttraditional transformations in Jewish life. Feminist academics who have focused their attention on the synagogue tend to emphasize either distant history or the current transformative challenge of feminism.[16] Even attempts by scholars of American Jewish history to be sensitive to the questions raised by feminist historiography frame such concerns as being relevant primarily to recent, contemporary, and future experience. Three definitive essays on the synagogues of the different American Jewish denominations, in an important volume edited by Jack Wertheimer, all describe how the evolving role of women in each movement will have a tremendous influence on the future course of their synagogues. Women's impact as a "new sociological force" is acknowledged at the very end of each of these essays, as if to suggest that the history of the American synagogue up to now has only peripherally been affected by the presence of women.[17] As Jonathan Sarna's essay on mixed seating in the same volume demonstrates, however, the challenge of finding a place for female religious expression has long been salient in shaping American Judaism.[18]

The present study takes the synagogue as its main focus. It attempts to explore the changing gender dynamics that were so critical to the creation of American Jewish identity and religious expression within the central institution of American Judaism. Identifying the early American synagogue as a meaningful site for the expression of female religiosity does not suggest that the institution became in any sense a women's sphere. In fact, one consequence of choosing to focus on the synagogue is that what purports to be a study of "finding a place for women" is often not about women at all. Yet whether or not women have been acknowledged, influential, or even present in any given setting or institution, study of that setting or institution can still yield important insights about the ways in which women's and men's roles are defined and structured in the culture of which it is a part. A culture may be defined as much by women's absence as by their presence. As Miriam Peskowitz points out, "even a womanless history is simultaneously and necessarily gendered."[19]

In this light, the synagogues created by American Jews warrant particular attention. It was in the synagogue that the centrality of women's absence in public Judaism became first explicit and then increasingly unacceptable. Peskowitz uses the metaphor of a construction site to convey how a complex grid of cultural assumptions and ideologies determines the shape of structures that may in their finished form appear to be seamless and natural. Jewish immigrants from Europe were remarkably active in establishing synagogues as the institutional expression of the traditions they were trying to recreate in the American setting. Yet in this process of removal to a new and unfamiliar setting, some of the tradition's underpinnings, some of its pillars, bars, and framing structures, were laid bare. American Jews had to confront the suddenly apparent awkwardness of gender arrangements whose balance had long been taken for granted.

Looking for stability on unfamiliar terrain, Jewish renovators worked to mask the suddenly exposed cracks in the foundations and walls of their religious culture as they sought to bring it into harmony with their new environment.

In the work of translating traditional identities into identities appropriate for the New World, the reordering of gender was central to the process of Americanization. American Jews confronted the conflicting gender ideals implicit in Jewish and American cultures most directly within the synagogue. The resulting transformations in synagogue design and organization reveal the extent to which the public face of American Judaism has been shaped by the space given to women's physical presence in the synagogue and to their presence in synagogue activity and life.

Public and Private

The religious institutions to which Americanizing Jews turned as models of more appropriate gender ordering reflected a culture shaped by its own assumptions about the proper roles and behavior for middle-class American women. Here too, men's and women's roles were defined by distinctive, if evolving, notions of public and private. Flattened portraits of both traditional Jewish and nineteenth-century American bourgeois cultures might offer parallel representations of societies in which men bore responsibility for the public world of communal organization and discourse, and women for a narrow sphere restricted to home, children, and domestic piety. The institutional stress implicit in adjusting Jewish institutions to the vagaries of American cultural expectations, however, illustrates the inadequacy of a simple dichotomy of public and private to describe either traditional Jewish culture or nineteenth-century American culture.

Historians of the 1960s and 1970s, trying to advance the narrative of women's history beyond that of anecdote and the stories of a few exceptional individuals, identified the illuminating notion that an ideology of "women's proper sphere" has determined the parameters and possibilities of women's lives through much of American history. More recently, historians have begun to question whether accepting descriptions by nineteenth-century social commentators of a world divided into "private" (female) and "public" (male) spheres misrepresents the lived experience of both men and women. Much scholarly work has been devoted to examining the ways in which women breached the bounds of the private and domestic to have an impact on the public world. In fact, organized women seem to have become a recognizable force in public life at the very moment when the emphasis on their domestic character was most precisely refined and most loudly trumpeted.[20]

Historians have tried to distinguish how a powerful and omnipresent social discourse decreeing women's "proper place" shaped women's experience and responsibility for domestic and family life and, at the same time, framed the social, benevolent, and reform work of women beyond the home. In this puzzle, in which engagement outside the home had to be justified according to recognized womanly qualities and virtues, which were grounded in the home, the public sphere of religion occupied, in Ann Braude's phrase, "an awkward indeterminate status."[21] Piety was a central component of the roster of virtues assigned to women by the prevailing ideology of domesticity, and women attested to its centrality not only by trying to create Christian homes but also by representing their piety through their presence in church. Here the inadequacy of the public-private dichotomy becomes clear. Some scholars have suggested that through involvement in church work and broader reform causes, women succeeded in expanding the boundaries of what was considered the private world. Others have seen that the expected, even required, presence of middle-class Christian women in the space of public prayer, discourse, and community served as a threshold or platform from which many women could collectively embrace public concerns and enter public life.[22]

The American synagogue provides an intriguing lens through which to view these questions about how public religion framed access to public identities for different groups of American women. Because women in the synagogue started from a place of marginalization, if not exclusion, efforts to integrate women into the physical space and organizational structure of the synagogue provide an extremely sensitive barometer of Jewish perceptions of American gender ideals. Many congregational leaders strove to create synagogues that middle- and upper-class Americans, whether Christian or Jewish, would see as worthy counterparts to nineteenth-century America's most respectable churches. They hoped to create an acculturated Judaism that, without abandoning the broad outlines of Jewish tradition, would still feel American. Thus, the extent to which the development of women's place in American synagogues replicated or differed from the gender organization seen in the country's affluent churches reveals much about what Jews perceived as necessary to the creation of a public American religious identity and the limits imposed upon acculturation by the constraints of Jewish tradition.

Ann Braude points out that it is a "narrative fiction" to speak of the "feminization" of American churches in the nineteenth century, because starting from the early colonial period, women's dominant presence characterized the public sphere of American religion at every juncture. It is, however, no fiction to speak of the emergence of women's presence in the American synagogue. The physical transformation of the synagogue to accommodate women's presence and the expectation that women would express their religious identity through synagogue attendance were something new. And against the backdrop of Jewish tradition, this innovation was very much about crossing a boundary between public and private, between a domestic religious world of female-centered observance (supported by communal institutions) and a public religious world of male-centered worship and ritual. American Jews, with Christian churches as their only guides to American religion, faced the daunting task of utilizing the available rhetoric celebrating women's domestic piety to justify the needful presence of women in a space that, in Jewish terms, could only be construed as public. Thus, as they built synagogues and shaped their worship, acculturating Jews were forced to explore the confusing intersection of the gender ideologies implicit in the different worlds in which they were trying to live.

Respectability

The nineteenth-century American synagogue was a laboratory where Jews, laypeople and rabbis alike, tested the components that would be necessary to build an appropriate American religious identity. American Jewish identities grew out of the tension between a quest for respectability, shaped by perceptions of American expectations, and an investment in distinctiveness, drawn from immigrant interpretations of Jewish tradition and history. Acculturating Jews had to negotiate a challenging terrain contoured by a broad range of expectations, choices, and assumptions. Because appropriate gender roles were fundamental to both American respectability and to Jewish tradition, attention to the gendered nature of American Jewish religious roles can help to make sense of this complex topography. All those, whether reformers or traditionalists, who hoped to create substantial American synagogues to serve prospering congregants had to reconcile the rigidity of familiar Jewish practice with the similarly fixed expectations concerning the proper treatment of women, which were a fundamental feature of American gentility.

Respectability has emerged as a compelling subject of historical interest, both for scholars examining how the American middle class assumed a distinctive identity and for those studying how outsiders, as either groups or individuals, sought inclusion and validation in mainstream America.[23] Karen Halttunen has examined the uncertainty engendered within nineteenth-century urban bourgeois society by the incursion of interlopers from the underclass or the country with pretensions of refinement and social grace. Kevin Gaines and Evelyn Brooks Higginbotham have looked at the attempts of those seeking the uplift of the black working class to approximate the manners and behavioral style of white Protestant America.[24] Social theorists have begun to look at all social behavior and self-definition as a mode of performance, through which individuals and groups attempt to determine who they are by clarifying who they are not and who they hope to be.[25]

Higginbotham describes how an elite group of African-American leaders sought to utilize a "politics of respectability" to validate their own efforts, to raise up their less cultured brethren, and to challenge those white Americans who dismissed the legitimacy of black American claims upon bourgeois respectability. Despite their own successes, the female leaders identified by Higginbotham were constantly frustrated by the refusal of most of their less cultured peers to subscribe to a code of refined behavior imposed by a society that refused to honor their aspirations. American Jewish men, by contrast, encountered a society that seemed poised, in a manner unprecedented in Jewish diaspora experience, to embrace and reward their economic, social, and political aspirations. Acculturating Jews hoped to prove they were worthy of the trust that these opportunities offered, seeking out identities that would secure their acceptance and respectability.

In this endeavor, American Jewish leaders repudiated the primitive-ness and lack of reverence that they ascribed to much of traditional Jewish worship. They attempted to disassociate themselves from the chaos, informality, and physicality typical of the traditional style of Jewish worship, commonly called "davening." Through the embrace of formalized worship behavior, American synagogue communities also distinguished themselves from the emotionalism and lack of control evident in the camp meeting type of revivalism that characterized so much nineteenth-century worship among lower-class white Protestant, immigrant Catholic, and African-American church communities.

Whatever the particular meaning of respectability for Jews or other groups in American society, American Jews had a deep investment in both approximating appropriate patterns of middle-class behavior and finding a way to retain distinctive Jewish content within them. As Jews began to explore the possibilities of an American Judaism, women's place in the synagogue and in Judaism became a marker of the division between traditional and Reform approaches to Jewish worship. Acculturating traditionalists hoped that an observant Judaism could be presented and experienced in a decorous and genteel fashion, but they maintained that the separation of men and women was a fixed aspect of what made Jewish worship Jewish. Those who wanted to reform Judaism did not believe that continued observance of Jewish rituals and traditions, governed solely by strict interpretations of Jewish law, could comport with an American way of life. Reformers came to the conclusion that a synagogue could still be Jewish if men and women sat together and, perhaps more important, that propriety demanded it.

Whose Story Is This, Anyway?

Following the attempts of Jewish religious and lay leaders to create religious congregations that would lead their fellow Jews to respectable American religious identities may not be the best way to track women's changing experience of Judaism. This study focuses on what it meant to find and define a meaningful role for women in the sphere of public Jewish worship, but it cannot provide a full account of how women personally experienced the religious changes implicit in becoming American. The main effort here is to examine the extent to which the need to reconstruct the parameters of women's religious lives, under the pressure of American middle-class life and expectations, was shaped by and gave shape to the construction of American synagogues and of American Judaism.

One of the drawbacks of highlighting a historically male-dominated institution is that, unavoidably, most of those who reflected upon the meaning of change within that institution were male. Despite the challenge posed by women's presence, the synagogue's organizational structure resisted any female encroachment upon lay or religious leadership until well into the twentieth century. The major agency ascribed to women in these pages is what they created by merely showing up; much of the discussion of these developments and their implications was left to men.

The lack of female voices commenting upon the American synagogue does not in itself establish the irrelevance of the synagogue as a religious sphere for women. Despite their silence, something was clearly happening to women who began to make synagogue attendance a central part of their religious lives. Having once found a place in the synagogue, acculturated American Jewish women would eventually build upon this presence to demand public recognition of their spiritual identity.

Despite trends that led one 1881 editorial observer to fear that congregations would soon become an "audience of old men, women and children with the nerve and fibre of the race, the brain and the marrow, persistently absent," leading roles in the creation of American Judaism rarely went to women.[26] Men effected the changes in synagogal space and organization and articulated the need for change. And although gender arrangements proved to be a powerful variable in the reformulation of American Judaism, such arrangements were often manipulated for purposes that had little to do with women's actual concerns.

The implications of these changes, moreover, resonated beyond the limits of women's religious lives. Because the separation of traditional and American Jewish experience was reflected so dramatically in the shifts of women's religious experience, reforms relating to gender often served as occasions for vociferous debate. Not surprisingly, polemics on questions of "women's rights" often became struggles over acculturation, textual authority, and the legitimacy of the American synagogue. The tension between traditional conceptions of female roles within Judaism and emerging American realities offered a focal point for the ambivalence with which many responded to the general decline of traditional Jewish life. Even amidst a general acceptance of American religious models, both traditional and reform-minded observers, in their different ways, questioned the direction of female religiosity among American Jews. Deep-seated anxiety over the shape of American Judaism found indirect expression in criticism of women's inability to recreate the romanticized ethos of the traditional Jewish home and community.

The ways in which American male Jewish leaders approached the question of women's presence in the synagogue also illuminate how American synagogues diverged from those of acculturating European Jews, who likewise had to face the conflicting definitions of public and private ideals for men and women in the societies in which they hoped to find posttraditional homes. Although these tensions were present for nineteenth-century Jews in western and central Europe, nowhere were the implications for public Judaism played out to the extent that they were in the United States. Although current scholarship on women in European synagogues allows for only speculation on this subject, any study focused on women in the emerging American synagogue must consider the ways in which these developments characterize a Judaism distinct from contemporaneous experiences of modernization elsewhere. Accordingly, this study will begin with a limited examination of the gendered experience of Jewish modernity in western and central Europe before moving on to a specific chronology of women's changing place in the American synagogue.

The changing religious lives of American Jewish women betokened a Judaism in the throes of transformation. Delineation of the contours of woman's role as a member of the congregation, as the possessor and conveyer of Jewish practice and belief, and, in many ways, as the embodiment of tradition, reveals the personal and communal costs and gains involved in the movement from traditional Jewish life to an American way of religion. Historical scrutiny of the efforts of American Jews to find a place for Jewish women in the synagogue illuminates the development of American Judaism.

Changes for women within American synagogues may often appear more subtle than momentous. The removal of physical barriers between the sexes and even the advent of mixed seating effectively did little more than offer women different views of synagogue worship. Such adjustments hardly turned the synagogue into a realm of gender equality. A gendered view of the synagogue uncovers neither the triumphant recognition of women in American Judaism nor a tale of unmitigated female subservience. But synagogues filled with women were profoundly different spaces than synagogues filled with men. This study explores the sources and consequences of that transformation.

It also delineates a new pattern of Jewish womanhood that emerged out of a complex amalgamation of traditional expectations, aspirations to acceptance as a respected American religion, and models of female Christian religiosity. By examining how gender came to signify tradition and modernity in the American synagogue, I hope to illuminate the shifting meaning of religion in the lives of nineteenth-century American Jews.

CHAPTER ONE

Jewish Women: Acculturation in Old and New Worlds

Tensions between the gender ideals of traditional Jewish culture and those of a broader society that acculturating Jews hoped to join were not limited to eighteenth- and nineteenth-century America, the setting for this study. In western and central Europe too, acculturating Jews sought acceptance in societies that seemed unsympathetic to the religious status and duties assigned to women within traditional Judaism. Yet a comparison of European and American Jewish attempts to address this tension reveals quite different responses to what may have seemed a shared problem of acculturation.

There is little indication that synagogue attendance became a central aspect of European female religious identity. European synagogues held to separate sections for women within their sanctuaries. The radical Reform congregation of Berlin, which seated men and women on the same floor, although in separate sections, was the only nineteenth-century European synagogue building to do away with the women's gallery.[1] In contrast, by the late nineteenth century, family pews in which men sat side by side with women became the hallmark of adaptation of American temples and synagogues to American culture.

American Jewish religious culture and practice, created as it was by European immigrants, must be understood against the background of European Jewish traditions and experience. Why did the American innovation of mixed seating and the phenomenon of largely female congregations not find contemporaneous parallels in European experience? How should these differences be understood? Conclusions about the gender order of Europe's Jewish communities must await further research on female participation in the public and private spheres of Judaism.[2] Still, despite the limitations of current knowledge, any inquiry into women's experience of Judaism in the United States must at least consider the ways in which American Jewish experience differed from that of Jews in the countries that provided America's immigrants. Such a preliminary consideration may suggest why public expressions of Judaism in America, but not in Europe, were so affected by the effort to incorporate new roles for women into the synagogue. Whether in the Old or New World, the shifting balance between the public and private aspects of Judaism helped to determine posttraditional identities for Jewish women and men.[3] Comparison of European and American attempts to reconcile Jewish identity with the gendered expectations and patterns of their host societies can help to identify the relevant structural dynamics that shaped these different versions of modernizing Jewish experience.

Beyond Tradition

Premodern Jewish experience, although often glossed here as "traditional Jewish life," was no less complex than the diverse experiences of modernity that supplanted it. Yet across the range of individual and collective experience, a general acceptance of the authority of Jewish law (halakhah), as interpreted by the constituted communal legal authorities of the time, helped to create a broadly shared framework for Jewish life. Laws and customs mandating distinct gender roles created explicit legal and cultural parameters within which individual Jews, male and female, lived their lives.

In accord with this pattern, a Jewish woman's religious identity found expression in her whole way of life. There is still much to be learned about the details of women's varied life experiences in pre-Enlightenment Europe, but few would have questioned a religious ideal that determined that every woman's primary identity should be as a wife and mother. With these roles, a Jewish woman accepted responsibility for providing kosher food to her family, maintaining the weekly and yearly Jewish calendar, preparing feasts for the Sabbath and other holidays, and removing all traces of leaven from her home before

Passover. She was particularly bound to observe the three laws assigned to women: lighting candles for the Sabbath *(hadlakat ha-ner)*, symbolically reenacting the tithe paid to the ancient priests by burning a small bit of the dough prepared for the baking of bread *(challah)*, and observing the laws of marital purity *(niddah)*.[4] In addition to her domestic duties, she also worked for her family's economic well-being, saw to her children's Jewish education, and at times took her place in the women's section of her community synagogue. These daily, weekly, monthly, and yearly responsibilities pervaded women's lives at the same time that they constituted the fabric of traditional Jewish culture.

In both western and central Europe, as well as in the United States, eighteenth- and nineteenth-century challenges to traditional Jewish culture disrupted this fabric as they undermined the accustomed authority of halakhic definitions of collective and individual identity. Cut adrift from the roles and rhythms of a shared communal framework, Jews sought out a workable balance between reconstituted versions of Jewish identity and the emerging possibilities of secular identity. Late-eighteenth- and early-nineteenth-century Jews in central and western Europe and in the United States confronted wide variations in political status, access to education, and the nature of local Jewish and non-Jewish society and culture. In every circumstance, however, they shared the problem of how to express Jewish identity and build Jewish community under drastically changed conditions. New roles for both men and women would be defined in a cautious negotiation between the demands of a traditional way of life and the demands of those cultures in which Jews began to find at least limited acceptance.

Emancipation or partial emancipation in western and central Europe broke down the distinctive legal definitions of the relationship between the Jewish collective and the state and advanced political rights for Jewish individuals toward those held by non-Jewish citizens. However limited, Jewish access to the political, educational, and economic resources of non-Jewish society had a profoundly disruptive effect on the internal dynamics of European Jewish community and life. In fits and starts, the world of non-Jewish culture and thought opened to the Jews of western and central Europe at the end of the eighteenth century and the beginning of the nineteenth.

The task of determining how to reconstitute Jewish identity in light of these changing circumstances was principally the enterprise of a small elite of male intellectuals. Their concerns were not those of the generally more traditional rural population nor of the acculturating, but not particularly self-reflective, urban Jewish population. Through their influence over the institutions of Jewish communal life, however, the efforts of early *maskilim* (followers of the Haskalah, or Jewish Enlightenment) helped to define the general patterns, including the emergent gender ideals, of modern Jewish life.

Moses Mendelssohn (1729–1786), the Haskalah's pioneer and paragon, insisted that Jewish religious law was still mandatory for Jews as a particular path to the universal standards of rational ethical behavior celebrated by the Enlightenment. For many acculturating Jews, however, if religion was chiefly an expression of universal ethical values, then it followed that all the observances, rituals, and minutiae that defined the practice of Judaism became secondary. Although Mendelssohn maintained strict adherence to Jewish ritual observance in his own life, few of his followers and none of his children were able to sustain a commitment to a religiously observant lifestyle.

Successors to Mendelssohn took up the theme that Judaism was a product of rational ideas. They argued that Judaism in its pure form, freed from the perversions and distortions imposed by persecution and isolation, promoted enlightened values, reasoned thought, and respectable behavior among its adherents. The emergence of Reform as a coherent ideology and then an organized movement in Germany in the 1830s and 1840s represented a self-conscious response to the challenge of modernity by Jews who wished to be both Jewish and part of the broader society. These Jews wanted to escape the restrictive bounds of Jewish law and community, but they also felt the continuing pull of Jewish identity and practice. By identifying religion with belief rather than with practice, Reformers hoped to distinguish the beneficial and admirable aspects of Judaism from the multitude of specific observances that had defined Judaism as a culture and a civilization, too many of which, they now feared, might be perceived as esoteric and primitive.

The Jewish Reform movement arose chiefly from a concern that the fixed observances of traditional Judaism were not compatible with the life of enlightened Jews who had moved beyond closed Jewish communities. German Jewish Reformers attempted to make Judaism into a religion that a modern German both could and would follow. If the religious aspect of their lives still rang with the accents of the ghetto and with traditions and sentiments that were appropriate to the experience of an oppressed people, would not modern German Jews simply abandon the pretense of Judaism altogether? Reports, perhaps exaggerated, of growing numbers of converts from Judaism seemed to bear out the relevance of such concerns.[5]

All those who were prompted by the lure of emancipation to demonstrate Judaism's compatibility with contemporary values implicitly challenged familiar Jewish models of female religiosity. Some Reformers, hoping to minimize the ways in which Jews could be shown to differ from their fellow Germans, approached certain characteristic observances of Jewish religious life with disdain. Rabbi Abraham Geiger, the most prominent of the German Reformers, suggested in 1837 that the religious duties at the center of women's domestic responsibilities may have been more demeaning than ennobling. He noted that the "three duties assigned to [women], niddah, challah, and the lighting of the Sabbath lights," were women's "central," but "truly not very lustrous jewel."[6] In the views of many like Geiger, those institutions and customs that shaped Jewish life outside the synagogue, like the *mikveh* (ritual bath), in which women were required by Jewish law to seek purification after their menstrual periods, or the many rituals associated with the maintenance of a kosher diet, were those most susceptible to criticism.

The observances most explicitly linked to female Jewish religiosity were among those most likely to undermine the Haskalah's claims to the utter rationality of Jewish belief and practice. Israel Jacobson, whose radical school for Jewish youth in Westphalia introduced the first example of a Reform prayer service and liturgy in 1810, noted that Judaism was "weighted down with religious customs which must be rightfully offensive to reason as well as to our Christian friends."[7] In a similar vein, Michael Creizenach, a Jewish educator associated with the Jewish reformers of Frankfurt, observed in 1839 that many avoided "observing Jewish rituals in their family circle" because such "rituals have a truly grotesque appearance for European, cultured people."[8] While Creizenach spoke of the possibility of altering these outmoded ceremonies "in a suitable way," reforming efforts found their central focus in the more public expressions of Judaism.

Proponents of Jewish Reform sought to create a Jewish version of a more universally acknowledged spirituality. In this redefined Judaism, as Michael Meyer observes, the synagogue was to become "for the

Jews what the church was for the Christians, the focus of religious life."⁹ Accordingly, much reforming energy was directed to increasing the respectability of public Jewish worship. How could Jews, striving for civil emancipation, defend the raucousness typical of Jewish public prayer? How could they pretend to find rationality and order in such chaos? By asking for the recasting of Judaism at the level of prayer, belief, and ritual, the Reform movement emphasized the centrality of the synagogue to the experience of Judaism.

Although nineteenth-century Jewish leaders were most intent upon refining public expressions of Judaism, Paula Hyman and Marion Kaplan have shown that the emergence of an ideology celebrating women's domestic religiosity was a cornerstone of the effort to portray Jews as respectable members of the bourgeoisie. Nineteenth-century German Jewish Reformers were indeed careful to celebrate and acknowledge the importance of domestic piety. This emphasis upon domesticity, however, did not translate into a Reform agenda for the home. Reformers did not envision a program for the modernization of Jewish domestic practice to parallel the process of synagogue ritual reform.

Many German Jews had already decided that questions regarding kashrut (the dietary laws), *niddah*, and the keeping of the Sabbath were extraneous to the acculturated way of life to which they aspired. Reformers did not expect to refine the laws of kashrut or marital purity in the same ways that they hoped to adjust traditional liturgy or synagogue customs to contemporary sensibilities. Those aspects of Judaism were, almost by definition, regarded as part of a backward lifestyle that was not even susceptible to reform. Although a Jewish woman's domestic role might be celebrated and redefined, it would not be because she found a better way to keep kosher.

In most European Jewish communities, the assumption presumably was that domestic ritual observances and customs would simply continue on their own as the private side of traditional Jewish life.¹⁰ Reformers did not actively promote the neglect or abolition of these observances, but they were little concerned about their preservation. By emphasizing those aspects of Judaism that had always been dominated by men, Reformers, consciously or not, largely ignored the world of religious practice and responsibility traditionally associated with female religiosity. This tendency to equate the boundaries of *modern* Jewish religious life with the walls of the synagogue meant that the Jewish religious world most familiar to women would be increasingly separated from the public Judaism propounded by Jewish communal leaders.

Women and the Reform of Judaism

Like their counterparts in the United States, European Jewish leaders who hoped to make Jewish religious identities compatible with emancipated bourgeois civil identities could not ignore the challenge that traditional female religiosity presented to their attempts to nurture a modern version of Judaism. At times, communal actions demonstrated an awareness that the apparent disregard for women displayed in Jewish public worship might prove embarrassing to Jews hoping for approval from non-Jewish society. In France an 1846 Central Consistory questionnaire to candidates for the position of chief rabbi solicited opinions about how to assure females a more pleasant and dignified position in Jewish worship.[11] A recommendation of the 1831 Strasbourg Consistory in Alsace suggested that synagogues be built so that girls might be able to enter through the front entrance.[12]

In England, tensions around fitting Jewish women to the demands of modernity found expression, not in questions of liturgical reform, but in the emergence of an unprecedented female Jewish literary subculture.[13] In his study of a remarkable group of nineteenth-century Anglo-Jewish women authors, Michael Galchinsky argues that while male Jewish leaders in England responded to contemporary religious challenges through traditional forms of rabbinic discourse, Grace Aguilar and her female literary compatriots were able to articulate nuanced critiques of tradition by adapting the popular literary genres of their era. These authors sought to counter the blandishments of popular conversionist literary romances that portrayed women oppressed by Judaism, who then became easy marks for both Christian suitors and Christian conversion. These female authors responded with historical romances of their own to show that Judaism could indeed provide sufficient answers to the challenges of a romantic and liberal age. Aguilar's notable 1844 work, *The Women of Israel*, attempted to counter popular assertions that "Christianity is the sole source of female excellence" by offering a series of inspiring sketches of biblical heroines.[14] The work of Aguilar and others reflected an awareness among acculturating Jews that Judaism was vulnerable to condemnation for failing to accord sufficient dignity to women as religious actors. Apologetic tracts like Aguilar's hastened to assure both Jewish and non-Jewish readers that Judaism in its essence, as reflected in the Bible, afforded nothing but respect and honor to what at least Aguilar agreed was still the weaker sex.

The most extensive discussion of women's place in traditional and contemporary Judaism was conducted by those engaged in the Jewish Reform movement in Germany. German Reformers attributed the apparent subservience of women in traditional Judaism to the "orientalism" they believed was still embedded in Jewish practice. Even though German Reformers argued for changes in the religious life of women along lines quite similar to those advanced in the United States, their efforts led to only limited practical results. The disparity between German and American outcomes is highlighted by the career of Rabbi David Einhorn, who called for the public religious equality of women at the 1846 Breslau Rabbinical Assembly—to little practical effect. In making a similar call in 1858, a few years after taking a rabbinical post in Baltimore, Einhorn not only condemned the "gallery cage" but also brought women down from the gallery in his own synagogue.[15] While German Reformers offered thoughtful, sometimes radical, critiques of the ways in which Judaism mistreated women, these analyses had only a limited impact on their practical agenda or on the religious status and behavior of women in their own synagogues. Only in the United States could Einhorn's call to abolish the women's gallery resonate as a central aspect of a broad movement of general liturgical and stylistic reform.

Abraham Geiger took up the subject of women's place within Judaism in 1837.[16] A pioneer in the effort to create a coherent and positive reform of Jewish practice, Geiger argued that despite its emergence "out of the womb of the Orient," Judaism had always treated women with great respect. According to Geiger, even as the Bible reflected certain oriental prejudices that might have led to the degradation of women, the Hebrew scriptures also introduced a "spirit of mildness" that mitigated many of the text's harsher edicts. He identified a continuing tradition in Judaism that, in its "truest expression," conveyed a profound respect for women, investing them with "the most beautiful, most elevated virtues." Thus he could conclude that historical Jewish values were actually consistent with contemporary bourgeois notions of the respect due to women as religious beings.

At the same time, Geiger acknowledged that despite this ennobling tradition, "the social position of women in Judaism remains unnatural, for it is surrounded with legal boundaries that are not found in nature," and he detailed the anachronistic and abusive restrictions created by this circumstance. According to Geiger, this unnaturalness, embedded in Jewish law, if not in Jewish life, ultimately prevailed in creating a religious practice that appeared to devalue women. Women, he pointed out, "in all religions . . . take such an active and lively part in all religious arrangements." It was only among the Jews, he observed, that women took a "minimal role" in religious life. Worse, Geiger described Judaism as a faith that "represses and strangles [women's] susceptible sense of religiosity." Geiger's evaluation reflects his general focus, which was directed not toward the manifold experiences and observances of Jewish life, where women were indeed central figures, but principally toward the synagogue. He pointed out that a worship service conducted in Hebrew, complete with its customary blessing of thanks to God for not being created a woman, effectively excluded women "from the thriving nourishment of the religious fervor of public worship." What incentive, he asked, existed to attract a woman to the house of prayer? How could the "noble seed of real religiosity develop" in a setting that treated her so ignobly?

Geiger proposed a reconfigured Judaism that would welcome women to the synagogue and would reject the laws that reduced the marriage contract to a purchase-and-sale agreement. Through appropriate adjustments in these public manifestations of Jewish values, Judaism could truly accord women the honor that was already a part of the tradition's ancient essence. For Geiger, it made logical and practical sense to try to involve women in the project of reforming the synagogue. As he observed, "our whole religious life will profit from the beneficial influence which feminine hearts will bestow upon it."[17] Toward this end, Geiger argued for revisions, like the introduction of more German into the liturgy, that would make the worship more accessible to women. Whether this reform was actually directed at women or at acculturated men whose Hebrew might not meet traditional standards, Reformers periodically pointed out the interest that women took in their innovations.[18]

The most notable attempt to address women's marginality in the synagogue in a programmatic way arose in the context of the assemblies of 1844, 1845, and 1846 in which German Reform rabbis gathered to consider "by what means the preservation and development of Judaism and the enlivening of the religious consciousness can be accomplished."[19] These meetings represented the German Reform movement's most determined efforts to reach a consensus on how tradition should be adapted to the spirit of the time. In introducing the subject of women to the 1846 assembly in Breslau, the radical Reformer David Einhorn observed that the issues under consideration by his committee were the same as those raised by the question of Jewish emancipation. He asked his colleagues to realize that the furthering of Enlightenment notions of equality could hardly be a dead letter to Jews, whose own status remained insecure. "A mere theoretical recognition" of women's disenfranchisement, Einhorn argued, "gives them as little satisfaction as . . . the Israelites are given in civic matters." Like the Jews of Germany, women had "received assurances of their capabilities for emancipation, without, however, being . . . permitted to become emancipated." The committee's statement emphasized that "for our religious consciousness, which grants all humans an equal degree of natural holiness, and for which the pertaining differentiations in the Holy Scripture have only relative and momentary validity, it is a sacred duty to express most emphatically the complete religious equality of the female sex."[20]

In line with this argument, Einhorn's committee offered a number of practical proposals: women would take part in religious instruction and be counted toward the quorum required for public prayer; the morning blessing of thanks for not being created a woman would be abolished; and women would take on the religious rights and obligations enjoyed by men—"so far as these *mitzvot* [commandments] have any strength and vigor at all for our religious consciousness." Einhorn and his committee suggested that women be given an equal part within Reform Judaism. Like Geiger, the Breslau report decried women's exclusion from public expressions of Judaism. Einhorn grimly observed that a Jewish woman found that "the house of God was as good as closed to her." Despite the urgency of Einhorn's report, no action was taken on its recommendations. Discussion of the report and the question of women's religious equality was put off until the following year's rabbinical assembly—which never took place.[21]

The most significant practical effort by European *maskilim* to redress the lack of public status granted women by traditional Judaism was the introduction of confirmation as a rite of passage for young Jews. The confirmation ceremony, in which a young person was asked to make a solemn declaration of faith, dates from at least 1803, and the earliest group confirmation from 1810. Early reformers intended the ceremony, drawn from Christian models, to mark the completion of a young Jew's religious education. It was meant to replace or complement the exclusively male bar mitzvah, which reformers dismissed as the mechanical recitation of Hebrew phrases by ill-trained boys.[22] Girls were included in confirmation rituals in German synagogues as early as 1817 and in French and English synagogues when such services were introduced in the 1840s.[23] The desire to include girls in the new confirmation ritual reflected changing attitudes toward the education of girls. As Paula Hyman has explained, the evolving expectation among assimilating Jews that mothers should bear primary responsibility for their children's religious training helped to reorient attention toward the education of girls. If Jewish education depended upon women's ability to convey knowledge, then, as the French *Archives Israélites* observed in 1852, "the health of our religion depends henceforth above all on the education of girls."[24]

Some community leaders took a particular interest in the education of young women, introducing schools devoted to instructing girls in academic and religious subjects, as well as in practical skills such as needlework and household management. Such schools were introduced for both the poor and the affluent. In both cases, the intention was to prevent exposure to alien doctrines, conveyed either by the attentions of Christian missionaries or by the allure of prestigious Christian schools. Among the acculturated Jewish population, however, the appeal of public education ultimately resulted in Jewish education being shunted into supplementary religious schools, which met only a few times a week. Nevertheless, the general commitment to girls' education by Jewish communal leaders contrasted sharply with the neglect that had customarily been accorded this subject.[25]

The Pull of Domestic Piety

Despite these shifts on issues related to the public status of women as Jews, German Reform leaders never actually extended the logic of their own quest for emancipation to improve the place of women in

Judaism. In part, Reformers were distracted by the prevailing celebration of womanly domestic virtues in German society. The influence of European romanticism, with its emphasis on woman's naturally domestic character and its glorification of the home and family, helped Jewish Reformers avoid the difficult task of creating new roles for women in the public sphere.[26] Since acculturating German Jews sought an appropriately domestic bourgeois identity for Jewish women, the creation of public roles for women did not rank high among shared communal concerns.

Calling attention to the outstanding models of domestic female piety in Jewish tradition became more important than welcoming women's voices in public prayer. The influence of romantic thought is seen in Geiger's portrayal of the nineteenth century's womanly ideal in his 1864 account of Jewish history. Geiger's history presented "noble pictures of women" drawn from a succession of biblical stories. Jewish tradition teaches, he noted, that the Israelites were delivered from Egypt "through the merits of their women." Yet in his praise for these ancient "mothers of Israel" who "guarded their homes, who attended to the morals of their children, who watched over the domestic hearth, who held up the standard of purity and charity," while their husbands were (literally) slaving away, Geiger might have been describing good German women.[27]

Geiger's most revealing identification of modern virtue in an ancient heroine appears in his portrayal of Deborah: "And again a beautiful figure rises before us, Deborah the prophetess and Judge, a brave and courageous woman, an enthusiastic leader, and yet fully conscious of her womanhood." When Israel was commanded to fight the Canaanites, Deborah did "not want to go into battle, amazon-like . . . But since he [Israel's general, Barak] will not undertake to fight without her, she consents to go with him and gain the victory."[28] In the biblical account of this exchange (Judges 4:8–9), Deborah hardly seems to be as diffident as Geiger would have us believe. When Barak asks that she accompany him to battle, Deborah responds rather brazenly, "I will surely go with thee; notwithstanding that the journey thou takest shall not be for thine honor; for the Lord shall sell Sisera into the hand of a woman." There is little hint of the concern for Barak's honor with which Geiger credited Deborah.

As recent historians have pointed out, the life course of acculturating Jewish women in Germany and western Europe was shaped more by the bourgeois feminine ideals reflected in Geiger's description of Deborah than by the Natural Law logic of inclusion and equality in public life. Even as Reformers found much success in the creation of more decorous and impressive synagogue services, the synagogue lost its accustomed primacy in the lives of many acculturating Jewish men. Although the new accessibility of social and economic opportunities in the secular world often distracted men from their traditional religious roles in the synagogue, women, who were still limited in their access to public space, developed their own responses to the new circumstances and expectations of modernity while remaining within the traditional framework of female Jewish life and observance. Recent historians of European Jewish women's experience in the era of emancipation emphasize that as the synagogue declined in importance in the lives of acculturating Jews, the domestic sphere overseen by Jewish wives and mothers became increasingly important as the primary locus of adjustment to non-Jewish society.[29]

In the context of acculturation, the emphasis on domestic religiosity among upwardly mobile Jews demanded more than merely updating traditional Jewish domesticity. In a society that invested middle-class women with responsibility for familial piety and devotion, the female stewards of domestic Judaism legitimated their own roles as women and helped to promote Judaism as a religion of bourgeois respectability. German middle-class society looked to women as moral exemplars and as the primary teachers of religious values. Paula Hyman has pointed out that the assignment of these particular identities to women found little grounding in traditional Jewish texts or experience. It was, however, from within the familiar (if redefined) sphere of the home that German Jewish women were able to connect their families to the emerging bourgeois values of *Bildung* (the acquisition of culture through education) and domesticity.[30] Consequently, the valorization of the home as a sacred site of religious expression legitimated the continuation of traditional observance by acculturated Jewish women and may have reduced the pressure on Jewish leaders to effect the sort of drastic reforms in public worship called for by Einhorn. Still, despite its apparent validation by bourgeois culture, a domesticated piety that seemed too Jewish, too governed by the minutiae of Jewish observance, remained an object of ambivalence and often disdain.

In emphasizing the need to make women active agents in the synagogue, David Einhorn's charge to the Breslau Rabbinical Assembly included a surprising dismissal of domestic Judaism. In arguing against the idea that women should be exempted from time-designated rituals, and thus from the obligations (and rights) of public worship, Einhorn expressed incredulity that this Talmudic exemption could be based on the urgency of women's domestic responsibilities. "If anybody should get this dispensation," he wrote, "it should be they [in other words, men] whose duties in supporting their families are indeed more pressing and time-consuming than the domestic duties of women."[31] Einhorn's depreciation of women's domestic vocation clashed with romantic evocations of women's holy role in creating virtuous households.

As in Einhorn's report, celebration of a Jewish bourgeois domestic ideal often succumbed to competing practical realities. While some husbands may have depended on their wives to create sanctuaries of bourgeois respectability within their homes, they often had little patience for the specific details of Jewish domestic practice. Even some of the examples cited as evidence for the continuity of home-based female religiosity testify to male repudiation of home observances. The women whom Marion Kaplan describes as resisting "the complete abandonment of their religious heritage" often did so in spite of husbands who rejected these religious practices. One woman quoted by Kaplan recalled that her mother strictly observed Yom Kippur with fasting and prayer, even as her father "found it easier to fast after a hearty breakfast."[32]

Shulamit Magnus's study of the life of memoirist Pauline Wengeroff illuminates the fragility of one observant woman's power to sustain a traditional household. Although Wengeroff struggled with the implications of the Haskalah as it emerged in Russia, her life poignantly reveals the painful tension between tradition and modernity endured by many Jewish women in acculturating milieus. Wengeroff, who was born in 1833, lived in Kovno and St. Petersburg, and died in Minsk, recorded her life story in a cultivated German. She grew up amid a rich and fondly remembered religious culture. After her marriage, however, she found that despite her own commitment to tradition, her husband, in his quest for assimilation, barred the observance of Jewish ritual in their home. From Wengeroff's account, Magnus concludes that the bourgeois world, to which Wengeroff's husband aspired, assigned women to the domestic sphere, but gave them little control over it: "Women were to be contained in homes whose course they could not set."[33] Wengeroff's example and the fragmented style of observance among those who did maintain their connection with tradition suggest that while observance of domestic Jewish culture continued among modernizing Jews, it often did so in new forms and under great pressure. For many, observance of the rituals that created a distinctively Jewish mode of domesticity yielded to a more homogenized, blander package of bourgeois piety and respectability.

The Persistence of Conservatism

The bourgeois domesticity cultivated by so many acculturating nineteenth-century European Jews left women like Pauline Wengeroff grasping for a meaningful connection to Jewish identity. Still, though a general breakdown in the structures and rhythms of Jewish community challenged the perpetuation of Judaism as a self-contained religious culture in nineteenth-century western and central Europe, the persistence of traditional communal institutions continued to shape evolving notions of female Jewish religiosity, even among acculturating Jews. The model of the organized local community *(Gemeinde)* among German Jews powerfully influenced popular modes of Jewish observance in the German states. With the beginning of emancipation, the local *Gemeinde* rapidly lost the authority it had derived from state sanction and the traditional commitments of its members, but the communal institutions overseen by the *Gemeinde* still retained their centrality in framing Jewish observance.

In a drawn-out and often regressive legal process that began early in the nineteenth century, the German Jewish community lost its political character and, consequently, its compulsory nature.[34] By the 1860s Jews in some German cities were free to refuse to associate with their local communities and their rights of residence were no longer restricted. (General emancipation was not finally achieved until German unification in 1871 under Bismarck.) In many cities Jews were free to choose whether they wanted to support the community or not, and they often had a choice of whether their synagogue would be Reform or Orthodox.[35] Many Jews found that, for the first time, they could choose whether or not they wanted to order their lives according to the strictures of Jewish community and ritual observance.

These circumstances could potentially have resulted in a situation akin to that in the United States, where acculturating Jews, supported eventually by Reform leaders, were able to reframe Judaism in the absence of those institutions that enabled a halakhically Jewish way of life. In contrast to the acculturated status of most mid-nineteenth-century American Jews, however, a significant proportion of Jews in western and central Europe continued to lead traditional Jewish lives well into the nineteenth century. Even in countries that had gone a long way toward acculturation, there was nothing automatic about the advance of social and religious change. Michael Meyer points out that "the majority of German Jewry—especially those in the country-side and of the lower middle class—continued to be observant for an-other half century [after 1792]." Steven Lowenstein likewise notes that the advance of Reform in Germany was far from total or com-plete.[36] Similarly, Jay Berkovitz and Paula Hyman observe that through much of the nineteenth century, the majority of Alsatian Jewry maintained a traditional way of life.[37]

Thus, despite the widespread decline of communal authority, the impact of disaffiliation and radical reform was limited by the resil-iency, persistence, and conservatism of the local Jewish *Gemeinde,* which continued to control the economic resources of the community. To shift the resources of a community away from the control of tradi-tionalists, Reform leaders, generally a small and elitist group, had to win over the majority of the local community. To do this, Reformers were forced to compromise their radicalism. Even when they gained communal authority, as they often did, they still had to meet the needs of those who would not vote for or support a Reform program. Gei-ger often lamented being forced to teach "a program of religious in-struction in which [he did] not believe" to serve a community that could not begin to comprehend his own radical theology.[38]

Robert Liberles points out that after the first swell of institutional success, Reformers began to doubt the viability of a nonobservant *and* voluntary Jewish identity.[39] Even in the many German cities where Reformers held sway in governing local religious and social Jewish institutions, they remained accountable to the needs of the more observant segment of the Jewish population. Reformers were thus often responsible for perpetuating the public institutions of tradi-tional Jewish life that were vital to a woman's strict observance of Ju-daism. Even as individual Jews found it possible to define themselves wholly outside of the Jewish community, communal institutions providing kosher food, ritual baths, and other services remained in place.

Despite an influential Reform movement in Germany that celebrated a creedal Judaism within the narrow bounds of the synagogue and a powerful bourgeois ideology that redefined notions of Jewish domesticity, the traditional institutions of Jewish community and observance remained intact. In France and England, the organization of Jewish life on a national level created a similar conservative dynamic. Even as they hoped to guide their communities toward civil acceptance and acculturation, chief rabbis in both France and England bore the responsibility of serving as national sources of traditional authority. Centralized leadership helped ensure that the institutions governing local communities would support traditionally observant versions of Jewish practice and ritual. Thus, while socio-economic and ideological transformations posed radical challenges to the traditional Jewish way of life throughout the world, the impact of these changes in European Jewish communities was mediated by the continued legitimacy of traditional institutions.

Implications for the Creation of an American Jewish Community

Traditional constraints on female Jewish religious expression did concern European Jewish leaders, especially German Reform rabbis.[40] German Reformers explicitly identified common innovations, such as confirmation services, regular sermons, and the use of German language in the service, as being offered to meet the needs of female worshipers. These efforts appear to have been matched by an increase in women's synagogue attendance. Still, despite these significant adjustments, it was only in the United States that public Jewish worship was structurally reconfigured to accommodate women's presence. Cultural tensions over appropriate religious identities for Jewish women, which found expression in both European and American settings, ultimately marked acculturating American synagogues far more than their European counterparts.

The most significant factor shaping the different avenues of acculturation traveled by European and American Jewish women seems to have been the inability of the American Jewish community to create institutions strong enough to frame a vital and observant Jewish domestic life. Compared to the embattled but venerable institutions of traditional communal life in even acculturated European Jewish communities, those that existed in the United States were weakly rooted. The 2,000 to 3,000 Jews who settled in North America in the eighteenth century and the 150,000 to 200,000 mainly central European Jews who arrived between 1820 and 1880 organized themselves into meaningful communities by establishing the necessary structures of Jewish communal life. Most nascent Jewish communities sought to secure cemeteries, create congregations, hire *shochetim* (ritual slaughterers), and build *mikvaot* (ritual baths necessary to fulfilling the laws of marital purity). The need to quickly secure a Jewish burial ground sparked the organization of many communities, and many early synagogue founders understood that creating a public religious institution helped to establish Jewish claims upon American identity. Yet communities were often slow or neglectful in building *mikvaot,* and the work of *shochetim* was open to constant question. If building synagogues added luster to Jewish public identity, the perpetuation of Jewish domestic practice only seemed to emphasize Jewish estrangement from the broader culture. In a society that seemed authentically open to Jewish civil and social equality, acculturating American Jews were not interested in creating a closed Jewish society so that they could follow their own exclusive customs and calendar. In many cities, communally run efforts to ensure kashrut and marital purity quickly dissipated with the first attempts at religious reform.

In these communities or in areas where Jews were few or not well organized, individuals did often find ways to observe the laws of kashrut and marital purity on their own. Without effective community sanction and support, however, such observances were only isolated individual acts rather than an expression of a collective religiosity. Lacking community-supported access to the basic observances of Jewish domesticity, an acculturated woman in the United States might preserve a memory or notion of traditional religiosity, but it is unlikely that she would see the observant lifestyle of a traditional Jewish woman as a realistic option or relevant pattern for her own life. In comparison, the sustained vitality of European communal institutions could preserve structures and expectations that made a traditionally defined collective female Jewish life possible and meaningful, even to those who had little use for traditional models of Jewish life. An acculturated German Jewish woman might not live an observant Jewish life, but continued access to a traditional religious communal framework would still shape her concept of what it meant to be a Jewish woman. Although they may not have chosen an observant lifestyle, European Jewish women knew and understood the ideal pattern of traditional female piety. As a result, there was less need within European Jewish communities to create alternative models for the expression of Jewish female religiosity.

Another critical difference between European and American synagogue communities was the extent to which congregations were willing to modify the practice and organization of Jewish worship.[41] German Reform leaders often called for radical revisions of Jewish ritual behavior and belief, whereas their American counterparts were less known for theological radicalism. In practice, however, German Reform congregations displayed tamer reforms of traditional worship than those introduced in American congregations. For a variety of reasons, including a lack of U.S. governmental interference in religion and the need of American synagogues for dues-paying members, American Reformers were able to push Jewish practice in directions that challenged many of the essential markers of Jewish ritual. Many American Reform congregations told male worshipers to remove their head coverings, introduced Sunday services to replace Saturday Sabbath worship as the week's primary religious service, and sat women next to men in the sanctuary of the synagogue. Whether or not these reforms found broad or permanent acceptance within American Judaism, they pushed American Jews to reframe their notions of what it was that made Jewish worship Jewish.

An 1898 article by Rosa Sonneschein, founder and editor of the short-lived magazine *American Jewess,* highlights the essential factors that defined the religious lives of acculturated Jewish women in America and separated them from the experience of European Jewish women. Sonneschein saw American Jewish women as cut off from the forms of Jewish identity that had shaped their mothers' lives. She pointed to "the destruction of belief in religious ceremonials" among American Jewish women. "The dietary laws were the first to succumb," she noted, and "with them disappeared other religious ceremonies in the home, of which Jewish women were the sacred keepers and safeguards from time immemorial."[42] Sonneschein's claim that the American Jewish woman of 1898 had "utterly discarded her religious mission in the home" may have been exaggerated, but she seemed certain that among her acculturated female readers, the rituals of a specifically Jewish domesticity were little more than hazy memories.

Sonneschein believed that American Jewish leaders widened the gulf separating the religious world of American Jewish women from the traditional world of their mothers by devaluing customs that had long been at the core of female Jewish religiosity: "The pulpit pointed out to the Jewess' mind as religious contradiction almost everything upon which her mother looked with reverence." The religious identity of her acculturated audience was dependent, not upon the domestic rituals and customs of their European forebears, but upon their contributions to the public world of American Judaism. According to Sonneschein, "the American Jewess is an important element in congregational life." Moreover, "the spacious and luxurious temples would be almost empty without her." Indeed, American Judaism depended on woman's contributions: "She furthers by word and deed the material and spiritual progress of the Synagogue, and is most remarkable for her devotion and ardent labors in the sphere of charity." As Sonneschein's comment suggests, for many acculturated Jewish women in the United States, the observance of a respectable Judaism within the synagogue and the practice of benevolence outside it had displaced the customs that had long been at the core of female Jewish religiosity.

Posttraditional Jewish communities in both the Old and New Worlds were challenged to formulate religious identities for women that would meet the expectations of the non-Jewish societies in which they lived. Women's marginalization within public worship constituted one of the most obvious manifestations of Judaism's resistance to such expectations in both American and European synagogues. In the United States, however, a society that especially celebrated both female piety and the centrality of the church to civic and religious life, Jews felt more pressure to respond to modernity's implicit critique of traditional Jewish constraints on women's religious expression. It was thus only in the United States that the need to address the question of appropriate roles for Jewish women resulted in the structural reconfiguration of the synagogue, remaining a constant dynamic in the evolution of American Judaism.

Even as America seemed to embrace Jews and their religion, the religious life of traditional Jewish women could not be readily adapted to the expectations of American society. As American Jews focused on shaping the synagogue into an American institution and Judaism into an American religion, Jewish men and women set out to develop a public female religious identity that would comport with their experience and understanding of American life.

CHAPTER TWO

Women's Emergence in the Early American Synagogue Community

American synagogue architecture offers a compelling physical record of the evolution of American Jewish female religious identity. Nineteenth-century Reformers consciously reshaped the synagogue through the introduction of mixed choirs and family pews in an attempt to align Judaism with the different, but equally rigid, gender assumptions of American religion. Even earlier, however, Jewish communities seeking simply to create synagogues according to traditional models had already redesigned the space assigned to women in the synagogues of the colonial and early national period. In their departure from European models, the women's galleries that graced many early American synagogues represented the first of many transformations occasioned by a desire to accommodate an American social reality that questioned the apparent subordination of female congregants.

Finding a Place for Women in European Synagogues

It is not clear whether any provision was made for women's attendance at worship services in European synagogues before the fourteenth century. Numerous synagogues built in the early Middle Ages had women's annexes added on in subsequent centuries. The two oldest surviving European synagogues, in Worms (built in 1175) and

Prague (dating from the thirteenth or fourteenth century), both exhibit women's sections that were only later added as adjoining annexes. In Worms, the annex was added at a right angle to the original structure in 1213. The Altneuschul in Prague did not gain its women's annex until 1732.[1] A women's section was added to Speyer's eleventh-century structure in the fourteenth century.[2] And in Frankfurt a room for female worshipers was built in the courtyard of the community's 1461 synagogue in 1603.[3]

Carol Krinsky observes that when synagogues did begin to include separate spaces for women, these spaces were often added as an afterthought, placed in whatever spare peripheral space adjoined the main, male-populated sanctuary. Improvised women's sections might have appeared in an extra room or aisle.[4] In the TaZ Synagogue in Lvov, Poland, built in 1582, it appears that a women's gallery was simply built into the original side wall of the building.[5] These sections may have been airless rooms overlooking the synagogue, connected by narrow windows or divided by thick walls from the main sanctuary. In some synagogues in the south of France, the women's section was underneath the floor of the sanctuary. Women in these sections could glimpse the main proceedings through grilled windows placed at foot level of the male worshipers.[6]

The lack of provision for women in the earliest synagogues may mean that women simply did not attend worship services. Alternatively, one could speculate that in early medieval synagogues women were in attendance but were not separated from men.[7] In some synagogues, curtains may have been used to create a women's section, not necessarily for use during worship, but for women who came to the synagogue to hear the sermons that were occasionally delivered on the Sabbath after the morning service.[8]

In some places, it seems that the women's section (often referred to as the *weiberschul,* or women's synagogue), with its thick walls separating women from the men's service, left women with their own almost autonomous sanctuary. One observer in eighteenth-century Provence reported that "below the synagogues in these communities there are synagogues for women, and there are holes in the floor of the synagogues through which the women see the Torah scrolls. They have their own cantor, a man who recites the prayers for them in French." Similarly, a Christian visitor to the Avignon synagogue in 1599 described how a blind rabbi preached to women gathered in the synagogue basement.[9] Elsewhere, particularly in eastern European synagogues, a woman known as a *vorsangerin* would follow the men's service and guide those in the gallery or women's section through the liturgy.[10] In 1897 Israel Abrahams took note of the thirteenth-century epitaph of Urania of Worms, which recalled how "she . . . with sweet tunefulness, officiated before the female worshippers to whom she sang the hymnal portions."[11]

In a pattern that would be repeated in American synagogues, the general evolution of architectural design in the postmedieval European synagogue intersected with the growing incorporation of women's presence. In seventeenth-century Amsterdam, Jewish synagogues, built as significant public edifices and designed by non-Jewish architects, displayed more regularized plans than earlier synagogues. The new design incorporated the classical pattern of galleried basilicas characteristic of churches of the Protestant Reformation in northern Europe.[12] Rather than trying to accommodate women only after the synagogue was built, the Christian architects of these buildings integrated galleries for women into the synagogue design and thus avoided the creation of often asymmetrical and awkward screened-off spaces that might block windows or entrances.[13] These integrated galleries overlooked the synagogue, though screens and grilles blocked men's view of the gallery's female denizens.

The first known lateral women's gallery appeared in a synagogue built for Amsterdam's Sephardic Portuguese congregation in 1639. This pattern was replicated on a grander scale in a building dedicated by the same congregation in 1675 and was soon echoed by the 1701 synagogue of London's Sephardim. The new style may have been one expression of the willingness of this relatively acculturated and cosmopolitan group to assimilate designs associated with Christian worship. Although the innovation spread most rapidly to other Sephardic congregations, the integrated women's gallery soon became a regular feature of European synagogue design.[14] Krinsky notes that by the mid-seventeenth century, both the Spanish and the German synagogues of Venice sported oval balconies to accommodate female worshipers.[15]

The American Ladies' Gallery

There is little evidence regarding separation of the sexes in the earliest American Jewish congregational gatherings, which were held in private houses or rented rooms. More information can be gleaned from the era in which Jews began to create religious spaces of their own—from the synagogue buildings themselves or from contemporary descriptions, often recorded in conjunction with the consecration of new synagogues. Given the limited presence of women in historical sources concerning colonial American Jews, an examination of the space assigned to female worshipers in the earliest American synagogues provides valuable clues to the religious lives of Jewish women in colonial America.[16]

The first North American edifice built explicitly as a synagogue was erected in 1730 by the Sephardic congregation Shearith Israel in New York City. It provided a gallery for women, described by a visiting Christian minister from Brookline, Massachusetts, in 1812, who noted, "The women are in the gallery, which has a breast-work as high as their chins."[17] As reports of numerous Christian visitors and press correspondents demonstrate, the separation of women in the Jewish synagogue as well as the barriers erected in front of them seemed worthy of comment to contemporary non-Jewish observers.

Separate seating within a religious setting was certainly not unknown to American Christians. "Men's sides" and "women's sides" were familiar aspects of colonial meetinghouses in New England and elsewhere in the English colonies. Mixed seating did not become common in New England churches until the mid-eighteenth century, and many denominations retained separate sections for men and women long after that.[18] In the non-Jewish cases, however, both sexes, though segregated, were seated together on the same level. The balcony and less desirable rear seats were reserved for those of lower status such as college students, teenage boys, indentured servants, black slaves, native Americans, and the town poor.[19]

Many synagogue visitors evidently found something disreputable in the apparent relegation of women to what they perceived as a subordinate religious space. Alexander Hamilton, a Scottish physician from Annapolis who visited Shearith Israel's Mill Street Synagogue in 1744, noted that the women, "of whom some were very pritty, stood up in the gallery like a hen coop."[20] Although Shearith Israel members may have wanted outsiders to take note of their community, this was probably not the sort of comment they sought. Synagogue members would have been troubled by the impression that the synagogue's treatment of women left on those who visited their worship.

Concern for respectability and acceptance was powerfully displayed in the building of the second synagogue in North America in Newport, Rhode Island, which was dedicated in 1763. This concern found expression not only in the design of the building's facade and sanctuary but also in its interpretation of the traditional women's gallery. For their synagogue the Jews of Newport called upon Peter Harrison, the first professional architect in the New World, who, in addition to having designed the most prominent contemporary buildings in Newport, was also the architect of Christ Church (1760) in Cambridge, Massachusetts, and King's Chapel (1754) in Boston.[21]

An account of the synagogue's dedication in the *Newport Mercury* described "an Edifice the most perfect of the Temple kind perhaps in America" and reported that "the Order and Decorum, the Harmony and Solemnity of the Musick, together with a handsome Assembly of People . . . could not but raise in the mind a faint Idea of the Majesty and Grandeur of the ancient Jewish Worship mentioned in the Scripture."[22] In keeping with Jewish custom, the Newport synagogue provided separate spaces for women and men. The gallery could only be reached through a stairway in the annex attached to the synagogue building's north side.[23] Reverend Ezra Stiles, the future president of Yale University, who attended the consecration, recorded that "a Gallery for the Women runs round the whole inside except [the] East End." He further noted that "the height of the Balustrade which runs around the Gallery" was equal to "the Depth of the Corinthian Pedestal" on the columns that ascended from the balcony to support the ceiling.[24] As can be seen in the building, now called the Touro Synagogue, which still stands in Newport, the height of the column pedestals and the balustrade railing is one that could easily be leaned over from a sitting position. From an aesthetic point of view, the open balustrade of the women's gallery matched the balustrade that surrounded the central reader's table, as well as the small enclosure around the ark. It is quite striking that, in contrast to Shearith Israel's Mill Street Synagogue, where the closed front of the women's gallery reached up to the chins of its denizens, Peter Harrison and the Jews of Newport decided to provide an open balcony for female worshipers.

The practical effects of this change may have been limited. Although the balustrade in the Newport synagogue was low, the gallery benches ran along the wall, about six feet away from the gallery front. According to Jacob Marcus, "It is not likely the women could be seen very well or could themselves see very much, since the bench they occupied was set back against the wall."[25] Still, this innovation certainly represented a departure from contemporaneous examples of European synagogue architecture.

It was in Amsterdam that the galleried hall of Reformation churches was first adapted to the needs of the synagogue by reserving at least part of the gallery for women. In the Sephardic synagogue built in 1639, as depicted in an engraving from the 1650s, the front of the balcony was blocked by a grillwork extending from the base of the otherwise open balustrade, past the balustrade railing, and up to the ceiling.[26]

Significantly, the two Sephardic synagogues most often identified as the likely models for the interior design of the Newport synagogue and other early American synagogues both carefully delineate the women's space with a distinct physical barrier.[27] At the new Portuguese Synagogue built by Amsterdam's Sephardic community in 1671–1675 and at London's Spanish and Portuguese Jews' Congregation, known as Bevis Marks, opened in 1701, women's galleries were integrated spatially and architecturally into the main sanctuary. In no sense do these balconies constitute separate or possibly autonomous sections of the synagogue. These areas appear much less cagelike than the women's sections of previous and contemporaneous synagogues, but the balconies of both these leading Sephardic synagogues of northern Europe were still screened by barriers of diagonal latticework.

As architectural historian Rachel Wischnitzer has observed, these seventeenth-century synagogues "made considerable headway . . . particularly with respect to more dignified accommodations for women worshipers."[28] Unlike the women's annexes of the past, the galleries in the Sephardic synagogues of Amsterdam and London afforded their female occupants a clear view of the sanctuary below. One twentieth-century visitor to the Amsterdam building (concerned, no doubt, that people might consider separate women's galleries discriminatory) was careful to point out that "the balconies, one in either aisle and across the west wall, permit the women-folk full and clear access to the service."[29] In other synagogues built on the Amsterdam model, the galleries retained distinct physical barriers. The presence of a lattice, screen, or grille defined the synagogue space reserved for European Jewish women of this period. As seen in Newport, early American synagogues did much more to open up the space around female worshipers, thus bringing new recognition to their presence in the congregation.

The screened-off women's gallery, which was never questioned in European synagogues before the advent of Reform ideology, quickly began to seem out of place in the American environment.[30] Subsequent early American synagogues, following the Newport example, also provided open galleries for women. A period painting of Charleston's 1794 Beth Elohim synagogue shows a low-fronted balcony with pillars from balcony to ceiling that seems to duplicate the plan of the men's seating area below, which is aligned along the side walls and marked by pillars from floor to balcony.[31] After the synagogue burned down in 1838 and a new one was dedicated in 1841, one observer noted that the "handsomely finished balustrade" of the

Interior of Bevis Marks Synagogue, London, dedicated 1701. Detail of watercolor by I. M. Belisario, ca. 1817. Courtesy of Spanish and Portuguese Jews' Congregation, London.

women's gallery was "much better adapted to our warm climate" than the closed paneling of the earlier building. Moreover, he pointed out, the new design "adds greatly to the harmony and beauty of the whole building."[32]

Although the open galleries of early American synagogues were a significant innovation in synagogue design, they may not have done much to change women's experience of synagogue worship. In Newport, as mentioned, benches positioned women against the wall of the building, about six feet from the balustrade. In the 1794 Charleston synagogue, as seen in a nineteenth-century engraving, the balcony appears to hang directly over a parallel alignment of benches for men on the main floor of the sanctuary. Although it is difficult to determine from the engraving, this suggests that it may have been possible

View of central reader's desk and open women's gallery, Touro Synagogue, Newport, Rhode Island, dedicated 1763. Courtesy of Society of Friends of Touro Synagogue and the American Jewish Archives.

to open up the forward and downward view of female worshipers without imposing their presence on male worshipers, at least when they were seated. During the many standing parts of the service, however, men and women would certainly have been able to see each other, unless the women stood with their backs against the wall (certainly not the practice at today's Orthodox services at Touro Synagogue in Newport).

The Mikveh Israel congregation of Philadelphia built a small synagogue on Cherry Alley in 1782. No pictures of this building survive, but instructions to the synagogue's builders explicitly detail provisions for a lady's gallery on three sides of the building. The seating was to consist in the "front part of the gallery" of "three plain rows of seats," with "two Rows of Seats in the sides, for the women, with a narrow strip of board to rest the back against." The instructions called for "the fronts of the galleries to be panneled, and have proper caping," but there are no clues as to how high the panels were to be. Elsewhere, for instance in noting the size of the reader's platform ("to be nine feet six inches, by seven feet nine inches"), quite precise measurements were given.[33] It seems likely that the builders were left to construct the height of the balcony railing according to their own concept of what a balcony should be. An engraving of Mikveh Israel's second synagogue, built in 1825, shows fashionably bonneted women quite in evidence, leaning over the gallery railing to follow the action below (see illustration on p. 53). In this case, where the male and female seats were arrayed in semicircles along the north and south sides of the building, it appears that men seated below would have had to be aware of the women seated in the recessed semicircle of the gallery on the opposite side of the building.[34]

In 1818, Shearith Israel, the oldest Jewish congregation in the New World and at that time still the only synagogue in New York City, dedicated a new edifice on the same site as their 1730 building. In planning for the new building there was some discussion over a resolution offered to the congregation's governing board that "the front of the Gallery be open work." A Mr. Levy dissented from this proposal and asked for a "close front Gallery."[35] Despite Levy's objections, the rest of the board determined to adopt what now seemed the American pattern of open galleries. Ultimately, the gallery was adorned by a "handsome, planed turned mahogany banister," apparently in keeping with the design of the rest of the sanctuary.[36]

The significance of this choice by Shearith Israel is highlighted by the design of a contemporaneous Reform synagogue in Hamburg, Germany. The Hamburg Temple, dedicated on October 18, 1818, provided 142 seats for men on a ground floor and 107 seats for women in a balcony unblocked by a partition.[37] Hamburg's accommodation for female worshipers was thus almost identical to that provided in New York (43 percent of Hamburg's seats were for women, compared to 44 percent at Shearith Israel).[38] The Hamburg Temple, however, was the creation of about one hundred young Jewish families whose intent was far removed from that of the New Yorkers. Simply by designating their institution a "temple," referring back to the destroyed Temples in Jerusalem, the German Reformers implied, as did their liturgy, that they looked forward to no greater redemption than the one they had found in Hamburg.[39] In this way, the temple's founders intended to set themselves apart from traditional Judaism, which looked forward to a future messianic redemption and the Temple rebuilt in Jerusalem. The Hamburg Temple's opening occasioned great controversy, as numerous traditional authorities condemned the congregation's use of an organ and its use of the vernacular in its prayer service. Conservative critics especially rejected the Reform liturgy of the Hamburg Temple's prayer book, which, among other innovations, omitted prayers for a messianic return to Zion. Likewise, the absence of a barrier in front of the congregation's women clearly distinguished the temple's arrangements from those of traditional synagogues. In particular, the open gallery was a nonverbal declaration by which the Reformers separated themselves from the traditional Jewish treatment of women and signaled their determination to end the subordination of women in the space of public prayer. Observers noted that the Hamburg Temple drew more women to services than did traditional synagogues.[40]

Unlike their contemporaries in Hamburg, the leaders of New York's Shearith Israel, conscious of their congregation's status as the leading and oldest synagogue in the United States, sought only to create an exemplary space for traditional Jewish worship. At that time, the possibility of a systematic reform of Judaism had not even been suggested in the New World.[41] The changed configuration of the women's gallery at Shearith Israel and other American synagogues had nothing to do with ideology. With the exception of Levy's dissent at Shearith Israel, the new design seemed to be quickly and quietly accepted wherever it was introduced, without much attention and without any accompanying rationale for the change. It appears that this innovation, in synagogues where the interior design was otherwise consistent with traditional arrangements for Jewish worship, represented an unspoken adjustment to new expectations in the American setting.

Outside the United States, synagogue designers were more constrained in their ability to adjust the physical space of traditional Jewish practice to emerging contemporary attitudes toward women. When the New Synagogue was dedicated at Great St. Helen's in London in 1838, a journalist observed that "on ordinary occasions the daughters of Zion are kept out of view, in the Asiatic fashion." At the New Synagogue, however, "the ingenuity of the architect has contrived a handsome screen, so tastefully perforated that the fair sex could see clearly all that was passing below, and at the same time those below could easily discover that the Jewish females of our time might vie with those so much admired in ancient times."[42] The design of the New Synagogue's gallery suggests that Jews in London, like Jews in New York, sensed that the barriers imposed between women and the conduct of public worship in traditional synagogues were better suited to the Orient than to the enlightened Occident. At the New Synagogue, however, awareness that the traditional women's gallery might prove an objectionable inconvenience to the "fair sex" resulted only in a more artfully contrived barrier. This London example again highlights the comparative ease with which American Jews addressed the problematic design of traditional women's galleries.

What led American synagogues to dispense with the traditional balcony partition screen? Written evidence on this point is lacking, yet the question demands some consideration. Those early synagogues designed by prominent Christian architects and builders presumably reflected their attempts to translate their ideas of religious space into a Jewish expression. Jewish communities selected designers and designs with an eye to creating edifices that would merit the regard of sophisticated and respectable non-Jews. These architects, of course, could have had only minimal contact with any Jewish religious space; their sense of what was appropriate would have derived mainly from what they were told by the congregations and from what they imagined should be Jewish.

Drawing upon European models, the interior design of all American synagogues built before the mid-nineteenth century displayed the distinctive and requisite features of Jewish worship space. All retained a central *bimah* (reading platform), an ark for the Torah surmounted by a *ner tamid* (eternal light), and a balcony used as a women's gallery. Except for the absence of gallery screens, all of these synagogues otherwise remained quite in keeping with traditional synagogue design. All seated their congregants facing the center along the north and south sides of the eastward-oriented synagogue.[43] All of the early American synagogues sought to maintain the traditional practices and rituals of Judaism. The absence of public discussion or notice concerning the disappearance of the traditional barrier surmounting the balustrade of the women's gallery in American synagogues highlights the contrast with continuing European practice.[44] The lack of controversy suggests that a change that came to seem almost automatic in American communities where Jews were organized and prosperous enough to build synagogues was not the product of any particular ideology.

Given the importance of the synagogue as an edifice that presented a public face for Judaism to the non-Jewish community, early synagogue leaders may have feared that cloistering women in a separate space behind a partition barrier would look barbaric and primitive to non-Jewish observers. Far from the centers of traditional rabbinical authority, American laymen could worry less than their Old World counterparts about the halakhic import of their adjustments of synagogue space. The change, in general, does not appear to have been the result of any grand decision making. Like the subsequent gradual shift away from seating in benches parallel to the side walls of the synagogue, or the seemingly more momentous transfer of the traditionally central *bimah* to the front of the synagogue, the shape of the women's gallery in the American synagogue resulted from a calculation as to what an appropriate American space of worship should look like.

Later in the century, when congregations began to respond to a conscious Reform ideology, part of the urge to appear more attractive and up-to-date was a function of the need to compete with other local congregations for members among a city's unaffiliated Jews. The opening up of the woman's gallery in most cities, however, preceded the advent of multiple Jewish congregations within one community.

When Shearith Israel changed the gallery design of its second synagogue, it was still the only congregation in New York, so the change was not made in the interest of appealing to potential members who might otherwise join other congregations. Still, by 1818 Shearith Israel's design probably would have been influenced by the style of synagogues in other American cities that provided open galleries for members' wives.

The shift to open balconies for women was not a universal development. The Lloyd Street Synagogue of the Baltimore Hebrew Congregation (dedicated in 1845) contained a curious amalgamation of traditional and innovative elements of synagogue structure. Isaac Leeser, the traditionalist editor of the monthly journal the *Occident*, recorded his surprise at finding pews at Lloyd Street rather than "open seats," an arrangement he described as "something unusual in our Synagogues." He also noted that the building contained no central reading platform (one was added in an 1860 renovation), but "merely a reading desk placed close in front of the ark."[45] Although the 1845 building, with its rows of men's seats facing the ark, thus departed significantly from the traditional and familiar synagogue model known to American Jews, its women's gallery was screened with latticework in the traditional fashion. Evidence of this is drawn from a subsequent objection to having the latticework removed.[46]

The reason for this divergence from the open-balcony style may, perhaps, be traced to the unusual presence in Baltimore in the 1840s of an ordained rabbi. Abraham Rice, generally recognized as the first ordained rabbi to arrive in the United States, did not have an easy time in Baltimore. He found that the members of the Baltimore Hebrew Congregation who had hired him were reluctant to follow what seemed to them his strict interpretations of Jewish law. Eventually they rejected his leadership. Still, it is likely that the congregation would have relied upon him for guidance when it came to the design of their synagogue. Thus, the placement of the reading desk and orientation of the seats may have resulted from Rice's judgment that the design, despite its similarity to a typical church sanctuary, did not threaten the halakhic propriety of the proposed worship space. At the same time, Rice may have argued that the halakhic separation of men and women in the synagogue demanded that an additional barrier be placed in front of the gallery.

The Emergence of Women in the American Synagogue

The transformation of the women's gallery in early American synagogues suggests that women's presence in the synagogue was gaining a new significance and meaning. Evidence from the records of early American congregations bears out this supposition. At Shearith Israel's first Mill Street Synagogue in New York, contentious discussions greeted a 1792 resolution proposing that "no unmarried lady except Rachel Pinto [who was almost seventy years old] be allowed to occupy a front seat" in the women's gallery. The resolution was defeated by a close vote of twelve to eleven. A similar resolution proposed in 1800, which would have barred any unmarried woman under the age of forty from a front gallery seat, was also defeated.[47]

These discussions may have been prompted by men in the congregation who were concerned about being distracted from their devotions, or by older folk who did not want to see the synagogue become a forum for flirting, or by married women who complained that young maids should not be allowed to usurp an honor that should come only with advanced age and status. Whatever the reason for the discussions, they reveal the salience of women's presence. Significantly, they also point to the presence of unmarried women in the synagogue. This presence distinguished Shearith Israel from European synagogues, where, according to some sources, no room whatsoever was provided for unmarried women.[48]

Shearith Israel's records suggest that the presence of these unmarried women challenged the community's orderly structure. Most synagogues in both Europe and America could accommodate more worshipers in their main sanctuaries than could fit into their women's galleries. Thus, it was possible to provide seats for schoolboys and presumably for unmarried sons of adult members in the main sanctuary, but not for their female counterparts. Female worshipers quickly outgrew the space allotted to them. At the early Shearith Israel building, demand for the seats originally provided in the gallery soon outran the supply. With New York's growing Jewish population, this shortfall was eventually matched by a shortage of men's seats as well.[49]

As with many adjustments attendant upon the establishment of synagogues in the New World, the need to provide places in the sanc-

tuary for the unmarried daughters of the congregation was unfore-
seen. In 1786 the *parnas* (president) of Shearith Israel informed the
congregation that the "want of proper regulations in the womans
Seats in Synagogue" had already caused "many inconveniences" and
"much Dissatisfaction," and he asked the board of trustees to "adopt
some decisive plan for the immediate regulation of said Seats," so as
to avoid the "Confusion" anticipated for the "ensuing Holy days."[50]
Although a decision was made giving married women first claim upon
the gallery's front row, the anticipated "confusion" still arose when
the three Judah sisters sat in unassigned seats on the second day of
Rosh Hashanah. In response, Miss Mincke Judah was actually sum-
moned to civil court in 1786 (and fined sixpence) for not sitting where
she had been told.[51]

A similar controversy, which occupied Shearith Israel's board
during the summer of 1760, was well documented in the congregation's records and illustrates the level of agitation that could be generated around a young woman's seat in synagogue. Mr. Judah Hays
complained to the board that Mr. Judah Mears had gone "into the
womens Gallary in time of worship last Sabath & turn'd Miss Josse
Hays from the seat, claimed by Miss Mears." Mr. Mears was fined
forty shillings for his indiscretion, and the board attempted to amelio-
rate the situation by lengthening the bench upon which Miss Hays's
mother sat so that Josse might sit next to her. When Mr. Hays still
found this situation unsatisfactory, the congregation threatened to
fine him forty shillings as well, if his daughter did not sit in the seat
that had been assigned to her.[52]

This sort of unrest was not limited to New York. An 1825 letter
from Abraham E. Israel, the *shamas* (caretaker) of Philadelphia's
Mikveh Israel synagogue, to the congregation's president recounts
how during services on the last day of Passover he ascended to the gallery "to inforse the Rules of the Congregation," informing "some Ladies" there that "the front seats cant be occupied by them." To the
Andrews sisters seated in the gallery, he gave specific instructions that
one of them "maight keep the front seat in place of her mother." The
sisters, however, refused to move or even respond to Israel's instructions. When the *shamas* returned to the first floor, he was accosted
by the young women's brother, Mr. Jos. J. Andrews, who not only
rejected Israel's request that he assist in getting one of the sisters
to move out of the front row, but, as Israel recounted, ordered the

shamas "never to go up Again to my sisters or I will Drag you down."[53]

Young women were willing to defy congregational authority in their desire for good seats. The same sort of imperative that had rendered the improvised women's annex obsolete forced congregational leaders to realize that it was no longer possible simply to leave it to women to find their space more or less between the cracks. The limited evidence available to us from early American synagogues suggests a changing pattern in female worship attendance. In 1825, for instance, Philadelphia's Rebecca Gratz wrote to her brother, "We all go [to the new Mikveh Israel synagogue] Friday evening as well as on Saturday morning—the gallery is as well filled as the other portion of the house."[54] Out of necessity, then, American congregations began to attend to a new constituency, whose needs had received little consideration in the original structuring of their communities.

Although the change in the nature of gallery barriers, along with the fact that any attention was paid to where individual women sat,

Undated interior view of Philadelphia's Mikveh Israel sanctuary (dedicated in 1825) with Torah procession and open balcony. From American Sunday School Union, *The Jew at Home and Abroad* (Philadelphia, 1845).

suggests that women's position in the synagogue was gaining greater importance, there was no noticeable alteration in women's religious practice in the traditional American synagogue. The prayer service continued to be the realm of men who served as its leaders, who monopolized all honors associated with it, and whose presence was required daily. Women may have attended, but apart from frequent requests for decorum among the ladies as well as among the men, their presence was still marginal to the congregation as a worship community.[55]

Members' Wives and Entire Strangers

The seventeenth-century bylaws of London's Spanish and Portuguese Jews' Congregation decreed that men's seats were to be assigned by the congregation's governing board, but that "the ladies shall sit in the synagogue in those [places] which they may find when they go to it."[56] Similarly, most synagogues in New York before 1860 did not bother assigning seats to women.[57] Yet, as experience at Shearith Israel demonstrated, Jewish women in New York cared too much about where they sat to be left to their own devices. Ultimately, the formal categories for inclusion in synagogue life had to be expanded.

Regulations for seat distribution in early American synagogues provided for the assignment of seats through sale or rent on an individual basis, as a means, in part, of garnering income. In a few congregations women's seats could be purchased separately. Shearith Israel's records document both widows and unmarried women paying for their own seats individually without any corresponding gentleman's seat.[58] At Mikveh Israel in Philadelphia, a listing of separate purchase and rental prices for seats "downstairs" and seats "upstairs" indicates that women's seats could be purchased separately from men's (at one-half the purchase price and less than one-quarter the yearly rent charged to men).[59] In most congregations, however, as indicated on a form for registering seat purchases at Philadelphia's Rodeph Shalom congregation in 1849, men's and women's seats were sold two at a time as one unit:

> It is hereby Certified that _____ has purchased a Seat in the Juliane Street Synagogue situated between Wood and Callowhill Street of the Germ. Hebr. cong. Rodef Sholem, to wit Male and Female Seats _____ in Class _____ and paid for the same the sum of _____ dollars.[60]

One's place in an American synagogue was not an automatic right assumed simply by virtue of one's birth or residence in the community, as had been the case in Europe. In the United States, synagogue membership was a privilege purchased, for the most part, by men. Thus, a wife's relationship to the congregation existed through her husband, and a child's through his or her father. These relationships did bring some specific privileges. For instance, family members of a synagogue member (in addition to wives, this generally included sons up to the age of eighteen or twenty-one and daughters until they were married) were guaranteed places in the congregation's burial ground.[61]

This system worked smoothly as long as anyone who was not an adult male was able to subsume his or her identity into that of someone who was. Early American synagogues, however, structured around the purchase of seats and rigid categories of membership, often proved unable to respond to circumstances that arose in the lives of individual Jews. Not all women were wives, and not all unmarried women lived with their fathers. How were these women to fit into the community? Presumably, arrangements were made for those who lacked the proper relationships so that they could acquire seats in a normal way, but independent individuals (especially women) and children who remained unmarried complicated the smooth working of seat assignments.

The rigidity of this system could affect men as well as women. Although congregations wanted single young men to become members, those same young men may not have wanted to incur the expense of a woman's seat for which they had no use. In 1849, a Cincinnati congregation discussed whether "a Gentm. [seat] with out a Ladies Seat can not be disposed of by itself."[62] In most communities, purchase of a seat required the acquisition of both a man's and a woman's place. Thus, difficulties could also arise for fathers who wanted to find seats for unmarried sons. At the Baltimore Hebrew Congregation, for instance, a Mr. L. Rosenstock purchased a seat in 1852 for his son, with the understanding that it would not be attached to the lady's seat that automatically came with it. Things apparently did not go according to plan, however, for Rosenstock had to make special petitions to the board of the congregation so that he could avoid paying for a gallery seat for which he had no use: "Mr. L. Rosenstock stated that the former Board rented out the Ladies seat of his son to Mr. H. Rosenthal for $4.75 but as Mr. Rosenthal refused to take the seat,

Mr. Rosenstock believes himself entitled to deduct this sum from the dues of his son." The board did subsequently vote to reimburse the $4.75.[63]

There may have been many unmarried adult women who chose not to belong to the synagogue community at all.[64] Nevertheless, many single women successfully found places for themselves in their local congregations and even appeared as regular contributors to synagogue fund-raising efforts. The unmarried women who formed the core of the powerful network of nineteenth-century Jewish women's philanthropy in Philadelphia—Rebecca Gratz, Louisa B. Hart, Ellen and Emily Phillips, and Simha Peixotto—were able, as members of the Mikveh Israel community, to maintain their own seats in the synagogue. At Congregation Beth Shalome in Richmond, Virginia, records report the regular contributions of five different Miss Meyerses, three of whom together ("the Misses Meyers") contributed $25 in the fourth quarter of 1868.[65]

Although some single women found places for themselves within their congregations, it was not easy for synagogues to adjust to the needs of individuals who did not fit conventional categories. An 1847 regulation at New York's Shearith Israel, for instance, decreed that a married woman could rent a seat only if her husband occupied a seat in the synagogue's men's section. At Philadelphia's Rodeph Shalom in 1850, a request by a Mrs. Cohen to rent a seat "was unanimously refused, her husband being a Member of an other Congregation."[66] In Cincinnati, when the former Mrs. Shonhaus married Moses Trounstine, the B'nai Yeshurun board informed Mr. Trounstine that he must either send in his own "petition for membership" or else "sell the pew owned by his wife in the Synagogue."[67] As illustrated in these cases, congregational boards found it difficult to accommodate women who did not fit within male-centered membership categories.

Even widows challenged American Jewish congregations. When a woman's husband died, she, whose identity had been encompassed within that of her spouse, suddenly became an independent entity in the eyes of the congregation and even gained access to the title of "member." But this was mainly for financial purposes. Most congregations allowed widows to pay dues that were one-half those of regular members, and in cases when women claimed hardship, congregations would often remit their dues entirely. Although widows sometimes were recognized as members, they did not carry the rights and privileges of male members. They paid dues, but they did not have the right to vote in congregational affairs. Nor did they gain access to the honors involved in the religious service, such as participation in the Torah reading, which was considered among the most important privileges that synagogues offered their male members. The most important right that widows retained as members of their congregations, along with their seats and possibly schooling for their children, was the right to be buried in the congregation's burial ground.

The conceptual problem involved in understanding the place of women and widows in a synagogue community is illustrated in the records of one Philadelphia congregation. At Rodeph Shalom in the 1840s, as at many congregations, much of the business of the board of trustees was taken up with trying to collect dues from members who were in arrears. After a certain period of nonpayment, each male delinquent would be informed that if payment was not forthcoming, he would forfeit "his right as a Member." It sometimes happened that the board of trustees would become aware of a woman attending services who was contributing nothing to the congregation financially. This was the case with a Mrs. Rosenthal in 1849. The board observed that she was "regularly occupying one seat in this Congregation without permission." Apparently realizing that withdrawing the privileges of membership from such a person would be a meaningless action, since a woman sitting in the women's gallery could neither participate in the worship service nor vote on congregational matters, the board resolved that a woman like Mrs. Rosenthal, a "widow who visit[s] our congregation and [has] not rented a seat in their own name," would henceforth "be considered as a Entire Stranger."[68]

This formulation of "entire stranger," which was never used to threaten men, did not mean the traditional sort of excommunication, which would have banned its target from any social intercourse with members of the Jewish community. Rather, the title seems to have been simply the board's attempt to define their relationship to someone who had some connection (either through her dead husband or by her own presence) to the community, which the trustees now wanted to sever. In this case, by the board's resolution, she was not to occupy a seat unless she paid for it.

Mrs. Rosenthal's case highlights the congregation's inability to incorporate women who did not fit within familiar categories. Like its traditional models, the American synagogue as a place of worship was built around the participation of male congregants. Likewise, the membership organization it was forced to become in the voluntaristic American setting was structured around the regular contribution of dues by its male members. American congregations could not afford to absolve independent women from paying dues, but they were not institutionally prepared to accommodate women as full participants in the community.[69]

Even women who fit securely within communal bounds could still pose challenges to synagogue leaders. When the trustees of Cincinnati's B'nai Yeshurun congregation wanted something from female congregants, they could adopt a coercive tone that was never used when seeking services from male congregants. Thus, when the board wanted women of the congregation "to sit up and watch in case of sickness or death of any members Ladys or childern," discussion focused on "making a law compelling members ladys" to do so, "and also to compell them to sew for the dead of the congregation."[70] The language of compulsion in this context contrasts with the language in which the board, more confident of its authority over the congregation's male members, could address men, indicating simply that "all Members [were] to sit up either with the Sick or at the Burial Ground."[71]

The difficulty of incorporating women into the community structure was exacerbated by the congregation's loss of control over its congregants' lives beyond the sanctuary. In accordance with traditional assumptions about the nature of Jewish community, the bylaws of Congregation Bene Israel in Cincinnati reflected the expectation that congregations would exercise a certain authority over the lives of their members. The belief that Jews should be able to govern themselves was reflected in an 1844 case in which a Bene Israel member was threatened with a $50 fine for "having sued Mr. N. Malzer in court, without having his complaint first brought before the congregation." The defendant, Solomon Samuel, did not contest the authority of the board in this case, yet in his response he radically challenged the limits of a voluntary community. He explained "that it was his wife who had sued Mr. Malzer, and that his wife was not bound to our By Laws."[72] In Europe, if it were possible that a similar case could have arisen, such an excuse would have been meaningless. There, a man's wife would certainly fall under the community's authority. But in Cincinnati a man paid dues to become a member in his own right;

the male-defined community contained no categories in which to incorporate its relationship to women. This lack of a structured place for women as individuals within the community meant that any input from women into congregational affairs would continue to be possible only on an ad hoc, noninstitutionalized basis.

Organizational Life

Despite women's marginal status in synagogue worship, they often constituted a powerful presence within the wider synagogue community. In most nascent Jewish communities in the United States, the synagogue was the starting point for a wide range of ritual and communal services. More than just a prayer hall, the synagogue also provided a base for the maintenance of traditional Jewish observances extending well beyond public worship. Communal services in early American Jewish communities included the administration of cemeteries and ritual baths, the supervision of kosher meat, and the provision of charity to beleaguered Jews, whether at the local, national, or international level. For many, public Jewish life included not only participation in synagogue worship and support but also involvement in a range of religious, charitable, and social activities associated either formally or informally with the congregation.[73] Both women and men took active roles in this sphere of Jewish life beyond the sanctuary.

The earliest identifiable collective work among American Jewish women actually consisted in bringing gifts to the congregation. A mid-eighteenth century blessing used at New York's Shearith Israel praised the congregation's women "for the mitzvah which they did in presenting to the synagogue the white decorations for the holy scroll of the Torah of the congregation, and the curtain of the holy Ark for use on the High Holy Days." Shearith Israel's historians suggest that the blessing referred to contributions to the congregation's 1730 building, the first synagogue built in North America. The women of Philadelphia's Mikveh Israel, led by Mrs. Jonas Phillips and Mrs. Simon Nathan, the wives of two congregational leaders, raised a subscription list of £13.7.4 for the congregation's 1782 synagogue, to pay for the curtains for the Torah ark, a silk covering for the reader's desk, and Torah scroll covers. Similarly, women of New York's B'nai Jeshurun congregation organized to make a curtain for the ark of their young congregation's new synagogue in 1827.[74] This role in making or buying many of the costly items that adorned ritual objects and the synagogue was one that individual women and women's groups continued to fill throughout the nineteenth century.

The growing network of American women's associations that emerged in the early nineteenth century was organized chiefly around religious and denominational identities.[75] Likewise, Jewish women's associational life would be carried on, for the most part, within strictly Jewish circles. The earliest documented involvement of American Jewish women in collective benevolence, however, illustrates the connections between the public life of American Jewish women and an emerging network of American women's organizations. In 1801 a group of twenty-three well-to-do women, including eight Jewish women—Mrs. Miriam Gratz with three of her daughters, Mrs. Deborah Cohen with her daughter, Mrs. Rebecca Phillips, and a Miss Levy—founded the Female Association for the Relief of Women and Children in Reduced Circumstances.[76] Participation in this effort to assist once-genteel Philadelphia ladies who had fallen upon hard times or in the Philadelphia Orphan Asylum (founded in 1815), which was also dominated by Presbyterians, immersed Jewish women in American models of associational life.[77] Thus, the future founders of America's pioneering Jewish women's societies found models and validation for their own denominational efforts in the religiously inflected, middle-class world of American female benevolence.

"On a stormy day in the autumn of 1819 . . . two benevolent ladies" sought, despite "their limited means," to respond to a deeply affecting "tale of distress" of a needy Jewish woman. According to an 1843 account, the two women "resolved to apply to other daughters of Israel for assistance."[78] The result was Philadelphia's Female Hebrew Benevolent Society, created by "the ladies of the Hebrew Congregation of Philadelphia . . . desirous of rendering themselves useful to their indigent sisters of the house of Israel."[79] This earliest of local Female Hebrew Benevolent Societies to offer relief to needy Jewish sisters included at least three women—serving in the roles of first directress, secretary, and manager—who had earlier helped to found the nonsectarian Female Association.[80] The founders of the Female Hebrew Benevolent Society hoped to aid impoverished Jewish women dwelling in their midst, and, echoing the earlier efforts of the Female Association, they included special provisions to attend to the needs of "reduced families" from their community "who have seen 'better days.'"[81]

Like this first communal organization, Jewish women's associations in the United States arose in response to the internal demands of the Jewish community but developed in accord with forms offered by the American environment. The major Jewish women's organizations in Philadelphia, including the Hebrew Sunday School Society founded in 1838 and the Jewish Foster Home created in 1855, were all inspired by familiarity with and commitment to the goals of similar non-Jewish models.

In 1820, the year after the creation of Philadelphia's Female Hebrew Benevolent Society, women at New York's Shearith Israel created their own Female Hebrew Benevolent Society, directed toward "the relief of indigent females and their families."[82] It appears in this case, as on many other later occasions, that the New York society drew inspiration for its creation from the earlier Philadelphia model. In fact, any discussion of Jewish women's organizations and benevolence in the nineteenth century must account for the unusual energy and communal influence of the Jewish "sisters" in the City of Brotherly Love.

Some authors have suggested that study of the public work of Philadelphia's Jewish women can provide insight into the general patterns of women's participation in American Jewish public life.[83] There is much evidence to suggest, however, that the creative, vigorous, and persistent benevolent efforts of Philadelphia's Jewish women, while extremely influential, were far from typical.

Rebecca Gratz, who, along with her mother and two of her sisters, belonged to the group that created the Female Association in 1801, was certainly the most prominent American woman identified with Jewish communal life of her day. She located her vocation in the work of benevolence. She was one of the founders in 1819 of the Female Hebrew Benevolent Society, which she served for many years as secretary. Nineteen years later, at the age of fifty-seven, she started Philadelphia's Hebrew Sunday School. In 1855 her urging and leadership keyed the founding of the city's Jewish Foster Home.

In name and content, Gratz's school, the first such educational effort among Jews, drew inspiration from the Protestant Sunday school movement, to the extent even of using somewhat modified Christian religious primers, Bibles, and catechisms when they were the only texts available.[84] The growing American Sunday school movement, with its large cadres of young female volunteer teachers of religion, would have been well known in Philadelphia, where the American

Sunday School Union was founded in 1824. By 1832 the city's Sunday schools served 11,735 students, almost 30 percent of Philadelphia's school-age children.[85]

Despite their own lack of formal religious or Hebrew training, Gratz and her coworkers were convinced of Jewish women's responsibility for the religious and moral training of children in their own community. Just as Philadelphia's female relief society was quickly followed by the creation of a similar New York group, the Hebrew Sunday School inspired a number of similar efforts in many of the locales where the Philadelphia women maintained personal connections. In a report on the progress of her new school in 1838, Rebecca Gratz noted that "this good work has already met with a reward. Our sisters of New York and Charleston . . . have determined to establish similar institutions in their respective cities."[86] The Jewish women of Augusta, Georgia, drew upon this model in 1845 when they created a religious school of their own. In the Augusta case, the women's effort constituted the very first local attempt at communal organization, and it "paved the way to this gratifying result," the creation of a congregation.[87] None of these schools matched the success of the Philadelphia effort, but more importantly, the women of Philadelphia's Hebrew Sunday School Society established an American pattern in which Sunday schools with female teachers became a familiar and accepted model of Jewish supplementary education.

In Philadelphia, Augusta, Savannah, Richmond, Baltimore, and elsewhere, Sunday schools provided a foundation for the expansion of women's work and engagement in the community. In Philadelphia and then again in New York, Sunday school work inspired school organizers to create Sewing Societies to replace the rags that too many of their impoverished students wore to school. Gratz's growing frustration at the inability of the Sunday school to address the crushing deprivation she saw in some children's lives, together with her own long-term involvement as secretary of the nonsectarian Philadelphia Orphan Asylum, pushed her to expand the sphere of Jewish women's benevolence even further, resulting in the opening of the Jewish Foster Home.

Along with Gratz's leadership, the ability of Philadelphia's Jewish women to learn from non-Jewish organizations, and the dynamism and continuity of their benevolent institutions, another characteristic of the city's extraordinary network of Jewish women's organizations was the extent to which it fostered and benefited from the contributions of unmarried women. In most nineteenth-century American Jewish communities, pride of place and position was generally accorded to married women, who often drew much of their own status from that of their husbands. There certainly were many wives and mothers in Philadelphia who stood out as leaders in Jewish benevolence, but one of the most striking things about the city's Jewish women's organizations was the persistent leadership of an energetic and talented core of unmarried women who devoted much of their energy to the community. Rebecca Gratz was only the most prominent example of a single woman able to win appreciation from her community through her dedication to benevolent work. She was one of many contemporaries, students, and successors to take leading roles in the Foster Home, Sunday School, and Benevolent Society. Many of these women shared a common social and familial background, creating a female network of closely connected benevolent workers that welcomed unmarried women, together with married women, and trained them for leadership roles.

Unlike in Jewish women's societies in many other American cities, the names of unmarried women in Philadelphia were not relegated to the bottom of membership lists below the married women. Rather, in a manner hard to imagine in any other American Jewish community, Philadelphia's unmarried female activists were judged worthy not only of admiration but even of emulation. Thus, in 1869 Matilda Cohen, one of Philadelphia's prominent Jewish matrons and activists eulogized the recently deceased Rebecca Gratz, describing her as a woman "just and virtuous," with a "pure and unblemished" life, "whose example may be commended to the imitation of the Daughters of Israel." Henry Morais's 1894 book, *The Jews of Philadelphia,* offered a similar assessment of three of the most prominent, if unmarried, female workers in Philadelphia Jewish charity and organizational life. Morais described Rebecca Gratz, Louisa B. Hart, and Ellen Phillips as "a trio of model women whose deeds Israelites may well hold in lasting remembrance."[88] Women like Mary Cohen, Simha Peixotto, Emily Phillips, Evelyn Bomeisler, Emily Solis-Cohen, and Esther Baum represent a few more of the ranks of unmarried Jewish women upon whom Philadelphia benevolence depended.[89] The community's ability to welcome and honor the efforts of these women fostered a communal activism that helped to keep women at the center of Philadelphia's Jewish communal life for many years.

These early organizations, oriented toward poor relief, education, and foster care, offered vehicles through which acculturating American Jewish women could invest their energies in community work, in models validated by their prevalence among middle-class Protestant women. As the country's Jewish population began to grow with immigration from central Europe in the early part of the nineteenth century and as the institutional dominance of the nation's Sephardic community receded, a different kind of women's benevolent society emerged. Many of the groups created in the 1840s revolved around the traditional Jewish obligations of sitting with sick and dying members of the community, watching over and ritually washing the dead in preparation for burial, and providing burial shrouds. In many communities, cash assistance soon came to replace personal nursing for sick members. Hebrew Ladies' Benevolent Societies in Baltimore, New York, Cincinnati, New Haven, Richmond, Albany, and Syracuse were founded for these purposes in the 1840s and 1850s.[90] Numerous other local women's benevolent societies may have served similar ends, but the contemporary newspaper accounts that note their existence and praise their "valuable and indispensable" work often neglected to tell what exactly they did.[91]

Like similar male societies founded around the same time, these "benevolent" societies were less concerned with charity to others than with the needs of the society's own members. These societies, often founded by immigrants from German-speaking lands, were in fact replicating, and were likely modeled on, the women's *hevrot* (societies) whose emergence Maria Baader has documented in German communities in the late eighteenth and early nineteenth centuries.[92] Many American organizations took on the same range of activities that seems to have characterized their German counterparts, although it is reasonable to suspect that the mutual aid aspect of these organizations served a different purpose for new immigrants than for those in more established communities. Many Jewish women's societies in this period were oriented toward the traditional ritual tasks of watching over the sick, dying, and dead, and they often carried German names replicating the formulation "Israelitische Frauen Verein" (Society of Jewish Women) used for such organizations in Germany.[93] Their English names, however, almost universally adopted the formulas of American organizations, as communities across the country created their own Female Hebrew Benevolent Societies or Hebrew Ladies' Benevolent Societies.

Whether for the funding of relief, sick benefits, Sunday schools, or sewing societies, antebellum Jewish women's societies were run as dues-paying organizations, often supplemented by income from invested capital and by occasional events intended to raise funds for charitable purposes. American Jewish women's organizations quickly proved themselves to be effective gatherers of capital, a role that often led them in new directions. One of the earliest of these efforts occurred in Savannah, where "the ladies of the congregation" organized a community fair in 1843 to enable the community to hire a religious leader. Before the fair took place, Rebecca Gratz expressed her doubts to her niece Miriam Moses Cohen, one of the fair's organizers, about "the success of a fair for that purpose [to hire a rabbi] in a Christian community. I would not venture on such an expedient here," she told Cohen, and she suggested that Cohen "consult with some of your Christian friends" to judge whether they felt a "more liberal spirit exists in Savannah" among the general populace than Gratz sensed in Philadelphia.[94] Despite the aunt's misgivings, she did collect and send her niece needlework "contributions of our Ladies for your Fair." Miriam Cohen even sought to bolster the fair's offerings by soliciting "fancy work" from the English author Grace Aguilar, whose romances and reflections on Jewish ritual in *The Spirit of Judaism*, published in 1842, were gaining growing American renown. Aguilar explained that, between teaching five days a week, writing, and caring for her family, she had "very little time for fancy work," but she promised to "gladly contribute my mite," including "two copies of a little work [book] of mine." Aguilar ultimately sent two reticules (purses), six needlecases, and twelve pincushions, along with needlework by others that she had gathered with "the help of some young friends."[95]

The fair proved a great success, raising $1,522.33 and establishing that Jewish women could indeed rely on the liberal spirit of their neighbors for generous interest and financial support. Subsequent Savannah fairs and investment added to this amount, so that in 1845 a local correspondent could report that $5,300 had been raised toward the employment of a hazan for the congregation, attributing "chief credit to [the] ladies of [Savannah], aided by those of New York, Charleston, and Bordeaux in France [who also likely provided needlework articles to be sold or auctioned at the fair]."[96] In Cincinnati, the Hebrew Ladies' Benevolent Society held an annual ball—among the "most decorous and splendid fetes of the season"—to meet the needs of those struggling to stay warm and fed through Cincinnati's winters.[97] In Philadelphia, the women's organizations funded their work through dues, contributions, and regular donations from the male-led Hebrew Charity Ball Association, which began to hold annual balls in 1843.[98] Many of the societies carefully invested their money and subsequently drew operating funds from the accruing interest.

With these resources, women's groups paid sick benefits to their members or provided relief to impoverished Jews, especially widows or deserted wives and their children. They also elaborated on the traditional women's practice of contributing to the ritual ornamentation of synagogue sanctuaries by offering monetary contributions to their congregations. Despite the relative sparseness of archival material documenting the existence of antebellum Jewish women's societies, the shadow of their presence can be seen in the records of the many male-led congregations that turned to their affiliated women's societies for critical loans or contributions that made land acquisition and synagogue building possible. All these activities spoke to their impressive fund-raising acumen. In Cincinnati the Hebrew Ladies' Benevolent Society lent $700 (at 10 percent interest) toward the Bene Israel congregation's purchase of a $4,000 building site in 1847. In 1851, when the city's B'nai Yeshurun congregation needed $2,520 to pay for additional property, the synagogue's leaders turned to the Ladies' Benevolent Society for $300 and the (German) Ladies' Relief Society for $200. Both loans were made at 8 percent interest. The congregation remained in debt to these societies well into the 1860s.[99] The women of New York's Shaaray Tefila Ladies' Benevolent Society contributed $400 to the congregation's 1845 building fund, apparently without interest.[100] Similarly, in Charleston in 1854, the Hebrew Sewing Society, founded to help liquidate the debt of the traditionalist congregation Shearith Israel, gave the "snug little sum" of $500 to the congregation for future use.[101]

By the 1850s, Jewish women's organizations that focused on poor relief and fund-raising activities appeared to be an integral part of the burgeoning religious and communal life of the nation's expanding Jewish communities. If women's organizations were not generally as central to the development of communal life as they were in Philadelphia, they showed great promise of becoming influential and permanent actors in the shaping of American Jewish life.

Judah Touro's remarkable will, with its intriguing portrait of the spectrum of America's institutional Jewish life at the time of his death in 1854, illustrates the extent to which women's organizations may have figured prominently within local communities yet remained much subordinate in public status to male-dominated religious and educational institutions. Although Touro became engaged in Jewish communal and religious affairs only toward the end of his life, his many bequests to Jewish organizations outside of New Orleans, ranging from $2,000 to $20,000 (totaling $143,000), provided the wherewithal to sustain a wide range of Jewish religious, educational, and benevolent efforts across the country.

Much of Touro's largesse was directed to organizations in New Orleans, where he made his home. He left a total of $120,000 to local non-Jewish recipients, including orphan homes and various Christian welfare organizations, with his single largest gift going toward "establishing an 'Alms House'" in the city. To New Orleans Jewish institutions, he left $108,000 in cash and property, benefiting two synagogues and an effort to create "the Hebrew Hospital of New Orleans."[102] He also gave $5,000 each to three other Jewish organizations, the Hebrew Benevolent Association, the Ladies' Benevolent Society of New Orleans, and the Hebrew Foreign Mission Society (an effort to help the Jews of China).[103] Although his New Orleans contributions do not appear to esteem the work of Jewish women's organization any less than that of men's, his bequests outside the city emphasize the lower public profile of women's groups.

Touro worked out the details of his will only a few days before his death, relying on the guidance of two close advisers who came to his sickbed to suggest worthy objects of Jewish and Christian charity. Gershom Kursheedt, a descendant of two prominent New York Jewish families, a strong supporter of the Philadelphia traditionalist Isaac Leeser, and a leader among New Orleans Jewry, had been instrumental in pushing Touro to engage, both philanthropically and spiritually, in Jewish religious life. Kursheedt did his best to help Touro create a will that would advance Leeser's vision of a strong and unified American Jewish community. He reported to Leeser, "If you knew how I had to work to get that Will made and how I strove to serve you, you would pity me." In regard to the specifics of the document, he indicated that as he stood by the sick man's bed, he made up "the list of Jewish Institutions . . . as well as [he] could."[104] Kursheedt's improvised list embraced thirty organizations in eighteen different cities across the Northeast, South, and Midwest but included only two women's organizations. The two women's groups may simply have been the ones about which Kursheedt had some knowledge. Kursheedt's personal connection to Leeser helps explain Touro's gift of $3,000 to Philadelphia's Female Hebrew Benevolent Society. The inclusion of $3,000 for the "Ladies' Benevolent Society of the City of New York" is readily explained in the will itself, which notes that "Mrs. I. B. Kursheedt" (Gershom's mother) served as "first directress" of that society in 1850.[105]

As suggested by Touro's will, Jewish women's public activities constituted a small part of the emerging community's institutional life at midcentury. Still, in women's galleries and in a variety of women's benevolent societies around the country, American Jewish women, building upon Jewish community needs and forms, and learning from the forms of Christian women's associational and religious life around them, were acting out new patterns for Jewish women's lives. By providing charity, mutual aid, and the creation of social spaces for women to gather as Jewish women, participation in women's associations provided an important arena for the elaboration of acculturated middle-class identities.

The *Mikveh*

At the same time that Jewish women were exploring new public identities, they were also redefining their own more private expressions of Judaism. Although this study will remain focused primarily on synagogue and associational life, it is important to direct some attention to the evolution in America of those institutions that framed Judaism as a traditional way of life.

In European Jewish communities, many communal institutions and arrangements beyond the synagogue sanctuary were peculiarly relevant to women's traditional religious roles. Ritual slaughterers (*shochetim*) were particularly important to wives and mothers who were responsible for providing kosher food to their families. For married women, access to a properly constituted ritual bath (*mikveh;* plural, *mikvaot*) was an absolute requisite to continued marital relations with their husbands. Men in traditional communities often used *mikvaot* to purify themselves before holidays. Ritual immersion was also a prerequisite for conversion. The essential religious requirement associated with *mikvaot,* however, was for women, who had to immerse themselves at a specified time after their menstrual period before they were allowed to resume sexual relations with their husbands.[106]

Study of the *mikveh* in early American Jewish experience will not yield a fully realized portrayal of the nature of personal piety among American Jewish women in this era. Still, an examination of the *mikveh*'s place in early American Jewish communities can indicate the extent to which the members of these communities followed the mandate of Jewish religious law in regard to one particular expression of personal observance.

In his magisterial history of New York's early Jewish community, Hyman B. Grinstein points out that in colonial and early national America, "the synagogue, which had been only one institution in the [traditional Jewish] community, came to include within its walls the entire range of community life . . . All the matters of religion, education, philanthropy and even social life became functions of the synagogue."[107] Thus, American congregations took on responsibility for hiring *shochetim* and building *mikvaot,* both of which, in principle, should have been among the immediate priorities of any Jewish community. Early synagogue records all mention the community *shochet,* but evidence of community *mikvaot* appears infrequently. Naphtali Phillips's nineteenth-century historical account of New York's Shearith Israel recalled the oral tradition associated with what was presumably America's first community *mikveh.* Phillips recounted that, according to tradition, "before the Synagogue was built, there was a fine run of water in Mill Street, over which a bathing house was erected, where the females of our nation performed their ablutions."[108]

Although necessary to the conduct of a proper Jewish way of life, organization of a *mikveh* did not seem to carry the same imperative as the establishment of a synagogue or cemetery or attention to kashrut. A *mikveh* generally required an organized community to see to its construction and superintendence, but by the time a community was organized enough to think about a ritual bath, local women may already have become habituated to neglecting what should have been one of their prime religious duties.

Jews in Philadelphia began to meet as an informal congregation in the 1740s. It was not until the Revolutionary War brought a number of Jewish refugees from other colonial cities, however, that a congregation was formally constituted as Mikveh Israel in 1782 and plans were made to build a synagogue. At that time, Jonas Phillips encouraged the congregation to save space in the small synagogue lot for a bathhouse, a school, and a residence for the hazan.[109] A 1784 petition submitted by Manuel Josephson to the congregation urged that a *mikveh* be built, and it pointed out the congregation's obligations in the severest terms, noting that "if we neglect our duty, [God] has denounced . . . severe and tremendious sentences against us," which could only be avoided by "endeavour[ing] with all our might to regulate our conduct in every respect conformable to His Holy Law."

Of "the many defects" that Josephson and his fellow petitioners noted that "this congregation called Mikve Israel in Philadelphia labours under . . . we find one in particular which strikes us most forcibly and cannot but affect with astonishment and horror every judicious and truly religious mind." They pointed to "the want of a proper *mikve* or batheing place, according to our Law and institution, for the purification of married women at certain periods." "Transgression of this ordinance" carried dire consequences for the community: "Children born from so unlawful cohabitation are deemed *bene niddot* [written in Hebrew, meaning children conceived during the period of ritual impurity associated with menstruation], which makes this offence the more Hoeinous and detestable, in as much as it effects not only the parents, but their posterity for generations to come." This crisis, according to the petitioners, undermined the Philadelphia community's legitimacy in the Jewish world: "Should it be known in the congregations abroad that we had been thus neglectful of so important a matter, they would not only pronounce heavy Anathemas against us, but interdict & avoid intermarriages with us, equal as with [a] different nation or sect, to our great shame and Mortification."[110] If Philadelphia's Jews did not attend to this crucial religious obligation, they would, in effect, cut themselves off from the Jewish people.

Given the momentousness attached to this issue by the petitioners in Philadelphia, what becomes surprising is the rarity of such emphatic expressions of concern. Many observances basic to Jewish life were inevitably neglected until American communities could organize to make observance possible. Some aspects of an observant Jewish life, even in the relatively scant institutional framework of a new society, could be established quickly. In localities without professionals or officials to do the job, individuals often slaughtered their own poultry or meat for themselves and their neighbors; laymen performed circumcisions and led their own prayer services. A woman, however, could not provide and oversee her own *mikveh*. Many women may have improvised ways to maintain their observance, taking advantage of streams or other bathing places, but if so, they did it without community support.

The 1784 petition's description of the urgent and immediate need for ritual compliance came, of course, after forty years of Jewish communal presence in Philadelphia without the benefit of a communal ritual bath. The petitioners, however, committed themselves without a trace of irony to "solemnly and Religiously" pay off their pledges toward the building of a ritual bath "without any hesitation or demur whatever." And they added, "We flatter ourselves that every married Man will use the most persuasive & evry other means, to induce his Wife to a strict compliance with that duty, so incumbent upon them." Paradoxically, the emphatic nature of this declaration seems to acknowledge their uncertainty about whether, if a *mikveh* were actually available, their wives would take advantage of it. Recognition that their wives might have to be convinced to use a ritual bath undercut the attempt to make *mikveh* practices seem central and crucial to Jewish life.

The apparent ease with which such a fundamental practice was neglected may reflect the Sephardic origins of the Jews who set the patterns for America's earliest synagogues. Sephardic Jews traced their origins to the expulsion from Spain; many came from families that were at one time secretly Jewish and which, under the pressure of the Inquisition, had been forced long ago to dispense with many of the outward, public practices that marked them as Jewish. Many Sephardic Jews had learned to get along without these practices and felt free to be selective in choosing which to reinstate.

As the influx of Jewish immigrants from central Europe accelerated in the first half of the nineteenth century, new Jewish communities arose throughout the country, and multiple congregations arose in cities with previously established Jewish communities. This migration introduced a population that was more attuned to traditional practice. In both New York and Philadelphia, formerly unified religious communities broke up, in part, because the newer immigrants sought stricter adherence to the letter of orthodox observance than was favored by native Jewish Americans. As Edwin Wolf and Maxwell Whiteman observe of Philadelphia's growing Jewish community, "although ritual practices were observed by individuals haphazardly and in accordance with the particular individual's piety, the religious practices of the formal congregation became increasingly more intense, better defined and more orthodox."[111] Even if some or most of the individuals in a given locale had acquired the habit of casual observance in their daily lives, they might adopt higher standards for themselves as an organized community. Thus, in Philadelphia, once a congregation was firmly established with a synagogue in place, it became more important to pay attention to the other requisites of Jewish religious life. In addition to the *mikveh,* the congregation started a school for the Jewish education of their youth and hired a *"shabbes goyah"* to light the synagogue's fires and kosher candles on the Sabbath.[112]

A description of a ritual bath site in Philadelphia was written in 1860 by Mrs. S. J. Cohen, who recalled the ritual, which she called a "baptism," attendant upon her conversion to Judaism in 1806: "A beautiful spot had been selected, some two or three miles from the city, where a natural stream flowed towards the east . . . And here a nice little bath-room had been built over this beautiful stream, with a flight of steps to descend." Presumably she was describing the *mikveh* facilities of Mikveh Israel, since the father of her intended groom served as hazan to that congregation. Mrs. Cohen described a ceremony in which, assisted by a female attendant, she disrobed and descended steps into "crystal waters," which "sported" with her "unbound . . . curls." At a signal from outside the bath, she wrote, "I was then pressed under the water, and allowed to rise. This was repeated three times, with responses from without. [The attendant] then assisted me to rise from the water, and robed me, the elders on the outside chanting the Hebrew hymn."[113]

A less evocative, but no less important, report of the creation of a communal ritual bath in New York appeared in Shearith Israel's minutes from 1759, where it was agreed on November 11 that "a proper bathing place shall be built of stone for the use of the Congregation."[114] As communities sought to establish frameworks for Jewish life, the creation of *mikvaot* often accompanied other communal milestones. A contemporary journalist's account of the Lloyd Street Synagogue of the Baltimore Hebrew Congregation, consecrated in

1845 under the aegis of Rabbi Abraham Rice, described "in the rear of the Church a building . . . erected for a dwelling," which "contain[ed] a room fitted up for the purpose of religious ablution."[115] The establishment of a *mikveh* in Cincinnati occurred in 1843, when a group of traditionalist Cincinnati laymen altered a "bath house, so as to have it in every way in accordance with the established custom as handed to us by our fathers." The city's Bene Israel congregation considered the possibility of renting "the frame Building next to shool for to Build a Mikwah," just as a second Jewish congregation was being founded in the city.[116] Bene Israel records of 1847 indicate that when one of Cincinnati's privately owned ritual baths closed down, the synagogue board considered how they might respond to "the necessity of establishing for the wives of the members of our Congregation . . . this requisite convenience." A desire to differentiate their congregation by identifying it with the "primitive holiness . . . of our holy Religion" may have led Bene Israel leaders to take on the cost ($1,000 dollars to get started) of maintaining a community *mikveh*.[117] In Rochester, New York, the first communal bath appears to have been established in 1856, when Congregation Berith Kodesh adapted the baptismal font of the Baptist Church they had recently acquired for a synagogue.[118]

More important than the existence of *mikvaot*, however, was the extent to which they were actually used. Where records exist, it may be possible to correlate the price of a *mikveh* visit with total *mikveh* income to determine how many women actually took advantage of existing facilities. Many variables, however, complicate this equation. For instance, the wives of members of a congregation that owned a *mikveh* would generally pay different rates than the wives of strangers, so total monthly income cannot be easily converted into number of patrons served. Still, some educated guesses may be instructive. Hyman Grinstein, in his study, recognizes that *mikveh* use could provide an important measure of the degree of religious observance or laxity in a community. Using the financial accounts of Anshe Chesed's ritual bath in 1851 as an indicator, he concludes that one hundred women a month took advantage of their facilities. Since Anshe Chesed was the dominant congregation in New York City at that time, he estimates usage at the other two baths, managed by two of the smaller congregations, at a lower level. With about 4,000 Jewish families in the city, he estimated that "some 200 women repaired to the New York ritual pools each month." Acknowledging the vagueness of his estimates, Grinstein notes that the only thing to be stated with certainty in regard to *mikveh* use is that it was lower among native Jews than among more recently minted Americans.[119]

Isaac Leeser's *Occident* often reported on the presence of *mikvaot* in synagogues, citing their existence as "proof that the ordinances of our religion yet possess faithful followers in our midst."[120] But the existence of a *mikveh,* although evidence of a communal commitment to the principle of traditional piety, could not be equated with actual observance. Leeser seemed to acknowledge this in his report of a Richmond, Virginia, ritual bath when he noted, "We also learn that it does not remain unused."[121] Such an observation reflected his realization that many *mikvaot* in the United States were not utilized to their capacity. By the 1850s, although *mikvaot* seemed to be widespread and available, the impression gleaned from published references, as well as from calculations like Grinstein's, is that the laws of marital purity, at least as expressed through *mikveh* use, did not play a significant role in the lives of most midcentury American Jewish women.

As Jewish leaders found increasing success in establishing synagogues as the primary site for the expression of Jewish religiosity, they no longer felt compelled to provide the community with institutions to support the observance of domestic religiosity. In many communities the provision of kosher meat became a privatized affair, losing the imprimatur of communal sanction and supervision. *Mikvaot* were also left to become private business concerns. The trustees of Cincinnati's Bene Israel, satisfied with the high-profile efforts of their new rabbi to create a worship setting of elevated devotion, withdrew their support from the congregation's own *mikveh* in 1857. Although they were later presented with plans to cooperate in sponsoring a new *mikveh* that would be jointly sponsored by four congregations within the city, congregational records indicate that they never took on this role and that they even refused to contribute "the materials of the old Mikpha gratis" to the new endeavor. The sheets and towels of the old *mikveh* were ultimately contributed to the city's Jewish Hospital.[122]

Mikvaot proprietors could not simply assume that local Jewish women would come to them out of a commitment to fulfill the demands of Jewish law. An 1853 advertisement promoted a "Mikvah Synagogue," overseen by a Mrs. Noot "(wife of the Rev. S. C. Noot)" at New York's "Green Street synagogue." After noting that the new *mikveh* was "fitted up with every attention to their comfort, and in strict accordance with the requirements of the Law," the advertisement addressed potential patrons in a more insinuating manner: "Mrs. Noot respectfully trusts wives and mothers in Israel will not take it amiss if she presumes to remind them of an indispensable religious duty incumbent on them, and which can only be performed in a Mikvah lawfully constructed, any other mode is unlawful, and therefore, in a religious point of view void and altogether useless."[123] Mrs. Noot apparently suspected that some women were trying to fulfill their religious obligations through uncertified means.

The contrast between the religious understanding of *mikveh* use as "an indispensable religious duty" and the somewhat apathetic attitude manifested first toward the provision of *mikveh* establishments and subsequently toward their use speaks to the restructuring of female Jewish religiosity in America. The emergence of women in the public sphere of the synagogue may have reflected a reality in which those aspects of communal life that provided the focus for a Jewish woman's religious life in traditional settings never found strong validation in American experience. From the eighteenth-century Philadelphia petitioners who encouraged one another to persuade their wives to attend the *mikveh,* to the promoters of the New York *mikveh* who, in 1852, assured potential patrons that their premises had been "refinished in a style of beauty, convenience and elegance" that would make them feel at home, to Mrs. Noot, who reminded women of the duties incumbent upon them, no one really seemed to think that attendance at a *mikveh* was something that American women would remember to do of their own accord.[124]

"Laidies Who Regularly Attend Divine Service"

This brief history of the early American *mikveh* suggests that individual Jewish women trying to sustain traditional modes of personal piety and observance found less support than they might have expected from the communal institutions of American Jewish life. Nevertheless, women's presence and actions appeared to demand increasing recognition within those precincts of Jewish life that had long been oriented chiefly around male presence and religiosity. In early American synagogues, arguments over who could sit in the honored front seats in the now open gallery were quite as impassioned as those over seating down below; Ladies' Benevolent Societies often made important financial contributions to congregations; and women's efforts were often central to whatever organized opportunities for Jewish education existed in a given city.

Important as some of these changes may have been, they did nothing to increase female access to any formal political or religious role in synagogue leadership. Still, as suggested by at least one unusual piece of evidence, by midcentury some women were willing to claim and defend their place in the synagogue. In 1853, fourteen women of the Bene Israel congregation in Cincinnati addressed a letter to the president and members of the congregation, which read:

> Gent'l, the undersigned laidies who regularly attend divine service in the synagogue respectfully inform the members that the curtain which is placed before the railing which divides their seats from those of the gent's was fastned down by them, but frequently torn down again. The intention of placing a curtain there is caused from the unavoidable necessity of having their seats on the same floor with the gent's and which exposed them to the public gaze & which is strongly forbidden by our holy laws they are also desirous to avoid, particularly in the house of prayers, the congregation will confer a particular kindness by their prompt attention to their request by having the curtain fastened, with the request that no person be allowed in anyway to misplace it &c Yours Respectfully [signed in English, Hebrew, and Yiddish.][125]

This letter indicates that its authors took their own synagogue attendance quite seriously. Identifying themselves collectively as the "laidies who regularly attend divine service," they testified to their awareness of themselves as a group with a voice, a point of view, and rights of their own. To them, the curtain separating them from the men of the congregation was evidence, not of disempowering segregation, but of the respect due them. Even as it demonstrated their respect for the custom of separate seating in Jewish devotion and thus for the traditional place of women in the synagogue, this letter also gave voice to the new identities women were finding in the American synagogue.

As Jews in the United States set about creating an American Judaism, they increasingly centered its expression in the synagogue. For women this process necessitated finding a new way to be religious. This examination of the increasing visibility of women in the synagogue, as well as of the apparent efforts of synagogue leaders and designers to recognize women's presence, has documented the beginnings of that process. American Jewish women had begun to define a major component of their religious identity in relation to the synagogue and the public sphere of worship.

In defending the traditional status quo in their 1853 letter, the women of Bene Israel articulated a subtle shift in the way they defined themselves as Jews. But a more explicit revolution was quickly approaching their community. Within two years Bene Israel would bring in a new rabbi intent upon introducing a range of synagogue reforms, including a mixed choir of men and women. These proposed innovations certainly constituted a challenge to the traditional conception of female modesty that the women seeking a fastened-down curtain had been so anxious to defend. Within ten years the same synagogue's congregants would be encouraged to construct a "House of Worship . . . which the demands of the present age require." Such a structure would contain "all the necessary improvements," including family pews, an organ, and a choir. Sixteen years after the Bene Israel women submitted their petition, their congregation would leave behind its sixteen-year-old synagogue to move into a grand edifice that featured family pews. The explosive progress of reform that gripped this congregation and many others like it in the 1850s, 1860s, and 1870s would continue to transform the place of women in the American synagogue.

CHAPTER THREE

The Quest for Respectability: Mixed Choirs and Family Pews

The arrival of between 150,000 and 200,000 immigrant Jews from the German states and elsewhere in central and eastern Europe radically expanded the geographic and institutional range of American Jewish life during the mid-nineteenth century. Filling a variety of economic roles in trade and commerce and benefiting from the growth of the American economy, this group quickly attained and often surpassed middle-class levels of economic and social status. As these Jews established congregations and built synagogues, their aspirations to individual economic success and social acceptance also shaped their collective efforts to create communal religious institutions. Mid-nineteenth-century American synagogues became sites for the reframing of ritual, worship conduct, synagogue space, and individual religious identities, as Jews sought to delineate the parameters of an appropriately American Judaism. In a society in which the roles and spaces assigned to women provided sensitive markers of social class distinctions, the status of women in Judaism and within the synagogue became one critical aspect of the general Jewish quest for respectability.

Numerous small and large Jewish congregations asserted their claims to public respectability and recognition as they built or acquired synagogue buildings in the 1840s and 1850s. In addition to serving as traditional settings for Jewish public worship, these synagogues offered Jewish immigrant communities an opportunity to make their own mark on America's urban and religious landscape. Jewish communal leaders sought out architectural styles and created physical structures that they hoped would command attention, impressing those who passed by with the solidity, grandeur, and substance of their synagogues and their communities. In design and execution, mid-nineteenth-century synagogue buildings, and the rituals conducted within them, embodied the qualities that community leaders wanted to associate with American Jews and their beliefs. Their aspirations may be seen in the adjectives that they used to describe their new synagogue edifices. Over and over again, the Jewish press reported upon the dedication of new buildings that were at least "neat and tasteful" and often "elegantly furnished [and] imposing."[1] Reports likewise directed attention to the orchestration of ritual and worship within these buildings. Jewish press articles described "impressive" worship services that "breath[ed] a spirit of true Judaism and real devotion," marked by "sublimity," and by "order and decorum," and conducted with "dignity, order and solemnity" in a manner "calculated to edify and to elevate our feelings towards our Creator."[2] Through their synagogues, Jewish immigrants of the mid-nineteenth century hoped to give concrete form to their aspirations for status and respectability.

From the late 1840s onward, attention focused on propriety in the conduct of synagogue ritual, as congregational leaders, both laymen and rabbis, sought to adjust the traditional Jewish worship style in such a way as to "render Judaism respectful with its votaries and the community at large."[3] The attempt to control and at times restructure Jewish liturgy would eventually crystallize into a self-conscious and systematic Reform program. Yet the effort to bring solemnity, awe, and reverence to Jewish worship echoed across the spectrum of Jewish religious observance. As the traditionalist Isaac Leeser affirmed, the pursuit of "order in the worship and public decorum . . . only tends to what all advocate."[4]

The "strong desire to render their congregation[s] respectable and respected" suffused the efforts of those who considered themselves representatives and leaders of the Jewish community in the mid-nineteenth century.[5] The impulse toward respectability was built upon their perception of a significant gap between the lack of refinement implicit in traditional Jewish religious life and the level of gentility sought by a developing American Jewish community. Through repeated emphasis on the uplifting visual, auditory, and emotional impact of worship in their new synagogues, observers highlighted the contrast between the elevated propriety found in these American synagogues with what might have been expected in more traditional settings. An emphasis on decorum, order, devotion, and edification conveyed the distance the American synagogue had moved from its more chaotic and disreputable antecedents. At the same time, such an emphasis established a Jewish claim upon respectability along an evolving American spectrum of refinement and propriety.[6] By aspiring to sanctuaries of staid orderliness, many acculturating American Jews sought to classify themselves with the congregants of the established and sedate churches of the country's affluent Protestant community.

As the restructuring of women's galleries in early American synagogues suggested, the gender order of Jewish ritual space would become a critical variable in the attempt to fit Jewish worship to the American environment. Even the earliest attempts by American Jews to create traditional Jewish institutions reflected a desire to adapt to American expectations of the place women should take in the sphere of public worship. In the 1840s and 1850s, the general expansion of American Jewish institutions and, in particular, the advent of Reform as a self-conscious ideology pushed acculturating Jews to incorporate middle-class American conceptions of female religiosity into contemporary Judaism.

Despite the reconfiguration of the women's gallery, early-nineteenth-century synagogue structures still violated the gender norms associated with bourgeois American Protestant religious practice. The continuing separation of women in synagogue galleries highlighted disreputable behavior among women and concretized male domination and female marginality. The apparent dissonance between women's religious status displayed in American synagogues and that prevalent among prosperous nineteenth-century Americans demanded resolution. The attempt to find an acceptable niche for women within the American synagogue continued to shape and distinguish the development of American Judaism through the middle decades of the century.

Acculturating Jews recognized that an American Judaism needed to honor women's place in public worship and affirm female spiritual equality. Both reformers and traditionalists accepted the importance of demonstrating respect for woman's religious nature. The question of how to express that respect within Jewish practice, however, became a subject of intense debate. The earliest efforts to make the synagogue into a sphere of respectability did not explicitly focus upon the reorientation of women's place within it. But the salience of women's voices and presence, at first indirectly and then directly, became integrally associated with the attempt to transform the synagogue into a haven for American devotion.

Respectability

The desire to be seen as practitioners of a respectable American religion accentuated the need for advocates of synagogue propriety to distinguish American Jewish worship not only from the embarrassing disorder of traditional Jewish worship but also from the excesses of Christian revivalism. The Protestant religious revival movement, marked by tent meetings, impassioned preaching, and the conversion of shaking bodies, was a ubiquitous religious and cultural force in the America encountered by Jewish immigrants at midcentury. Although the revivalists made a powerful impact on the American religious scene, Jewish immigrants, aspiring to social respectability, recognized this socially marginal movement as something to define themselves against. Although the intent and focus of Jewish worship was far removed from that of Christian revivalism, the chaotic behavior and swaying movements that characterized traditional synagogue deportment may have seemed uncomfortably similar to the uncontrolled nature of some revivalist worship. Those experiencing God's saving grace at a revival, like many traditional Jews, did not bother to stay in their seats, and they might speak or cry out as the spirit moved them. Revivalist gatherings were intended to generate spontaneous, sometimes overwhelming, responses to the spirit of God. Acculturating American Jews believed that although Jewish ritual might also appear chaotic, even frenzied, to the uninitiated theirs was a ritual with a clear rationale informed by reason. The possibility of being seen as enacting worship behavior that could be equated with the unsophisticated followers of the revivals gave American Jews all the more incentive to ban uncontrolled religious behavior from their midst.

Early attempts to regulate American synagogue behavior, for instance, focused on reducing extraneous movement or expression in an effort to create one harmonious and unified congregational voice.

With varying degrees of success, synagogue leaders tried to legislate the chaotic style of much traditional Jewish worship out of existence. They attempted to rein in those who treated the synagogue sanctuary and service as an arena for coarse, everyday behavior. Efforts to create an American Judaism that would distance its practitioners from the confusion of the traditional synagogue, as well as from the emotional excesses identified with Christian revivalism, focused on the creation of the American synagogue as "a place specialy dedicated to the Service of the most high, where a feeling of deep Reverence and devotion must actuate our Boosom and characterize our deportment & where every act of impropriety, indecorum & disorder becomes sinfull."[7]

Records from medieval synagogues indicate that the attempt to silence talkative congregants was hardly an American innovation. American Jewish leaders in the eighteenth and nineteenth centuries, however, displayed an intense concern with controlling the voices of worshipers in an effort to produce harmonious prayer. This concern emerges in some of the earliest documentation from American synagogues. At the consecration of Philadelphia's first synagogue in 1782, for instance, congregants were warned "to be particularly carefull not to raise their Voices higher than the *Hazan's* who will endeavor to modulate his Voice to a proper Pitch so as only to fill the building."[8] The 1791 constitution of Congregation Mickve Israel in Savannah, Georgia, mandated "that a decent behavior be observed by every person during services no person to raise his voice above or disturb the Reader or hold any conversation either in the Synagogue or places adjacent."[9] And at New York's Shearith Israel, which was renowned for establishing a model of respectable decorum for American congregations, bylaws adopted in 1805 mandated that "every member . . . previous to the singing any psalm, or prayer, remain silent until the *hazan* shall signify the tone or key, in which the same is to be sung, and those who are so inclined may then join therein, with an equal voice, but neither higher or louder than the *hazan*."[10]

As congregations of new immigrants in the 1840s and 1850s sought to make their own claims to respectability, they too sought to organize the congregation's worship around one central authoritative voice. Regulations introduced at Cincinnati's Bene Israel congregation in 1848 mandated that "no person shall interrupt, or correct either the Hazan during the service or reading the Torah." If someone did have a concern about "any mistake made by the Hazan or Parnas," they were instructed to make it "known to the B[oard] of T[rustees] at their meetings."[11] The emphasis of these resolutions was to subordinate individual prayer to the collective voice of the congregation as defined by the central voice of the hazan. In 1844, resolutions at New York's Anshe Chesed proposed fines for "everyone who reads prayers aloud or chaunts with the choir without being authorized to do so."[12] As at many other congregations, further resolutions at Anshe Chesed banned all conversation in the synagogue and offered a plan to train some of the congregants in "the way the prayers are required to be read." All other worshipers would be "requested to read the prayers silently until they have learned the way to read them," and then to "read their prayers with solemn voice and be particular not to interrupt the *hazzan* either by praying or singing before him."[13] Provisions like these sought to unify the community's voice and thus counter the more individualistic style of worship most familiar to America's Jewish immigrants.

Such regulations indicate the kind of worship behavior that congregational leaders came to find objectionable and, at the same time, suggest that many within the congregation resisted the leadership's attempts to impose order. Most of those coming from traditional communities were accustomed to communal prayer in which a prayer leader loosely governed the outline of the service but did not loudly verbalize every word of every prayer. Worshipers were left to pray in their own voices, according to their own rhythms. The effort to unify the community's voice or to silence or sing over the chanting of a tone-deaf congregation inevitably brought synagogue leaders into tension with the customary and familiar style of Jewish worship and, consequently, with many in their congregations. Many congregational leaders during the 1840s, like those at Anshe Chesed, hoped that trained choirs would help guide synagogue worshipers to modulate their voices and respond to prayer in unison.

Women's Voices

Attempts to alter musical expression in the synagogue in keeping with evolving aesthetic concerns challenged the traditional order of the synagogue on a number of levels. Synagogue organ music, for instance, first introduced in the United States in Charleston in 1840, overturned established worship practice, which had long banned instrumental music on the Sabbath. Although choral music represented an innovation to many in the context of the synagogue service, it was not in itself religiously objectionable. The inclusion of women's voices in many of these new synagogue choirs, however, blatantly violated halakhic prohibitions against women's voices in public prayer.

The movement to introduce mixed choirs into Jewish worship grew more from aesthetic concerns than from an ideologically driven challenge to Jewish law and tradition. Congregational leaders hoped that the formality and elegance associated with four-voice choral harmony would foster the spiritual uplift and reverence appropriate to the cultured adherents of a respectable creed. The introduction of choral music as well as organs helped bring American Jewish congregations into conformity with the style and aesthetic that Jews could observe in the churches of their affluent Protestant neighbors.

In addition, and perhaps unintentionally, the introduction of mixed choirs raised an explicit challenge to women's segregated and subordinate position in the synagogue. Tradition decreed that women's voices, as a potential cause for men of improper and distracting thoughts, should not be heard during worship. Various interpretations have been given to the initial dictum against hearing woman's voice *(kol isha)*, but over the years it came to be seen as a prohibition against women singing in public worship.[14] Consequently, the gradual acceptance of women's voices singing out in public synagogue choirs revealed the willingness of a portion of the American Jewish community to opt for a pleasing aesthetic over maintenance of the traditional gender order of Jewish worship. Ultimately, the introduction of mixed choirs reframed the position of women within Jewish worship, validating their voices and redefining the role of the worshiper in ways that had important implications for the future place of women in American synagogues.

Mixed choirs were first used by American Jewish communities in the dedication of new synagogue buildings.[15] Congregations presented consecration ceremonies as singular and auspicious moments.[16] Before the eyes of the community, Jews dedicated monuments of their distinctive faith in a manner worthy of general celebration. The whole Jewish and non-Jewish community, as represented by its political and spiritual leaders, was invited to these public celebrations. One Cincinnati lay leader noted proudly that "the crowd of our Christian friends" at the 1836 consecration of the city's first synagogue "was so great that we could not admit them all."[17] Not surprisingly, congregations invested consecration ceremonies with all the impressiveness they could muster. Since these events were not observed as traditional worship services, they were not subject to the usual restraints of Jewish public worship. Thus, for these ceremonies, halakhic constraints against the participation of women's voices were relaxed. Orthodox congregations apparently saw no problem in organizing choirs of men and women for their consecration celebrations. Mixed choirs performed at the dedication ceremonies of both the 1818 Mill Street Synagogue in New York and the 1825 Mikveh Israel synagogue in Philadelphia.[18] Because these consecrations were intended to represent Jewish congregations in the most favorable light possible, the regular presence of mixed choirs of men and women became a requisite part of such ceremonies, even for the most traditional acculturated congregations.

At times, the desire of congregations to show off the respectability and stature of their new edifices and of their assembly became an end in itself. When the members of the New York congregation Shaaray Tefila laid the cornerstone for their first synagogue in 1846, for instance, press accounts of the ceremony made it seem as if they were building a temple dedicated principally to decorum, "where 'Worship, Order, and Respectability' would be the graces." S. M. Isaacs, the congregation's spiritual leader, explicitly identified "the leading essentials—order and decorum"—necessary to "secure devotion" and called for the cooperation of the entire congregation "in carrying them into execution."[19] Presumably it was in keeping with these goals that a mixed choir of men and women performed at the synagogue's dedication, although the same group would not have been allowed to perform at the regular worship service of the strictly traditional congregation.[20] Despite the popularity of these ceremonies, some observers questioned their halakhic propriety. In response to an inquiry from America in regard to the anticipated performance of the dedication choir at Shaaray Tefila, England's chief rabbi, Nathan Adler, declared that "it is by no means correct to permit ladies to assist with their vocal powers at the consecration of a synagogue." Adler's concern seems to have been that should women begin to sing in nonreligious rituals, they might more easily become a part of the worship itself.[21] Nevertheless, despite Adler's ruling, Shaaray's Tefila's consecration choir performed on June 25, 1847.

Adler's prediction was not ill founded. The recollections of Joseph Jonas, a founder of the Bene Israel congregation in Cincinnati, suggest that at the far western reaches of Jewish settlement in the early nineteenth century, restrictions on women's participation and voice were not initially taken too seriously. The "glorious occasion" marking the dedication of Cincinnati's first synagogue on a Friday afternoon in 1836 was accompanied by a band and a choir "of about twenty of the ladies and gentlemen of the congregation." Although the coming of the Sabbath silenced the instrumental music being played for the dedication, the women and men of the chorus apparently continued to accompany the service, and the whole "was concluded by one of the ladies leading in the splendid solo and chorus of *Yigdal* [a Hebrew hymn]."[22]

According to Jonas, however, the subsequent numerous arrival of "our German brethren" helped push this flexible frontier congregation back into accord with more traditional practices, at least in relation to the synagogue. Indeed, in 1852, before the consecration of the congregation's second synagogue, Samuel Bruel, generally recognized as one of the more learned members of the congregation, "moved that ladies be prohibited from singing at said consecration."[23] Although Bruel represented the most conservative faction within the congregation, the committee assigned to consider the matter validated his objections when they reported their conclusion that "it would be wrong for ladies to participate in the ceremonies."[24] Nevertheless, the silencing of women's voices on these occasions was rare. In fact, wherever congregations began to take an interest in adapting their synagogue worship to the demands of respectability, suggestions for the establishment of a choir were among the earliest proposals.

The first synagogue choir to perform regularly at American synagogue services was a voluntary group of men and boys organized in 1845 at the newly established Emanu-El congregation in New York. This innovation marked the congregation's attempt to devise a more up-to-date synagogue ritual.[25] When the congregation moved into an old church on Chrystie Street in 1847, innovations for the new synagogue included an organ and women choristers.[26] The second choir in New York City was organized at Anshe Chesed in 1849, when that congregation moved into a new building. At first the choir consisted of men and children (gender unclear), but when Leon Sternberger arrived in the same year to serve as hazan, he created a choir of sixteen adults, both men and women, as well as eleven children.[27]

Allowing men and women to sing together in the Anshe Chesed choir generated little congregational discussion of religious legalities. The only difficulties involving the choir to surface in the congregation's records were complaints "that it was not proper of the *hazzan* to sing with the ladies in one choir and to run in and out twice during the service." Hyman Grinstein explains that the congregation objected to the hazan, Jonas Hecht, serving as both service reader and choir director, running back and forth between the *bimah* on the floor of the sanctuary and the balcony where the choir performed. His movements apparently were seen as out of keeping with developing notions of propriety for behavior at a worship service. Hecht's reply to the congregation's complaint is itself instructive. The minutes record him as saying, "The singing by the *hazzan* with the ladies in one choir was not prohibited by our Jewish laws but that the singing of ladies itself was not in accordance with the rites of the Jewish religion." The congregation ignored Hecht's identification of the questionable legality of their practice; the choir continued, but Hecht was dismissed.[28] Mixed choirs were not universally embraced, however; the choir at New York's B'nai Jeshurun in the 1850s, for instance, remained restricted to men and boys.

Attempts by Cincinnati's two leading synagogues in 1848 to address synagogue "disorder," which was attributed "partly to the manner and conduct of the service itself," point to the expectation that choirs could transform congregations into settings for devotion.[29] Both communities proposed the introduction of choirs as a way to silence individual voices within their congregations. At B'nai Yeshurun, the congregation was instructed to "be perfectly silent" when the hazan was praying and was otherwise forbidden from "chimn[ing] in with the Chasan or [newly mandated] choir except in making the Responses . . . in conjunction with the choir." Bene Israel also planned the creation of a choir as new regulations instructed that all worshipers were to recite their prayers "in a low tone of voice so as not to interfere with the Hazan or Chorus, and in no case to disturb the worship." The congregation carefully stipulated that although a choir was to be formed, "no alteration or diminishment shall take place in our present form of Divine Service or Prayers" as a result. The Cincinnatians hoped to change the style of public worship while keeping the service itself intact.[30] Yet as their caution suggests, the members recognized that the introduction of more order into the service threatened the integrity of the traditional ritual. With the new rules, the aggregation of individual voices would no longer constitute public worship. Instead, the individual's voice became a potential disturbance to the harmonious unity of centralized communal prayer. If these adjustments did not necessarily "alter" or "diminish" the prayers themselves, they certainly changed the worshiper's relationship to the liturgy—taking it out of the individual's control and putting it into the mouths of others.

The introduction of choirs thus potentially changed the relationship of women in the congregation to the worship service in two important ways. First, by giving women a role in articulating the prayers of the congregation, the introduction of choirs offered women important symbolic participation and leadership in the prayers of the community. Second, as the prayers were taken from the control of those in the congregation, the position of women as congregants grew closer to that of men. As the emphasis on ordering the service silenced or carefully channeled the responses of individual worshipers, male congregants lost their proprietorship over the service, and their individual contributions to the service diminished in importance. Thus even without changing the position or religious responsibilities of most women who prayed in the synagogue, their status as congregants shifted as what it meant to be a congregant was redefined. Innovations that were mainly intended to bring order to the sanctuary resulted in a transformation of the basic assumptions about what worship could be, who could participate in it, and how it was to be conducted.

Choir Debates

As congregations introduced mixed choirs to provide measured, orderly, and "edifying" religious expression, few communities gave much attention in their deliberations to the proper place for women in Judaism. In fact, as many congregations began to hire choristers for their services, the issue became, not whether Jewish women should sing out in the worship, but how much to pay Christian singers who were hired to perform in the choirs. Nevertheless, while the congregations appeared unconcerned, the nation's nascent Jewish press conducted an extended theoretical debate about the propriety of women's voices in worship, in light of the larger question of the appropriate role and place for women in the American synagogue.

The discussion about mixed choirs in the national Jewish press was one of many among nineteenth-century Jewish leaders that focused on the contest between the demands of tradition and the demands of contemporary values and expectations. This debate, like later discussions on the introduction of mixed seating in American synagogues, reveals that questions about women's rights and status were also part of larger discussions about the public appearance of Judaism and the legitimacy of reform. In the choir debate, arguments about the rights of women were mixed together with familiar community concerns about bringing devotion and decorum to Jewish worship. Central to these discussions was a debate over the legitimating authority of traditional texts.

At the center of this debate stood Isaac Mayer Wise. As the new rabbi of Cincinnati's B'nai Yeshurun congregation, he started the weekly newspaper the *Israelite* in 1854 as a forum for his views on the reform of Judaism, as well as for news of the Jewish world. Wise had introduced a choir of boys and girls in his Albany congregation in 1847 and upon his arrival in Cincinnati, pushed for the creation of a mixed choir as one of his first priorities.[31] Wise's 1855 article "Does the Canon Law permit Ladies to sing in the Synagogue?" provoked an extended debate in both the *Israelite* and the *Occident* from 1854 through 1856, focusing on the religious legitimacy of women's voices in prayer.[32]

In making his argument for mixed choirs, Wise played upon the growing awkwardness of the traditional gender divisions of Jewish worship in a society that so valued and emphasized female religiosity. He suggested that objections to female participation in synagogue choirs would "appear ridiculous" when exposed to the light of contemporary sensibilities. "In our days," he argued, only men who lacked "full command over their intellectual faculties" could countenance the "queer notion of prohibiting ladies to sing in the choir."

In this debate, as in many others, Wise was not afraid to advance somewhat contradictory arguments. On the one hand, he was careful to show that an accurate reading of the Talmud would support women's inclusion in synagogue choirs. On the other hand, he also satirized Talmudic judgments and dismissed their relevance to modern life. He started by arguing that the traditional silencing of women in the synagogue was based "upon a misunderstanding of the original passage in the Talmud." According to Wise, the relevant passage from the Song of Songs says only that the voice of woman is "pleasant," but this passage was misused to support the much more extreme Talmudic claim that "the voice of every women is lubric, or engaging impure affections." Furthermore, Wise claimed that Talmudic judgments were meant to be taken as law only when they were based upon texts drawn from the Pentateuch. Since in the silencing of women's voices "the proof is brought from the Song of Solomon . . . none can imagine for a moment that this could be intended to be a canon law." Wise thus read the Talmudic prohibition as a discussion, not a legal proscription.

Having argued that the Talmudic observation about women's voices was never intended to be law, Wise went on to show that, in any case, such texts were irrelevant to present-day realities. He thus carefully demonstrated his own rabbinic credibility by citing a myriad of traditional texts yet concluded that no Jew was compelled to live in accord with Talmudic judgments that in modern days "can have no meaning and no application." The Talmud's view of women, after all, had been influenced by "the oriental custom of hiding and imprisoning the women in harems." As Wise pointed out, "In this and all European countries women sing, and we are accustomed to hear them; hence there is not a shade of a prohibition, that they should not sing in a Synagogue choir." Although Wise based the bulk of his analysis on his reading of rabbinic texts, in comments like these he framed the question of women's status in the synagogue in relation to their status in contemporary society.

Wise also presented the choir question as a means to expand women's presence and influence in the synagogue. "It is most desirable and recommendable," he observed, "that our ladies should take an active part in the synagogue." Such a development would advance the transformation of the synagogue that he sought by adding "to the devotion of the heart, the solemnity of the ceremonies, and the decorum of the divine place of worship." Wise recognized that allowing women to participate in the service would transform the nature of woman's relationship to the synagogue. "Let them consider themselves bound in duty to participate in the worship of the Almighty," Wise declared. The implication was that under the old dispensation, with no actual or potential role for women in the service, everyone understood that women's presence was irrelevant both to what went on in the synagogue and to their own spiritual needs. Once they were brought into the service itself, he argued, women would no longer be able to regard their presence as more or less optional. Finally, Wise suggested that the integration of women's voices into the formal praise of God would transform the ethos of the synagogue itself. "We have long enough sung methaphysics and prayed logic," he observed; "let heart and sentiment come into our liturgy by song and music, by the female voice and the female heart."

Most of those who penned articles in response to Wise's far-reaching arguments wrote as if the questions raised in regard to "ladies singing in the synagogues" were purely issues of Talmudic interpretation. Thus, Solomon Jacobs felt compelled to refute Wise in order to prevent him from leading others astray: "I am ready to confess that your views are sufficient to stagger any one at first sight. If this be really the case with those who have some Talmudic information, what must it be with those who have none?" Jacobs thus sought to "intercept" Wise's "onward course" by proving that the Cincinnati rabbi's arguments were "unfounded on Talmudical grounds."[33] Even when a sympathetic rabbinical colleague of Wise, Isidor Kalish, joined the debate, he too sustained the rhythms and requirements of Talmudic argument. Kalish went so far as to ridicule Solomon Jacobs for not recognizing a standard mode of Talmudic argumentation.[34] Kalish, like his opponent, argued on the basis of Talmud, seeking to prove definitively that "even on rabbinical grounds are no objections against the singing women in the synagogue."[35] While debating whether the Talmud's discussion of when a woman might publicly read the Book of Esther meant that the Talmud legitimated the presence of women's voices in a synagogue choir, the two men battled over whose interpretation of the text was authoritative. Both wielded traditional texts to justify their points of view and reminded each other, as Kalish instructed Jacobs, "not to contradict any longer the Talmud, the best and safest authority in religious matters."[36]

Neither side in the discussion wanted to cede the other's right to draw authority from Judaism's traditional authoritative texts. This conflict, expressed in the 1854–1856 newspaper discussion about choirs, reflected the issues at stake in a lay–rabbinical conference convened in Cleveland on October 17, 1855. Called by Wise and presided over by Kalish in his capacity as host rabbi, the Cleveland conference was attended by Reformers and traditionalists from eight cities. Wise's avowed goal in organizing the meeting was to promote cooperation and unity among American Jews. The document promulgated by the conference sought to realize this end by compromising on a statement that agreed upon the "immediate divine origin" of the Bible and the basic authority of the Talmud in its "logical exposition of the biblical laws." Condemnations of this Cleveland compromise were immediate and passionate. Traditionalists berated their usual champion, Isaac Leeser, who had participated in the program, for believing that he could work with Reformers. David Einhorn, a leading radical Reformer in Europe who had recently arrived in America, blasted Wise for kowtowing to the claims of traditionalists and Talmud.[37] This larger debate about the place of textual authority in American Judaism determined the framework for discussions over choirs and other reforms involving women's place in Jewish worship.

Nonetheless, most communities considered or instituted mixed choirs, not on the basis of Talmudic authority, but on considerations of order and dignity in the worship service. Congregational records rarely reveal any halakhic or Talmudic concerns when the idea of a choir is advanced. Such discussions seemed to emerge only when someone objected after the fact, and they seldom affected the final outcome. Debate in the Jewish press about the introduction of mixed choirs ignored the question of what purpose such choirs would serve, apparently accepting the notion that their introduction would ensure more solemn and decorous devotion. Opponents, seeking to convince readers that such innovations could not be reconciled with strict standards of Jewish observance, tended to concentrate much more on the legal and textual objections to such innovations.

Consequently, the extensive wrangling over Talmudic interpretation had little effect on congregational decisions about mixed choirs. Moreover, such a dialogue was possible only so long as both sides were willing to conduct it according to the same authorities. The controversy that erupted over the conclusions of the Cleveland conference demonstrated that many Reform leaders were no longer interested in this discussion. In fact, as Samuel Bruel, who had already seceded from a reforming Cincinnati congregation over the issue of women's voices in the choir, observed, the question had to a certain extent already become moot. In his response to Wise's initial article, Bruel inquired, "Why ask a question, to which you have replied by word, act and deed." Wise had, after all, as Bruel put it, "been . . . most active in the formation of a choir including ladies." Further discussion only masked what was effectively a foregone conclusion.[38]

The Next Stage—Mixed Seating

Although the issue of mixed choirs continued to be a source of contention in many congregations, by 1855 the vanguard of Reform had already passed on to the next gender frontier in the synagogue. The first generally acknowledged introduction of mixed seating in the modern synagogue occurred in 1851. When Isaac M. Wise was banished from Albany's Congregation Beth El after disagreements that began over ritual and doctrine had ended in fisticuffs, he was joined by followers from Beth El in founding a new congregation, Anshe Emeth.[39] As Wise recalled in his memoirs, the Baptist church that the seceders bought in 1851 to serve as their new synagogue "contained everything necessary for a temple, except an ark for the *Torah* . . . It was well furnished, had an organ and family pews, schoolroom, vestry-room, dwelling etc." The group consecrated their new synagogue in October 1851 and, according to Wise, "resolved unanimously to retain" the family pews. Wise described the "innovation [as] an important step, which was severely condemned at the time," and claimed that "the emancipation of the Jewish woman was begun in Albany, by having the Jewish girls sing in the choir, and this beginning was reinforced by the introduction of family pews."[40]

Wise's claim to being the bold emancipator of Jewish women was exaggerated. Jonathan Sarna has pointed out that the only record of the bitter opposition or "the cry of horror [that] rent the heavens" or the "gallons of ink . . . wasted in denouncing it as an 'immoral' innovation" recalled by Wise were a few restrained comments from Isaac Leeser.[41] Throughout his tenure as editor of the *Occident*, Leeser was the foremost advocate for traditional Jewish practice and observance in the United States. In December 1851 Leeser commented on a report in the Albany *Evening Journal* that Wise's congregation "numbers about eighty families, each family occupying a pew." Leeser observed that "our readers will easily recognise in this another reform of the Doctor's, one by no means to be commended."[42]

In 1854 Temple Emanu-El in New York City also adopted an old church as their new synagogue building. Like Wise's congregation in Albany, Emanu-El's leaders decided to retain the family pews of the existing structure. As in Albany, it was not clear that the Emanu-El congregation meant to highlight their radical spirit with this seemingly startling innovation of seating men and women worshipers side by side. In both cases, Jonathan Sarna has argued, the family pew was adopted principally as a matter of convenience, so that the existing church buildings could be utilized with less expense and trouble. In this reading, neither congregants nor observers experienced the introduction of mixed seating as such a striking departure. Sarna suggests that the ideological and religious divide that came to be associated with family pews developed only after their initial introduction.[43] Yet even if the introduction of mixed seating was governed principally by convenience, such a change would have been possible only if it fit with the world view of those who would occupy the pews.

Wise, for instance, had introduced a number of ritual changes into the worship service at his first congregation in Albany, yet the congregation still saw these innovations in the context of the traditional synagogue. When he urged the introduction of a boys' and girls' choir in 1847, for example, some insisted upon maintaining "the old singsong" in prayer, but the only serious discord arose in determining where the new choir would sit. Space within the synagogue was limited, and the young women in the choir objected to having to sit among the men. The congregation rejected Wise's suggestion "to apportion the seats anew, and to set apart half of the floor, as well as of the gallery, for the women." Instead, the board determined to build an extension to the gallery on the north side of the synagogue for the choir's use. This suggestion, however, led to what Wise later termed "an uprising of the Amazons," because it incurred the wrath of those women who lost their front-row gallery seats because of the extension. In the end a separate "handsome perch" was built on the west side of the gallery exclusively for the choir, "for the girls objected strenuously to sitting among the men [on the sanctuary floor]."[44] Thus, in Wise's first American congregation, those involved in his innovations tolerated the introduction of a choir but refused to allow it to alter the synagogue's prevailing gender order.

It was only when members of the old congregation joined Wise in starting a new congregation that they were ready to adapt a new pattern of Jewish worship. In the new congregation, members were prepared to accept the new framework for Jewish community being defined somewhat improvisationally by their unconventional rabbi. Family pews represented one aspect of their freshly defined religious space and community. In the same way, members of New York's Temple Emanu-El understood that the creation of their "temple" separated their community from previous expressions of Judaism. Again, the introduction of family pews was one aspect of many within the new pattern of Jewish religious life they hoped to realize in their new temple on Twelfth Street. With the dedication of the new edifice, the Judaism of Emanu-El became the prototype for Reform worship in the eyes of many American Jews.

A correspondent to the *Asmonean* in April 1854 wrote "to inform your readers in what the reforms of the Emanu-El Temple service consists." "S." noted the omission of some prayers and repetitions in the service. He also described the reader's slow and distinct enunciation of the prayers, the contributions of organ and choir, the lecture by the Reverend Dr. Leo Merzbacher, and the elimination of inappropriate synagogue business from the conduct of the service. "So much in

Sanctuary with family pews, Temple Emanu-El, New York, adapted from a former church building and dedicated as a synagogue in 1854. © Collection of The New-York Historical Society.

a few words," he concluded, "for the reform of this Congregation, but," he continued, "allow me . . . to say something in regard to the material affairs thereof." S. then described how "instead of galleries for Ladies," the synagogue was "divided into pews for families . . . so that each member sits with his family." This observer saw in the seating innovation neither redress of the status of women in Jewish worship nor a striking aspect of the "reforms" introduced by the congregation. He identified the family pew simply as an "arrangement" that "prevents a great deal of confusion complained of in the Jewish synagogue."[45] An October 1855 *Asmonean* commentary, "On Jewish Reform," cited Emanu-El's "splendid temple in 12th street" as an exemplary model of the Reform congregation, "with choir and organ and all the appendages," but did not even mention the family pews.[46]

Mixed seating, then, was apparently not perceived as the most striking innovation among the complex of reforms enacted at Emanu-El in 1854 and had likewise drawn limited notice when introduced in Albany. Nevertheless, the prominence of Emanu-El and its elite congregants helped to bring the question of mixed seating into public view and associated it with the Reform agenda. The most significant public debate regarding seating at Emanu-El appeared in the *Asmonean* in December 1855 and January 1856, between the Reverend Henry A. Henry and Leo Merzbacher, the spiritual leader at Emanu-El. Their argument picked up on the themes at play in the mixed-choir discussion and elaborated on the issues at stake in the conflict between traditionalists and Reformers. Wise had asked, in August 1855, "Does the Canon Law permit Ladies to sing in the Synagogue?" Henry, in December, asked, "Does the Canon Law permit ladies to sit in the synagogue next to the gentlemen during time of divine services?" Although the two men agreed upon the relevant question at stake in synagogue innovations, they came up with opposing answers. Henry argued that Jews should take the Talmud as their guide, rather than its would-be interpreters: "If a new Minhag America [form of worship or custom that would be American] is really requisite, let it be based on more solid principles, than those advocated by the self constituted rabbins of America."[47] Like Wise and Kalish before him, Henry sought to claim the imprimatur of rabbinic tradition to validate his claims.

By contrast, Merzbacher declined in his response to build his case on textual authority, thereby undermining the shared premise of the debate.[48] In Merzbacher's view the authority of tradition could not legitimate outmoded practices. Although he did not ignore the traditional text, Emanu-El's leader made a virtue out of refusing to build an argument by piling on textual references. He cited "numerous passages" in the Talmud in support of his case, but in asking his audience to "save us, for mutual benefit, the trouble of quoting and perusing," he implied that neither he nor his readers wanted to be dragged through the tedium of Talmudic disputation.

Merzbacher's case paralleled Wise's argument in denying that the segregation of women in the synagogue had anything to do with canon law. In fact, according to Merzbacher, although Henry "regaled" the reader with much Talmudic discussion, he "could not point out a direct precept, ordinance or statute" against the innovation. Merzbacher portrayed the "present would-be Talmudists" as searching "against every innovation, however wise and proper, for some objection in any obscure book." He argued that contemporary Jews should be guided, not by the minutia of outdated laws, but by the original intent of the lawmakers.

In the case of family pews, Merzbacher pointed out that the separation of men and women in the ancient Temple arose because it was "unanimously considered as conducive to decorum." To assert that the need for decorum rather than for separation should be the basis for defining the appropriate place of women in the synagogue raised troubling questions about existing synagogues. Merzbacher was not meek about exposing contemporary practice in an embarrassing light. He questioned how well the "present adopted principle of the modern orthodox builder of Synagogues" accorded with the desire to preserve decorum in public worship. In so doing, he painted an evocative picture of the American synagogue of his day:

> The gentlemen are ranged on benches, in the lower part, to the left and right, corresponding with the amphitheatrical seats of the female order in the gallery above so as to present to the gaze of every one the whole array of female beauty in the upper region; and *vice versa*, to take under consideration from on high the rank and file of the male order below; affording also the opportunity of a constant telegraphic communication, at the twinkling of an eye, to all parts of the house.

The conclusion to be drawn from this spectacle was obvious to Merzbacher: "Do you earnestly believe that this mode of arrangement is conducive to decorum and devotion?"

Merzbacher suggested that the only way to reinstate the original principle of decorum intended by the tradition was to revert to the practice as "you have certainly seen [in] some old Synagogue . . . where the partition wall of the ladies' department was surmounted by a close lattice-work, with curtains attached there-to, so that no glances could penetrate the interior, and no captivating look find egress from within." This system had certainly been more effective in preserving decorum than the present "perversion of principle," which seemed to invite "opposite parties to a mutual consideration and attention!"

Despite its title, Merzbacher's article "Women-rights in the Synagogue, or Ladies and Gentlemen on equal footing in the Place of Worship" expressed little interest in the cause of women's rights. Only in satirically suggesting that the reintroduction of the traditional synagogue's closed-off women's annex might be the best guarantee of decorum within the sanctuary did Merzbacher refer to contemporary protofeminist sensibilities. Strict segregation, he suggested, was, after all, hardly an option at a time when "the ladies of our day claim more liberty, and equal rights even, and will not submit to the restrictions of former times and return to the ghettos of the synagogues of old." Given the changed expectations of contemporary women, Merzbacher claimed that "the most conservative plan for decorum is to place on the side of every gentleman the guardian angel of his choice, and to surround him with the members of his family, a mode applied with the best success by our neighbors."

Despite his allusion to women's rights, Merzbacher did not focus on the injustice done to women in the traditional synagogue nor emphasize the respect finally accorded them in his own new temple. He seemed to assume that the absurdity of the old custom must be so obvious to all that it need not be mentioned explicitly. In his reading, the inappropriateness of segregating the sexes derived, not from its original intent, but from its impact on the contemporary American synagogue, where it was more a cause of impropriety than a guarantor of decorum.

The mixed choirs and mixed seating introduced into American synagogues during the 1840s and 1850s were only two aspects of a wide range of changes that Reformers hoped would transform Judaism into a suitably modern and American religion. Other reforms, like organ music, sermons in German and English, and the removal of hats from male worshipers' heads, were also introduced in the interest of bringing a greater measure of respectability and devotion to the public expression of Jewish worship. In this general effort, however, the problems generated by the traditional gender order of the synagogue demanded particular attention. Leo Merzbacher may have cared little about women's rights, but his indictment of vertical flirting indicated his awareness that Jewish claims to respectability could not be separated from attention to women's place and status in the synagogue. As long as women's galleries recalled the ancient practices of primitive religions and as long as the alluring remoteness of galleried women disrupted efforts to sustain orderly worship in American synagogues, Jews would fall short in their drive to secure their claim to refinement and respectability in the American spectrum of religiosity. American Jews could not aspire to the social and religious status they imagined for themselves until they altered the gender order of their public worship so that Jewish women could become the "guardian angel[s]" of the family pew, rather than the beautiful temptresses of the gallery.

CHAPTER FOUR

The Trouble with Jewish Women

As at most mid-nineteenth-century banquets, the toasts delivered at the 1858 gala of New York's Hebrew and German Hebrew Benevolent Societies included one in honor of "the Ladies." On this occasion R. J. De Cordova, Esq., acquitted himself well, delivering a tribute that left no room for doubt that the "women of Israel" not only matched but surpassed every feminine ideal that mid-nineteenth-century American society could hold up: "If he were to tell them [his male audience] that no women in the world were more chaste, more loyal or more true than the Jewish women—if he told them that they were the tenderest and best of mothers, the most affectionate and dutiful of daughters in the whole family of man, he only said what they all knew." De Cordova cited the works of the "poets and novelists of Christendom" to attest to the outstanding examples of courage and motherly excellence set by Jewish women and the conviction that "Jewish beauty was the purest and most delicate in the whole world."[1]

De Cordova's excess of superlatives, his insistence that "the most eloquent orator in the world might pile word upon word, trope upon trope, metaphor upon metaphor and yet fail to do justice to the millionth part of the claims which the Jewish women had on the affection, the admiration, and the esteem of mankind," was typical of a society that viewed women as exemplars of pure and earnest piety. The "loud applause" that interrupted his words testified to his audience's awareness that successful American identities could not be built solely upon economic success and convivial celebrations of benevolence. Acceptance as refined and respectable members of American middle-class society depended as well upon successful emulation of that society's gender ideals.

However much Jewish community leaders in the first half of the nineteenth century might have yearned for the respectability associated with lofty rhetoric, fine buildings, and increasingly prosperous congregants, their quest was complicated by synagogue structures that continued to marginalize women. As De Cordova's anthem to female virtue made clear, the arrangement of gender roles was a crucial component of any religion's claim to refinement and respectability. In the Jewish case, traditional gender structures were problematic from a number of perspectives. Not only did American synagogues depart in appearance from respectable American churches, but even more egregiously, the structure of the traditional synagogue actually seemed to encourage and exhibit disreputable behavior among its female worshipers. Rather than offering a view of the chaste and retiring femininity boasted of by De Cordova, the galleries too often displayed a spectacle of irreverent behavior and an implied exotic sexuality.

The standards of middle-class gentility in antebellum America demanded that women clothe themselves with modesty and reserve. Refined ladies were expected to see to the respectability of their men, who might otherwise tend to cruder and less polished behavior.[2] The genteel model of respectability and refinement represented by affluent Protestant congregations featured the fashionable and pious presence of their female members. In this context, breaches of propriety among women seated in synagogue galleries cast a particularly embarrassing light on the state of American Judaism. Furthermore, praise of the "dark oriental beauty" so often attributed to the denizens of the gallery was hardly the kind of admiration that Jewish leaders sought for their communities.[3] Jewish claims to American respectability were confounded by galleries seemingly filled with dark-eyed, raven-haired, exotic maidens. Propriety demanded that Jewish women, like their bourgeois Christian counterparts, embrace the role of decorous matrons and moral guardians. As long as Judaism sequestered women in separate galleries, however, communities could do little to domesticate either their behavior or perceptions of their collective presence.

Misbehavior associated with the women's gallery was not limited to the "constant telegraphic communication" between men and women noted by Emanu-El's Merzbacher. Instead of serving their communities as paragons of refinement, gallery occupants created their own brand of disorder and commotion. Early attempts to impose order on the synagogue were frustrated by the difficulty of legislating female conduct within existing synagogue governing structures. In the general effort to subsume individual voices and movements within the orchestrated unity of a formal worship service, congregational leaders were stymied by community structures in which women had no official status. In addition to being separated from the male congregation and kept from direct participation in the worship ritual, women were also excluded from the organizational framework of the community. Because women, unless they were widows, were not considered members of the congregation, congregational officers could not press female worshipers into obedience as a condition of membership. The rules and bylaws issued by many congregations regarding synagogue behavior added the footnote that "the ladies are also respectfully required to comply with the above regulations" or the reminder that "the forgoing rules apply equally to the Ladys as the Gentlemen."[4]

Sometimes, congregational boards addressed specific instances of disruptive behavior arising among the female congregants. Occupants of the gallery in Easton, Pennsylvania, in 1846 were scolded for not sitting in their assigned seats and fined for using the front row of the gallery as a passageway and a perch from which to get a better view of the congregation seated below.[5] At the Baltimore Hebrew Congregation in 1852, regulatory announcements called out at Sabbath services reminded parents that they were responsible for the behavior of their children and directed that "the ladies are requested not to change their places during divine worship & that the gentlemen are responsible for their ladies."[6] Similarly, at Cincinnati's Bene Israel in 1849, a resolution was discussed that would declare "that all ladies attending divine service shall not be permitted to leave their Seats or talk with each other until the service is completed, unless they retire from the Gallery." The board further proposed that the congregation's president "shall fine the Husband of any lady who disturbs the Worship by talking or otherwise."[7] Although this resolution was tabled, disorder in the gallery was clearly a concern at Bene Israel, even if its trustees were unsure of how to deal with it.

These repeated admonitions and discussions reflect the ambiguous and indirect relationship between the congregation and its female congregants. Although women were a regular presence in the synagogue, it was difficult for male officers in the sanctuary to control the behavior of those in the gallery. The trustees at Keneseth Israel in Philadelphia asserted their general communal authority by resolving that "all laws for peace and quiet and decorum apply to men, women and children alike." Yet the trustees, recognizing that they could not truly legislate for all, added the provision "and the men are responsible for their women."[8] Because women had no official status within the congregation, attempts by the board to assert authority over female worshipers had to be mediated through their husbands.

Whether the behavior of women congregants was any worse than that of their male counterparts, disorder among the "ladies" was regarded as a distinctive threat to the aura of gentility sought by proponents of congregational decorum. Acculturating Jewish leaders recognized that the model of refinement and probity on display in prosperous Protestant congregations featured the sedate presence of pious female worshippers. Thus, when women resisted the imposition of order within the synagogue, they undermined congregational attempts to establish the respectability of the synagogue as a religious space. Baltimore's Rabbi Abraham Rice never grew accustomed to the practices of American Jews and was appalled by the behavior of American Jewish women. "As long as the President and Officers of the Congregation find it necessary to repeatedly remind you to maintain decorum and proper conduct during worship and to request the women to cease the constant disturbances in the Ladies' Gallery, we have the clearest proof that we have lost our self-respect," he observed.[9]

Merzbacher's condemnation of flirting in the synagogue introduced a related concern, which troubled both Reformers and traditionalists. As early as 1845, Reverend S. M. Isaacs had complained in the *Occident* of the many "evils" and "continual disorder" that prevailed in the synagogue, making particular reference to "our eyes being constantly employed gazing on the tenants in the galleries, instead of contemplating our deplorably sinful condition."[10] Leeser, too, deplored the behavior of those who spent their time in the synagogue craning their necks upward toward the gallery.[11]

The flirting problem emerged as a result of the open gallery front characteristic of the antebellum American synagogue and its typical "gay array of blooming faces with which the galleries were crowded."[12] The situation was further exacerbated by another, little-documented trend in synagogue gallery design. The increasingly elaborate synagogues of the 1850s featured what Leeser, reporting on the 1847 Shaaray Tefila building, described as "the declivity of the galleries" and which Merzbacher identified as "the amphitheatrical seats of the female order in the gallery above."[13] The arrangement of gallery benches or pews in tiers (rather than in rows of benches all set on the same level) lessened the degree to which women were cut off from the service and gave everyone a better view. From a practical perspective, elevating the back rows of the gallery may have decreased some of the competition for front-row seats. A contemporary description of the dedication of B'nai Jeshurun's Greene Street synagogue in New York in 1851 indicates that the tiered seating arrangements were indeed designed with some concern for women's interests: "The galleries, side

Women in tiered seats at the consecration of Shearith Israel, New York, 1860. Courtesy The Jewish Museum, New York/Art Resource, N.Y.

and front are remarkably pleasant, the arrangement being such that the whole of the persons in them, have a full view of the body of the Synagogue."[14] A portrayal of the consecration of a new synagogue for New York's Shearith Israel congregation in 1860 shows at least four ranked rows of women attentively following the proceedings below.[15]

Giving women a better view, however, also gave those in the main sanctuary a better view of the women. By the end of the 1850s, equating the still segregated synagogue with a "matrimonial mart" had become a standing joke.[16] A young woman, writing to the *Jewish Messenger* under the name "Enfante Terrible," attributed the presence of young men in the synagogue to the opportunity offered them of "sauntering into the house of worship when the service is three parts finished, and then instead of reading your prayers, ogling all the girls who may be within reach of your vision."[17] "An Observer," responding to this accusation, acknowledged that there were some young men "who pay more attention to the gallery than to the service," but pointed out that "if it were not for the circumstance that the gallery was tenanted by the 'Enfante Terrible' and her compatriots, the eyes of those below would, with much greater attention be fixed on their prayer books." He further noted that "the young ladies are not in the least indisposed to encourage the attention paid them, whereas they should be the very ones to set the example of devotion."[18] When women, who were supposed to be the guardians of propriety, actually became the focus of misbehavior in a public religious setting, they called into question whether this community could merit either the "self-respect" mentioned by Abraham Rice or the respect of others.

Decency

One 1855 Jewish visitor to a traditional synagogue wrote disparagingly of male worshipers who "congregated round two stoves" while engaged in loud conversation and disorderly behavior. When he turned to the women, however, he observed "among some of the females far (if possible) more indecorous conduct than that of the men." He reported seeing women seated in the synagogue who behaved as if they were attending a low-class entertainment, describing "conduct . . . that would not have been allowed in the boxes of a two shilling theatre." In addition to noting "continued talking and laughing" in the women's gallery, the visitor reported that "one of the *ladies* . . . was actually engaged with an opera glass during the whole time of divine orthodox service in making 'observations' about the synagogue." The "pious females" around her, he observed, enjoyed "a hearty laugh over each piece of information conveyed."[19] The author of this article contrasted this scandalous behavior with that of women in Reform places of worship. If the women at Reform temples were not "over full of religion," he reflected, at least they attended houses of prayer where "decency and propriety of conduct is strictly observed."[20]

Another 1855 critic of "the antiquated form of synagogue worship" pointed to the "sad spectacle" presented by traditional synagogues. According to this observer, a "dispassionate and reasonable" look at the synagogue would reveal "families separated—women above—men below—some standing up—some sitting down—prayers read without reference to the performances of the Hazan—and the devout interrupted by talking, running in and out &c." To this author, the women's gallery was one of a series of clearly disreputable "customs and usages of the past" that "do not suit the present." He was of the opinion that the segregation of men and women contributed to the infelicitous behavior that marked traditional synagogues. Yet, as the example of Emanu-El made clear, solutions were at hand: "Now, if the prayers were shortened—if families sat together—if the congregation were required to assemble at a given hour—to rise and sit at appointed prayers, and to accompany the Hazan, or sit still and listen to him, any man must see that confusion would be avoided, and quiet and devotion preside over the assembly."[21]

Many synagogue practices appeared illogical and anachronistic to this observer, but his challenge to the women's gallery was particularly pointed: "Why should families be separated? Tell me, ye self-styled orthodox, the sense, the propriety, the *decency* of this custom."[22] This author clearly viewed the division of the family unit in the synagogue as a heinous offense, though he failed to articulate precisely what made it so outrageous. He expressed no particular concern about women's treatment in the synagogue. What seemed to be at stake for him was the way the custom of separating male and female family members at prayer publicly exposed the outdated gender organization of Jewish life. In his view, no contemporary rationale could justify continuing the antiquated practice of separation, which so flaunted current notions of civilized public behavior.

As acculturating American Jews became more concerned about how their public worship comported with the values and aspirations they expressed in the rest of their lives, they cast increasingly critical eyes upon the practices of the traditional synagogue. Assessments of the aesthetics, decorum, and propriety of American synagogues became evaluations of the social and moral worth of Jewish worship. In challenging the *decency* of those involved in traditional Jewish worship, both the observers cited above applied the standards of bourgeois respectability to the exercise of religious devotion. They highlighted those aspects of the worship ritual that might offend the sensibilities of visitors. In fact, their plea that readers take a "reasoned and dispassionate" look at the "spectacle" provided by Jewish worship defined the synagogue as a performance space for the presentation of Judaism. In the synagogue ritual, Jews submitted not only the substance of their tradition but also their claims to respectability for evaluation by the outside world.

Seen through the eyes of others, many of the customary practices associated with synagogue worship appeared confusing and disreputable. The position of women in the synagogue, however, offered a particularly sensitive barometer of the synagogue's aspirations to respectability. As acculturating Jews took on the identity of the "dispassionate and reasonable observer" for themselves, they began to question the suitability of gender arrangements that had long been taken for granted within Jewish culture. Under the scrutiny of bourgeois sensibilities, the unintegrated, sometimes unseemly presence of Jewish women seemed a glaring anomaly. The synagogue could never lay claim to a respectable American identity until it found a way to recognize the critical role assigned to women by middle-class culture in matters of refinement, decorum, and gentility.

The Public Gaze

Acculturating American Jews at midcentury were intensely concerned about being seen and judged by non-Jews. In January 1856 a letter to the *Asmonean* described the progress of San Francisco's two synagogues. "May both congregations succeed," the correspondent implored, "so that we no more need be ashamed when a gentile enters our places intended for worship—that we no more need have to lament the want of all devotion and decorum—and no longer drag out an ignominious existence of obstinate ignorance and mental petrifaction."[23] Although few Jewish observers would have put it quite so strongly, the desire to avoid disgrace in the eyes of outsiders often determined the rhetoric and behavior of both Reformers and traditionalists. In this context, the seemingly dishonorable and anachronistic treatment of women in the synagogue proved a highly visible and sensitive issue.

This concern with the views of outsiders increasingly came to shape the construction of synagogue practice and ritual. The elaborate consecration exercises staged by congregations ranging from rigidly traditional to radical Reform were one overt indication of Jewish concern with their public image before the non-Jewish community. An even more telling display of sensitivity to external judgment and standards might be found in repeated admonitions within the Jewish community to adopt the perspective of "a person unaccustomed to Jewish worship" and consider what *they* might see "upon entering the Synagogue."[24] Implicit in this advice was the expectation that Jews themselves would begin to identify with a synagogue visitor's shock in encountering "the careless and undevout behaviour of those engaged in the solemn act of addressing the Almighty."[25] In adopting the outsider's point of view, insiders found themselves needing to justify traditional Jewish practices and modes of observance not only to others but also to themselves.

Observing that "we are fast losing ground in our own estimation, and especially in the esteem of those who think not as we do in religious matters," S. M. Isaacs, editor of the *Jewish Messenger,* asked his readers to join in taking dispassionate measure of the synagogue ethos. "Let us take a fair view of the interior [of the synagogue] as it is presented to us on Sabbath mornings."[26] Were a critical eye directed toward synagogue behavior, Isaacs implied, its incongruity with middle-class standards of behavior would be obvious. One aspirant to "Rational Worship" asked those in attendance at worship services to "observe attentively what usually transpires." An objective visitor would encounter little but confusion and hypocrisy: "apparently unfelt responses, so indecorously uttered . . . boisterous and rapid chanting . . . the want of time and harmony . . . one standing up, another sitting down; one walking in, another running out. Some mumbling prayers quite audibly while the Hazan should be reading alone."[27]

Isaac M. Wise declared that the Jew who had adopted the "taste, views and inclination of the American" could only respond with disgust to rituals and ceremonies that "once touched his heart." Now, according to Wise, "he thanks God, if no stranger hears it."[28] S. M. Isaacs noted that American synagogues revealed "a complete want of spirituality, a total absence of that devotional feeling which should animate the beings who assemble in God's house." To Isaacs, this situation was all the more disgraceful when displayed "in a land where we stand on equal ground with all men." Those who had lifted the yoke of oppression from the shoulders of the Jews rightfully expected that America's Jews would show themselves worthy of the respect of a civilized society: "We are bound to manifest to them that we are impressed with the decorum due to God's house."[29]

Both traditionalists and Reformers who looked critically at the American synagogue saw a sanctuary in embarrassing disarray. Isaac Leeser, writing in 1848, decried the lack of punctuality in synagogue attendance, marked by the "loud and boisterous slamming of the door, and with a searching afterwards for prayer-books and the like, and then superadd a somewhat noisy manner of taking the seat: and we leave it to the candid judgment of any one to decide whether there can exist proper devotion among so much disturbance!"[30] Leeser asked his readers to compare this behavior with that of the gentiles: "Look . . . how they hasten to their churches when the time for meeting is about to arrive . . . and then behold the Jews dropping in at the Synagogue before or after the commencement of the service, as it may suit their tastes or convenience . . . What would a disinterested spectator imagine," Leeser asked, "but that Christians went to church with their whole soul . . . whereas Jews went because it was a sort of duty . . . but which is . . . very disagreeable to them."[31] Similarly, one of Leeser's correspondents urged, "Now contrast our Service with that of the gentiles only see how decorous every part of their service is performed, when you enter into some of their churches we are struck with awe."[32]

The concerns of Leeser and his colleagues that Jewish worship might be seen as a crude and hypocritical exercise resonated with the sensibilities of the society in which these Jewish leaders sought inclusion. Karen Halttunen has pointed out that bourgeois antebellum society was so filled with seekers after gentility that hypocrisy was construed as a "major social threat," through which "confidence men and painted women" might deceive and betray those who were truly genteel.[33] In bourgeois American society, recent Jewish immigrants were very much the unknown outsiders who had to establish their credentials to belonging. The possibility that Christian outsiders might perceive some fundamental hypocrisy in the expression of Jewish worship was of great concern to Jewish lay and rabbinic leaders. In response, they emphasized their belief that Jewish worship should "touch the heart, . . . lift the thoughts to God, and . . . purify and satisfy the cravings of the soul," and not simply parade as a mask for gentility.[34] For a community in search of legitimating authority, the stranger's eye and judgment, as well as the comparison with respectable non-Jewish assemblies, came to serve as a measure of propriety. Constant worry "whether it is not humiliating to us, were a stranger to enter our shrine" inevitably had a significant impact on the shape of Jewish worship.[35]

Christians did take an interest in Jewish practice, as well as in Jewish women, with results that must often have been disturbing to Jews concerned with their public image. Secular press accounts of synagogue dedications usually reported "neat" and "tasteful" buildings and described the "peculiar" and "interesting" rites of the Jews. Many observers came to synagogues seeking a taste of the exotic Orient.[36] These observers often directed their attention toward the women's gallery. Walt Whitman was one of many synagogue visitors who found himself distracted by the gallery's array of oriental beauty. After an 1842 visit to New York's Shearith Israel, he recorded his impressions of the synagogue's gallery, "filled with women—dark-eyed Jewesses . . . by no means the most unpleasing sight in the whole proceeding . . . We found ourselves casting our glances thither quite frequently."[37]

In 1841 the noted author and social critic Lydia Maria Child published an account of her own visit to Shearith Israel.[38] Child was surprised by the "heterogeneous jumbling of the Present with the Past," which she found quite jarring. Approaching the scene with romantic notions of "Israel's wandering race," Child found her "spirit . . . vexed with [the] incongruity" of the appearance and behavior of the worshipers: "I had turned away from the turmoil of the Present, to gaze quietly for a while on the grandeur of the Past; and the representatives of the Past walked before me, not in the graceful oriental turban, but the useful European hat! It broke the illusion completely."[39] Similarly, Child reported herself "disappointed to see so large a proportion of this peculiar people fair-skinned and blue-eyed. As no one who marries a Gentile is allowed to remain in their synagogues, one would naturally expect to see a decided predominance of the dark eyes, jetty locks, and olive complexions of Palestine."[40]

Absorbed in her reverie on the strange spectacle, Child was taken aback when she was approached by "one of the masters of Israel," who "somewhat gruffly ordered me and the young lady who accompanied me, to retire from the front seats of the synagogue. It was uncourteous; for we were very respectful and still, and not in the least disposed to intrude upon the daughters of Jacob." Although Child had noted that "the women were seated separately, in the upper part of the house," she evidently attributed the separation to the vagaries of the Orient and hardly expected that such strictures could be applied to herself, a modern and respectable Christian woman.[41]

Although Child was critical of the "cold, mechanical style" of worshipers dressed in incongruous "modern costume" and though she could not but bemoan Jewish blindness to the light of Jesus, her observations were, on the whole, sympathetic. Other accounts of Jewish worship, often part of campaigns to convert Jews to Christianity, were much more critical. In these descriptions, the place given to women in the practice of Judaism came in for close examination. *The Jew at Home and Abroad,* an 1845 publication of the American Sunday School Union, presented the "actual service of the Jews" as "generally speaking, a round of empty and profitless rites."[42] In detailing the public worship "of this remarkable people," the work noted that "females are not reckoned of the congregation. While the males worship in the synagogue, they are in the gallery." This account described the "lattice-work" that denied women "a distinct view of what takes place" and observed that while women were allowed to "join in the prayers, . . . their voice must not be heard in the synagogue." This portrayal suggested that the separation of women in the synagogue should be understood as indicative of the low esteem accorded women by Judaism. An anecdote is included about a visitor to a Prague synagogue. Seeing that the women's section afforded access to the sanctuary only through "certain rents or apertures [in the partition wall] about an ell long, and inch broad," the visitor remarked that "they will hear but little there." Judaism's lack of concern for female religiosity is reflected in the "ungracious reply" attributed to the visitor's "Israelite" guide: "Oh! quite enough for a woman."[43]

Herman Baer, presumably a Jewish convert to Christianity, wrote

The Ceremonies of Modern Judaism for publication by the Methodist Episcopal Church, South, in 1856.[44] He too had little sympathy for retrograde Jewish customs. Baer observed that unmarried ladies generally did not attend the synagogue, that women commonly did not attend Friday night services, and that "even the married ladies are not very regular in their attendance. This must seem surprising to a Christian," Baer continued, "who is accustomed to see twice as many ladies in a church as gentlemen." According to Baer the disparity arose, not because Jewish women were less religious than Jewish men, "but because it is thought a matter of minor importance whether the [ladies] attend service or not." He also pointed out that "in all synagogues, even among the somewhat heterodox Israelites of this continent, the ladies occupy the gallery; in Europe they are moreover completely screened from view by a kind of lattice-work." Baer attributed the custom of separate seating to its origins in "the more eastern clime of the harem."[45]

While Baer's narrative attempted to detail and explain (sometimes sympathetically) the peculiar practices of Jewish life, his ultimate purpose was to show that Judaism had become outmoded and irrelevant. Description of women's role served him well in this endeavor, especially since his portrayal focused more on the traditional synagogue of memory than on the American synagogue of the mid-nineteenth century. By associating the women's gallery with the harem, Baer left little room for doubt in the minds of his readers that the gender arrangements of the modern synagogue were premised on the religious and sexual subjugation of women. He noted that women were invested with great responsibility for the complex system of Jewish dietary laws but received little religious education. After listing the numerous disabilities imposed on women by the Talmud, Baer concluded that "the great theological and psychological problem, whether a woman has a soul, seems to have been solved in the negative by the old Talmudists." Baer asserted that even though "the spirit of the times has rendered many of these doctrines obsolete, yet even at this day, and in the United States of America, every Jew says in his daily prayer: 'Blessed are thou, O Lord, our God! King of the universe, who hast not made me a woman!'" Evincing outrage that such a sentiment could be expressed on American shores, Baer concluded, "What a chapter of woman's wrongs!"[46]

Conversionary novels, likewise, registered shock at the relegation

of women to the far regions of the synagogue, even as they found a seductive fascination in exotic beauties who might have walked through
the pages of the Bible. An 1867 tract portrayed the surprise of a synagogue visitor unfamiliar with Jewish practice when he "saw with astonishment" that the young girls he was with were "committed . . . to
the care of a woman who took them up to the gallery," while he was
directed to enter "the body of the house." These novels, while pity-
ing those who "fruitlessly wait[ed] for the coming of Israel's King,"
could also incorporate romantic notions of modern-day Israelites, especially as personified in dark-haired maidens: "His eye wandered to
where—bending from the latticed galleries as eager, earnest listeners
to the truth—sat a bevy of young girls, whose dark oriental beauty
was so unlike the blondes of the Gentile world . . . [T]here sat one, he
thought, who might represent Miriam of old . . . Another might have
represented Rebecca so sweet and gentle was her expression." [47]

Jewish authors who presented Judaism to the non-Jewish community had to address the place of women in Jewish practice. In his 1854
guide to Jewish practice, entitled *The Stranger in the Synagogue*, Simon Tuska acknowledged that "the method of praying in the synagogue seems very confused to the stranger." [48] Tuska, the eighteen-
year-old son of a Jewish minister in Rochester, New York, hoped to
show that with a little instruction, the proceedings would begin to
make sense even to the uninitiated: "By understanding its peculiari-
ties, much that seems irregular will appear to be methodical." [49] Although Tuska sought to validate traditional synagogue practice, he
expressed approval of those synagogues that had modified "some un-
social customs ordered by the Rabbins" and rejected "the vain traditions of the Talmud." [50] His concern was particularly evident in his
discussion of the role of women in the synagogue. He noted that "females are not admitted as *members* of the Congregation, nor are they
reckoned in forming a Minyan." Thus, no woman, "however pious,"
could ever be counted toward the minimum of ten Jews needed for
the conduct of public worship, whereas any man, "however impious,
provided only he is a son of Israel, would be allowed and even en-
treated to complete the Minyan." Tuska realized that this custom
would violate the sensibilities of even his most sympathetic readers
and did not try to justify it. "In the present age," he acknowledged,
"to lay such restrictions as these on the privileges and dignity of
woman, is far below the standard of civility, and it would therefore

seem proper to have no regard for old customs in any respect similar to the above."[51]

Both Tuska and Baer recognized that there was no way to defend the synagogue's traditional gender order in American terms. Even non-Jewish observers like Lydia Maria Child who entered the synagogue hoping for a glimpse of the romantic oriental past looked for practices that reflected their own bourgeois nineteenth-century values when evaluating how women were treated within this unfamiliar space. An 1856 commentator in the *North American Review,* for instance, appreciated the ancient echoes of the modern synagogue setting, where a "visitor . . . sees substantially the same arrangement, and hears substantially the same prayers and chants, as the Hebrews of Syria saw and heard in the days of Hillel." At the same time, this author also expressed his hope that the "grave Rabbins," in deciding the ongoing dispute as to whether women should be allowed to sing in public worship, would recognize that whatever the "seductive power" of women's voices, "they would soften and improve very much the songs of Zion, and add to the attractiveness of the service, at least to a Christian ear."[52]

Women's Rights in Collision with the Prayers

The message from such observations was clear: Quaint tradition was appealing; sultry oriental beauties were seductive and alluring. But much as these qualities might add to the interest non-Jewish observers took in Jewish worship, they undermined the likelihood that Jewish ritual would meet the stringent standards of acceptance set by polite, bourgeois society. As long as women were separated and their voices silenced, their presence remained seductive and sexualized. If women were allowed to become a part of the service, their presence could become a modernizing and harmonizing force—their participation could remove the rough, exotic edges that continued to jar the Christian eye and heart. Sequestered in the gallery, women served as a prominent reminder of the synagogue's oriental past. Integrated with men in the sanctuary, the distracting, flirting women of Merzbacher's typical women's gallery could become "guardian angel[s]," seated safely beside their chastened husbands and surrounded by the members of their families. The presence of Jewish women in the synagogue was sexualized by separation, but domesticated by integration.

Both traditionalists and Reformers agreed that the American synagogue sanctuary should become a home for decorous piety. The success of Reformers in identifying certain innovations, such as mixed
choirs and family pews, with the advance of decorum and respect for
women left traditionalists stranded without viable strategies for opposing these reforms. Like Reformers, traditionalists tried to make
their arguments consistent with contemporary discourse and values.
The effort to justify practices that had become identified as antiquated
and primitive, however, could only be made with a degree of awkwardness. Bound to reject innovations they believed were contrary
to Jewish law and custom, traditionalists strained to find a synthesis
between Jewish and perceived American values. A. Abraham, in an
1847 report on the consecration of Shaaray Tefila in New York, used
conventional laudatory phrases to refer to the women present. In describing the new synagogue, he noted "wide-spreading arches, between which were seen the galleries, filled with God's best gift to man,
the real ornaments of creation, the mothers, daughters, and sisters of
Judah."[53] But with growing criticism of the traditional synagogue as a
structure that exiled female bodies and voices (if not their souls) to the
galleries, on the margins of sacred space, such praise came to sound
increasingly hollow.

Traditionalists quickly realized that if they were to justify the traditional treatment of women, they would have to employ the rhetoric of
secular society. Even Samuel Bruel, a Cincinnati conservative who
was dismissed as an "upholder . . . of bigotry" and as "wedded to
noise & confusion" by traditionalists within his own community, was
sensitive to the need to acknowledge the respect due to women and
the importance of decorum within the synagogue.[54] Bruel admitted
that under Isaac M. Wise's choir plan the ladies were encouraged "to
participate in the worship of the Almighty and the edification of the
human heart," and he even commended Wise for "the zeal and also
the gallantry which you manifest in favor of the daughters of Israel."
Bruel was then left with the difficult task of justifying traditional limitations on women's participation in the synagogue: "Let me assure
you, Rev. Sir, that in this particular [urging women to participate]
your orthodox friends fully agree. Witness their prompt attendance
and the overflowing of their galleries." Despite Bruel's claims that
women had not been disenfranchised by orthodoxy and that the orthodox did "teach them [women] the precepts of the Lord and

train them to be rational beings," he still had to justify the traditional status quo. In this effort he equated change in the synagogue with radical attacks on society's gender divisions: "At the same time they (the orthodox) are not such staunch hyperaspist champions in favor of woman rights, as to desire them to take an active part in our religious service."

The awkwardness of Bruel's position became even more apparent as he attempted to explain why allowing women's voices in the prayer service detracted from the "great devotion" that all desired. Bruel focused particularly on the injunction against being distracted by a woman's voice during the recital of the "Shemang Yisrael," as he referred to the Shema prayer. Bruel observed that "the reader commences *Shemang Yisrael* at the top of his voice, and the sound of the female voice above it again creates a shrilling sensation in the ear and mind to the end of the prayer, our sages and casuists knew the frail nature of mankind; they directed their efforts to remove all temptation, that were like to inflame the passion, or to divide the attention during prayers."[55] Bruel's curious pseudoscientific explanation only exposed his cause to ridicule from Reformers like Wise, who observed of those opposed to mixed choirs that he "did not know whether to pity their ignorance, detest their hypocrisy, or laugh at their childish fear to differ with the notions of the vulgar."[56]

Others attempted more sophisticated appeals. Henry A. Henry, in his polemic against mixed seating, understood that he could not simply cite the authority of Talmud and tradition; he had to address his fellow Jews as rational and discerning Americans. "Reader!" he inveighed, "Do not imagine for a moment that we are arbitrary in our conclusions, and that we wish you to adopt an old custom because it is old, far be it from us. We wish you to exercise your reasoning powers." Despite this assurance, Henry was unable to demonstrate the relevance of ancient arguments to contemporary concerns. Ultimately, having concluded his Talmudic case, Henry could only admit, "It is not our purpose here to argue the right or the wrong of these customs . . . [O]ur purpose is only to show the points of law and then we have done our duty."[57]

Traditionalists did not want to be seen as denigrators of woman's religious or spiritual being. Even for Henry, it was hard to argue that it was objectively *right* to separate women from men in the sanctuary. Similarly, Solomon Jacobs, contesting Wise's arguments in favor of mixed choirs, admitted that "with respect to the abstract question itself, whether there is any actual sin, on mere rational grounds, in hearing a female sing in Synagogue, I am not prepared to offer an opinion, neither do I consider myself bound to look at the question in that light. We are dealing with it on talmudical or rabbinical grounds."[58]

The title of an 1857 *Occident* article, "Women's Rights in Collision with the Prayers," encapsulated the intractability of the conflict between traditional and contemporary values. In this article, "B." sought to demonstrate that although the morning blessing in which a man praised God for "not having made me a woman" provided an easy target for critics of Judaism, in no way did it mean that Judaism devalued women. B. assured his readers that Judaism accorded women the highest measure of equality: "As a being belonging to the spiritual world, woman . . . stands on the same elevation with man, and has claims to the same rights." Such views, he wrote, were intrinsic to Judaism from the start, when "the complete emancipation of women in the department of religion [was] fully pronounced in the Bible." According to this writer, the controversial blessing simply recognized that nature had made women "*physically* weaker." In his reading, male worshipers were thanking God for creating separate vocations and constitutions for men and women, invoking the notion of separate spheres that framed nineteenth-century gender thinking. "Both sexes," B. wrote, "acknowledge thereby that they are fully conscious in spirit of their respective positions and relations, and are ready to follow their destiny in the spheres pointed out to them by the God of nature, and in accordance with the rules prescribed to them by nature."[59]

B. recognized that American society itself hardly demanded gender equity. Most contemporaneous writing about social gender roles emphasized two separate but complementary spheres for men and women.[60] The problem for traditionalists like B. who tried to use this argument in defense of Judaism was that the two most prominent fields ceded to women in American ideology were the home and religion. In a society where women were celebrated for their spiritual influence and piety, it was difficult to defend practices that seemed to deny the fullness of female spirituality. Ultimately, despite his attempt to use contemporary gender ideology to justify Jewish custom, B. was unable to reconcile traditional practice with the contemporary expectation of the respect due to women in the public religious sphere. He could only conclude that "should we ever desire to grant to the spirit of the times its full and due importance, we should still have to decide that, in cases of collision, the spirit of the times must yield to that of eternity."

An 1856 contribution to the family pew discussion by a writer calling himself "Lara" also attempted to identify a contemporary rationale for the traditionalist position. Lara acknowledged that the separation of men and women in the synagogue reflected the customs of an oriental society in which "women were not admitted to the society of the men in mixed company" and in which women were "regarded . . . as inferior to men." Like Henry and Jacobs, Lara refused to "enter into the discussion whether they were right or wrong in this respect." Lara, however, was brasher than his colleagues in proclaiming that applying contemporary values to the synagogue would show that "the indiscriminate mixing of men and women in places of worship [was] an evil," while separating the sexes was "wise and prudent."[61]

Like other commentators, Lara feared the intrusion of sexuality into the sanctuary, but he insisted that it was integration, not separation, that presented the greatest danger. In his view, "the eye that ought to be uplifted to Heaven, ought not to be turned away to meet the eye of woman." Lara quailed at the thought of the house of God becoming "a matrimonial mart" or a home to the distracting "feelings as the presence of female youth and beauty cannot avoid engendering." Significantly, he pointed out that the Reform Jews of London, as well as those of Hamburg, had not adopted the latest American fashion of mixed seating. These groups, according to Lara, kept the separation not "out of respect of the Rabbinical authority" but, like the Quakers, out of motives of "reason, common sense, decorum and devotion." Even if Lara was accurate in his assessment of the motivations of Europe's Reform Jews, however, he was unable to sever the connection that acculturating American Jews were increasingly making between decorous devotion and the "indiscriminate mixing" that he so deplored.

The growing distance between traditionalists and Reformers on the issue of respect for women was captured in an 1856 exchange between Isaac Leeser and Rabbi Max Lilienthal. A German native, Lilienthal had come to Cincinnati from New York in 1855 to serve as rabbi of Congregation Bene Israel and as a reforming ally of Isaac M. Wise.[62] Lilienthal characterized Leeser's approach to Judaism as a "retrogression" and claimed that general acceptance of his traditionalist positions "would make our religion a contemptible laughing stock." As an example of the absurdity of trying to preserve traditional Jewish strictures ("Would you not run the risk of being laughed at when calling such customs 'religion'?"), Lilienthal raised the question of Jewish women's hair: "You know, that the married women in Israel were forbidden to show themselves without a cover of their hair; that hence they were used not only to wear hoods but even a kind of wigs."[63]

Traditional arguments for the covering of married women's hair revolved around the sexual allure of a woman's uncovered hair and the possibility that she might attract the interest of other men, when she should be an object of desire for her husband alone. Lilienthal realized, however, that within the bounds of mid-nineteenth-century discourse, it would be improper to even suggest that a respectable married woman could become an object of general sexual interest. Where modesty and restraint had been naturalized into inherent feminine qualities, explanations of traditional Jewish restrictions meant to control female sexuality might themselves seem to impugn the character of respectable Jewish women. Lilienthal was confident that no one writing for an acculturated Jewish readership in 1856 could credibly defend forcing married Jewish women to wear wigs. He noted that "this custom now-a-days has been done away with . . . and everyone gave his silent consent to this change." Lilienthal challenged Leeser to "dare now to step before the American public of Israelites, and argue the necessity of re-introducing this custom."[64]

But even on this point Leeser refused to concede any ground. Appropriately, he tried to argue on the grounds of modesty, suggesting that to question this traditional custom was to cast aspersions on the character of countless female forebears. Leeser asserted that the "present general neglect of this ancient custom does not prove that it is either wrong or absurd" and wondered about making "the custom of our mothers" into a "subject of ridicule." Leeser further asked "whether, on the whole, we have gained in the modesty of our women, by their neglect of ancestral manners and rules. Formerly, such a being as an unchaste Jewish woman, married or single, was unheard of . . . And now—!"[65]

Leeser could reasonably hope his argument that constraints on women were consistent with contemporary social ideals for feminine behavior would make sense to Jews concerned about being seen as good Americans. Unfortunately for Leeser, whatever the state of chasteness among his female contemporaries, the rules of public discourse determined that it was inappropriate to draw attention to even the potential sexuality of respectable young women, except to affirm its purity. As the observance of Judaism became skewed toward the public sphere of worship in a society that celebrated female religiosity and modesty, it became increasingly difficult to defend an arrangement that highlighted women's continued marginalization in the most visible arena of Jewish expression. The association of this separation with the oriental institution of the harem drew attention to the exotic sexuality associated with Hebrew beauty. Thus, Max Lilienthal could argue that traditional restrictions on Jewish women's religious expression were an outrage to civilized notions of decency. In his view, a prohibition against displaying one's own hair, for instance, could only be justified by the most obscure, primitive, and outdated reading of Jewish sources.

Reformers were able to portray traditional Jewish practice as denigrating and sexualizing women in the very sphere of life where middle-class Americans celebrated women's presence, piety, and modesty. With the widespread introduction of mixed choirs and the introduction of family pews in a few settings, constraints on female religiosity became increasingly synonymous with uncivilized and disreputable behavior. Attempts to justify these practices only further undermined efforts to portray traditional Judaism as a legitimate expression of American religion.

American Jews, wishing for middle-class respectability for themselves and for their religion, were extremely sensitive to the way that non-Jewish outsiders would perceive the public performance of Judaism. As acculturating Jews adopted the perspective of the imagined objective onlooker for themselves, they realized that the traditional and gendered structure of the synagogue could not stand. If Jews were to achieve the class and racial identities that they associated with secure American respectability, they would have to show that Judaism and Jewish worship could adapt to the gender order of bourgeois American society.

CHAPTER FIVE

Women in the Reforming Synagogue: Resistance and Transformation

One index of the growing salience of family pews can be found in Isaac Leeser's evolving response to their emergence in America's reforming synagogues. In November 1855, four years after expressing only limited interest in Isaac M. Wise's use of family pews in Albany, Leeser showed greater concern when he reported that in Rochester "the silly reform notions which have invaded the West of the Union had also found adherents . . . to the extent of some contemplating of doing away with the ladies' gallery and seating men and women together after the Gentile fashion." He predicted that such a course would "endanger the peace of the community, as there are a great many who are not yet ripe to follow the lead of the new-school teachers."[1]

Leeser's mention of the invasion of the West by "silly reform notions" was presumably a reference to Wise's 1854 engagement as a rabbi in Cincinnati, where he continued to champion Reform causes in his new congregation and in the weekly newspaper, the *Israelite*, that he founded soon after his arrival in the city. Although Leeser was rightly concerned about the potential influence of Wise's reform notions, Cincinnati's new rabbi had not yet brought the practice of mixed seating he introduced in Albany to his new home. The apparent model for Rochester's would-be reformers was, it turned out, not

Cincinnati's B'nai Yeshurun, but the new sanctuary of New York's Temple Emanu-El, consecrated in March 1854. For when Leeser wrote with some relief in December 1855 that he had apparently been "misinformed in regard to reform measures which had been contemplated" in Rochester, he noted that there were "some, indeed, [who] would have liked to have a mode of worship similar to the Emanuel Temple at New York; but they will not desire to introduce any reform which might lead to disunion." Although Leeser's informants told him that the only reforms sought by Rochester's Jews were "order in the worship and public decorum . . . and nothing beyond it," Leeser remained concerned that some in Rochester still "wanted a thorough reform." This phrase apparently had become associated with whatever was done at Temple Emanu-El. Fortunately, he declared, according to his latest informants the Jews of Rochester had finally recognized the divisive dangers lurking in such notions and determined that when they did purchase a synagogue, "the house [would] be supplied with a *gallery*."[2]

By 1861, when Congregation Tifereth Israel in Cleveland resolved to introduce family pews, Leeser no longer dismissed this sort of reform as a "silly" notion. In reporting "the introduction of family pews for seating males and females together," Leeser referred to the proposed innovation as "this last extremity." He described "this last radical change" as "so shameful and outrageous an innovation on our worship as the converting of a Synagogue into the style of a Christian church." What at first perhaps seemed to Leeser an odd folly, attributable to the whims of an obscure minister in Albany, had become the hallmark of radical Reform, distancing America's Jews from "such as are known to be the peculiar and individual characteristics of the Jewish faith by the intelligent and learned of the whole civilized world."[3]

Although Leeser appealed to the civilized world to validate his notion of synagogue design, in fact his ideal religious setting, with its apparent banishment of women, brought forth an image that was increasingly untenable to those seeking the creation of an *American* synagogue. As Leeser indicated, the question of where women sat in the synagogue was a defining characteristic of the Jewish religious setting. Allowing women into the main sanctuary entailed a willingness to revise fundamental assumptions of what it looked like to be, or to pray as, a Jew. In Rochester, Cleveland, and elsewhere, such notions were being challenged and redefined. Case studies of the history of a few congregations during this era illustrate the symbolic power of gender issues to advocates of tradition and reform alike.

Resisting Reform in Cleveland

In the 1850s both of Cleveland's Jewish congregations were solidly orthodox. They utilized traditional liturgies in their worship services, they provided the requisite communal services (cemetery, ritual slaughterer, and ritual bath) necessary to an observant Jewish community, and their prayer services were conducted in a style characteristic of traditional worship. Like many midcentury American synagogues, both Anshe Chesed (founded in 1846) and Tifereth Israel (founded by seceders from Anshe Chesed in 1850) had made some efforts to regulate the behavior of their congregants. Rules adopted by Anshe Chesed in the 1850s included the typical prohibitions against speaking to one's neighbor during the service, going in and out during the Torah service, or gathering "on the sidewalk before the synagogue or on the steps thereof."[4] Cleveland served as the site of the 1855 rabbinical conference called by Isaac M. Wise, but a lack of consistent rabbinical leadership in the city apparently slowed progress toward even stylistic reform.[5]

With changes emerging through lay initiative, it took until 1859 for controversies over reform to have an impact upon Cleveland's congregations. In that year the members of Tifereth Israel, as part of a proposed plan to merge with Anshe Chesed, discussed the possibility of securing "the services of a preacher or lecturer of reformed principles."[6] The congregation's proposal suggested that "in order to accommodate and meet the advanced views; the *united* congregation would require a new house of worship, a lecturer, . . . a Chazan, . . . and teachers." The new synagogue, according to the plan, was to be "constructed into pews" but was to provide a "gallary for ladies."[7] Thus, it would appear that in 1859 Cleveland Jews did not yet consider mixed seating an integral part of "advanced views" regarding Judaism.

Although the proposed merger was rejected, Tifereth Israel did begin the contentious process of reform by introducing resolutions to omit some traditional prayers.[8] The influence of the Reform movement in Cleveland was also evident at the 1860 rededication of the Anshe Chesed synagogue, presided over by Isaac M. Wise. Despite

Wise's visit, it was Tifereth Israel that continued to take the lead in pushing toward reform.[9] In 1861, when it appeared that another proposed merger with Anshe Chesed would not succeed, Tifereth Israel sought to raise $1,000 to "furnish and refit [their own] Synagogue." As was often the case with the building of new synagogues or even with the refurbishing of old ones, this suggestion provided the opportunity for the congregation to redefine itself. The proposal to renovate the synagogue was adopted with an amendment providing for "family pews in the body of the Synagogue." At the same meeting, resolutions to introduce a choir and an organ were also agreed upon.[10] When the congregation rejected Benjamin Franklin Peixotto's suggestion that the plan for the renovated synagogue be adopted "with the exception of pews," Peixotto, treasurer of the congregation and superintendent of its Sunday school, submitted his resignation.[11]

A native-born American from a Sephardic family, Peixotto came to Cleveland as a boy in 1836, when his father took a position at the Willoughby University Medical School. Peixotto was willing to accept other innovations in the synagogue but apparently considered the introduction of mixed seating to be too extreme a change. In a letter to Isaac Leeser written in November 1859, when the congregation was first considering how to accommodate "advanced views" of Judaism, Peixotto raised his concern that the congregation wanted not only to introduce "family pews—for male & female" but also to "adopt a new minhag—engage a reform preacher & in a word go the whole figure *a la Dr. Wise.*"[12] Peixotto pledged himself to resist any "departure from the limits of enlightened orthodoxy" and swore to Leeser that he would be found "among those who will resist to the utmost this wholesale system of innovation"—if need be, by legally preventing the reformers from selling any synagogue property.

He appealed to Leeser to provide him with some kind of rationale to justify the position he wanted to take on the issue of "Pews." "I believe neither the Pentateuch nor Prophets speak advisedly on this point," Peixotto wrote, suggesting that he was familiar with the Reformers' argument that the practices to which they were objecting had no basis in the most fundamental texts of Judaism. Despite his public stand in defense of traditional practice, Peixotto made it clear to Leeser that he had little personal sympathy for the practice of separate seating or for whatever (presumably obscure) explanations might be behind it: "The only reason for the seperation of the sexes I have ever heard advanced & have entertained myself have been with reference to cleanliness & the reverse at certain periods in the other sex."

It is striking that even the congregant in Cleveland who took the most principled stand against mixed seating and claimed to "study the law constantly" brought no genuine conviction to his public opposition to the proposed innovation. Informing Leeser of his reservations, Peixotto added, "While I say this to you privately I maintain publicly an observance of the old custom that is I have already done so in more than one speech on the subject." Peixotto was clearly torn between his ability to "see much [in the way of change] that might be adopted with benefit" and his fear that too much change "would cause Israel to depart eventually from the ancient faith." He appealed to Leeser for help in arguing his case: "I want your advice on this point and arguments to sustain my public position for my private conviction rather favor the mingling of both sexes in the Synagogue on [?] an equality." He admitted in regard to mixed seating, "It is true it assimilates in form to Christian mode of worship, but certain [?] devotion if only apparent, is not wanting in the appearance of their Congregations. Give me some good solid reason or law why they should not sit together." Yet despite his apparent sympathy with arguments for reform and even mixed seating, Peixotto stood firmly in defense of what to him constituted a proper Jewish place of worship.

Although Peixotto was apparently able to forestall the introduction of family pews in 1859, less than two years later the momentum of a growing national Reform agenda overcame his personal authority within his congregation. Peixotto was willing to tolerate the introduction of an organ and a (presumably mixed) choir, but he could not countenance mixed seating in a synagogue, no matter how reasonable the practice seemed. Family pews represented too extreme a transformation of the synagogue and presented a dividing line that Peixotto, for the moment, refused to cross.[13] When Peixotto resigned from the congregation in 1861, he informed Leeser of "the grand metamorphose of the Tif Israel Kahal [congregation] into a demi-semi-Gentile and Jew church."[14]

The Cleveland discussion suggests that at the congregational level, as in the more intellectual newspaper debates, the attraction of the mixed-seating innovation lay in its promise of more serious devotion. Family pews would help to achieve the same decorous atmosphere sought in the introduction of organs and choirs. Peixotto's letters to

Leeser indicate that he was unable to locate any fallacy in this logic of decorum, even to convince himself. What arguments did exist could only be construed as archaic and embarrassing, were they to be publicly articulated. Peixotto was probably the most Americanized member of Tifereth Israel—he later would serve as one of the most prominent Jews in public service, when he became consul to Romania under President Grant.[15] If Peixotto, an important member of the community who was certainly more secure in his Americanness than his foreign-born coreligionists, could not convince his fellow congregants that his position was consistent with American values, it is unlikely that anyone else in the congregation could devise more effective arguments.

Although most Cleveland Jews could hardly be considered active Reformers, Peixotto's letters indicate that "a very large number if not quite a majority of the members of both societies [the synagogues] are ready & anxious to adopt these views & prospects unless speedily enlightened as to their apostasy." Peixotto hoped that the others in his community would come to understand the great threat he saw embodied in family pews. Because he felt sure of his own identity as an American, Peixotto may have been more willing than his fellow congregants to preserve synagogue traditions that could weaken Jewish claims to a position of respectability in the American hierarchies of race and class. Few, if any, others joined him. One other member resigned on the same day as Peixotto, but his membership had already been in arrears.[16] The loss of Peixotto's leadership and participation was obviously costly to the congregation, but they were probably consoled by the application of ten men to be new members the following week.[17]

Resisting Reform in Cincinnati

In Cincinnati, changes in women's synagogue roles very quickly drove a wedge into the Jewish community. In 1855, soon after Max Lilienthal arrived as the rabbi of the traditional Bene Israel congregation, a group of outspoken traditionalists, incensed at the new rabbi's determination to introduce a mixed choir, seceded to form a more traditional congregation. Not all of those who remained behind at Bene Israel, however, were content to follow Lilienthal on the path to Reform. Joseph Abraham, the only Jewish lawyer in Cincinnati, sympathized with the traditional position but was put off by the "noise and confusion" that he associated with the new congregation.[18] Like Peixotto in Cleveland, Abraham hoped to prevent his own congregation from sliding further toward Reform. Abraham believed that, despite the Reform tendencies of its rabbi, Bene Israel could maintain both quiet and good order while preserving traditional liturgy and practice.

Peixotto had appealed to Leeser for "confirmation of assistance of counsel of authorities etc. etc." to help him in his attempt to defend tradition. Abraham's situation was even more difficult than Peixotto's. In his struggle he had to face down two newly arrived reforming rabbis who, by virtue of their positions and their purported learning, easily projected authority for the legitimacy of the changes they advocated. Referring to Isaac M. Wise and Max Lilienthal, Abraham noted that "the hold which the two Drs have here upon the people is astounding as it is appalling, it strengthens with its growth . . . [T]hey cling to these modern reformers with a tenacity it is impossible to avert. Some say these are learned men know better than we, they are plausible and reasonable." Abraham described the atmosphere in 1859 Cincinnati as being "so filled with reform doctrines, that it requires a strong body & mind not to inhale the pernicious vapors."[19]

In 1860 a plan came before Bene Israel to spend $10,000 for the repair of the synagogue, which had been built in 1852. The proposal included a recommendation "to make pews in the Synagogue for males & females indiscriminately." In this challenge to the gender arrangement of the synagogue, Abraham saw a crisis that would force the congregation to clarify its position on religious change: "The propriety or impropriety of the pew system for the mixing of the sexes will bring in question, the whole of the theological questions above named." Predicting that Lilienthal would "prepare a written opinion in favor of the pews," Abraham asserted that "to the best of my feeble ability," he would prepare a counterattack to challenge Lilienthal's "whole purposes & views." Abraham believed that the question of mixed seating would be the one to call the whole program of the congregation's reforming rabbi into question. "I will not give up to the minutest change in our present service," Abraham declared. He asserted that if the congregation were to break apart over the issue of "pews and Reforms," other leading members would join him in forming "a congregation upon orthodox principles combined with decorum & order."[20]

Abraham valued decorum and order, but not at the expense of what he considered to be authentic Judaism. He grudgingly acknowledged the appeal of Reformers who advocated the notion "that all which is troublesome or irksome is obsolete & not now Judaism, all that is pleasing to the senses, and gratifying to the mind alone need be observed."[21] Like Peixotto, Abraham took on the role of defender of the faith, but he too needed to be convinced of the points that he steadfastly sought to represent in his congregation. "And yet altho' opposed to them [the Reformers] to the fullest extent," Abraham told Leeser, "my opposition is mainly grounded upon the fact that they are not competent to determine disputed points, to enact new customs and laws, and to abolish old ones." He even hoped that Talmudic principles could be found to support some aspects of the new order. "There are very numerous doctrines they advocate," he admitted, "to which I would also be willing to subscribe if carried by competent authority." For instance, Abraham questioned why, if in Jerusalem Jews celebrated just "one day of the holy days . . . we could not be doing wrong in" doing the same. He also noted that "I have never seen a satisfactory reason for preventing ladies joining in the choir service, tho I have heard much clamor."[22]

The correspondence of both Abraham and Peixotto with Leeser indicates the lack of orthodox authority in the United States at this time. These individuals, among the most Americanized Jews in their communities, hoped to institute respect for tradition together with modern expectations of order and decorum.[23] Both men were confident that their arguments rested on the authority of tradition, but they lacked the language and knowledge to back their beliefs. Presumably they shared the resentment, described by Leeser in 1857, of those in New Haven who found that "the innovation [of family pews] seems to throw odium on the conservatives for resisting a movement which," in Leeser's opinion, had "actually nothing to recommend it."[24] In fact, by 1866 Abraham was begging that Leeser do nothing to indicate that the two men had any connection or correspondence with each other, even asking that his name be deleted from the subscribers' list published in the *Occident* for fear that he would be "pointed out" for the "henious offence to do aught which may in any way reflect on Reform or Reformers."

The Rise of Reform and Family Pews   *Mixed seating.*

These accounts from Cleveland and Cincinnati suggest that by the early 1860s family pews had emerged as a defining aspect of the Reform program. If the agenda and challenge to traditionalism that came to be identified with the mixed-seating innovation was not fully present at the time of its introduction at New York's Emanu-El, its presence in such a prominent setting helped to invest it with larger meaning.[25] Although few congregations adopted the practice in the first few years of the innovation, mixed seating quickly became associated with the American Reform agenda. In August 1856 a correspondent to the *Israelite* noted that "family pews hitherto have been introduced but in a very limited number of synagogues" and suggested that the next rabbinical conference should consider whether the practice was "illegal or in accordance with our laws."[26] An 1857 article in the *Jewish Messenger* reported that although a new synagogue in London "had abridged some of the service, the women are separated from the men in the house of God."[27] While the 1856 query suggested that Reformers needed to establish their position on the question of mixed seating, the 1857 report seemed to assume that family pews had already become a part of the Reform program, at least as it was understood in America.

Although at least one congregation closely identified with Reform (Keneseth Israel in Philadelphia) did institute mixed seating in 1858, many more contemporaneous synagogues—including new buildings in Philadelphia, Mobile, Alabama, New Orleans, and New Haven— were dedicated with the traditional gallery.[28] During this period, however, the connection between mixed seating and the religious emancipation of Jewish women came to be more explicitly articulated. In sermons on the position of women published in 1858 and 1861, David Einhorn, now rabbi at Baltimore's Har Sinai, spoke out against the Jewish customs that deprived Jewish women of full religious expression. He advocated granting women an equal range of religious rights, duties, and instruction with men and condemned the "gallery-cage" of the women's gallery.[29] Einhorn brought the women of his own congregation downstairs, though apparently they continued to sit separately from the men for a few more years.[30] In 1859 Sinai Congregation was formed in Chicago on a platform that banned "everything that is contrary to the convictions of the congregation," including "bombastic words, exaggerations and bad taste," as well as "customs and rites which are . . . based on erroneous views." One of its founding principles was that "in the public worship of the congregation, there should be no discrimination made in favor of the male and against female worshippers."[31]

As family pews were introduced in Chicago and Cleveland, the tide began to turn. With acceptance of the family pew reform accelerating, Isaac Leeser continued to protest that "the conclusion is inevitable, that the change in question is against the spirit of our ancient times." Yet even he seemed to realize he had lost the battle with the spirit of modern times. His 1863 argument that a practice so long sanctioned by custom "acquired the force of law" seemed an admission that there was no real textual mandate for separate seating. The standard claim of the traditionalists that they were the true advocates of decorum in the synagogue echoed without conviction. Leeser acknowledged that "men will appeal to our gallantry," but he insisted that "this has nothing to do with the question; the gallery for the ladies is no mark of impoliteness, it is simply the result of all experience that we shall best promote devotion by placing the people so as not to introduce disturbing causes."[32] Increasingly, however, family pews were associated not just with decorum but also with the rhetorical affirmation of women's religious and social equality demanded by American middle-class culture. When family pews were introduced at the Indianapolis Hebrew Congregation in 1863, the president confidently remarked that "Ladies & Gentlemen are seated together, which is nothing more than civilization demands."[33]

When in 1862 Wise commented on a discussion over the *mechitzah* (the curtain divider separating the women's section in the synagogue from the men's) that had appeared in the *London Jewish Chronicle*, he was able to claim that this was "a question long ago decided with us . . . The fun of the discussion is the absurdity of the question."[34] Ironically, although Wise's arrival in Cincinnati in April 1854 quickly led to synagogue renovations to accommodate a choir and an organ, it did not prompt any moves toward mixed seating. In fact, Wise's new congregation in Cincinnati did not actually institute permanent family pews until 1866, when it dedicated a grand new temple.[35] As at Wise's B'nai Yeshurun synagogue, the introduction of family pews often had to await the construction of entirely new structures. With new synagogue buildings, congregations often instituted broad programs of reform in the interest of creating a ritual and practice in keeping with their grand and elegant temples. Thus, traditionalists like Peixotto, Abraham, and Leeser had not been underestimating the profound transformation that the introduction of family pews would bring in its wake.

By 1869, when postwar prosperity brought a surge of new and grandiose synagogue construction, mixed seating suddenly seemed to be de rigueur. In that year Cincinnati's Bene Israel congregation finally dedicated a building that had been proposed in 1863 as "a temple with all the necessary improvements viz. family pews, an organ, a Choir."[36] Different congregations offered different rationales for the introduction of family pews. At San Francisco's Sherith Israel, also in 1869, it was explained that "the existing custom of separating the sexes during Divine Services in our synagogue is a cause of annoyance and disturbance in our devotion," and thus was unacceptable in the place of "Divine Worship [which] should and must be attended by the strictest observance of order and decorum."[37] In an unusual case, despite the introduction of family pews, Sherith Israel remained otherwise orthodox in its practices, continuing to bar the use of organ or mixed choir.[38]

At B'nai El in St. Louis, again in 1869, it was proposed that in the interest of a more dignified appearance, women should be allowed to sit in the main body of the synagogue during the winter months, when attendance was not that numerous. B'nai El's records reveal that a year earlier on consecutive Saturdays there had not been enough men present to give the standard number of seven blessings over the Torah readings.[39] Presumably, this congregation and many other congregations like it wished to avoid the odd spectacle of balconies crowded with women overlooking deserted sanctuaries.

Such evidence suggests that in some congregations the establishment of family pews may have been a practical attempt to fill a vacuum left by male congregants who were otherwise engaged. Julius Freiberg, president of Cincinnati's Bene Israel, often bewailed Sabbath attendances so small that he declared himself "disinclined to state the number, which consisted with slight exceptions of old gray headed men and a few who had no occupation to take them elsewhere. Even of our trustees, very few are seen in the temple during the year." He also bore witness to the practical benefit of bringing women downstairs when he noted that "were it not for the women and children—God bless them—and thanks to the introduction of family pews . . . our large and costly temple would be nearly empty." In his many years as president of Bene Israel, Freiberg frequently expressed appreciation for female attendance, as he deplored male absence: "Of course we often have a goodly congregation of women and children, and I must confess that I am always delighted to see them, but at the same time, I would have been delighted much more if I had the pleasure of seeing our members in the Temple, if only occasionally."[40]

In the 1870s the movement for mixed seating spread to those congregations that embraced an American style of worship but rejected the full extent of the Reform program. In some cases, as at B'nai Jeshurun and Shaaray Tefila in New York City, agitation for change emerged following the death of a long-time traditional leader.[41] In other communities, congregants convinced conservative rabbis that the time had come to adjust to the tenor of the times. In 1867, as Philadelphia's Rodeph Shalom congregation considered plans for building a new synagogue, a committee in consultation with the rabbi, Marcus Jastrow, recommended that in the new synagogue "the Ladies shall occupy seats upon one side and the Gentlemen those upon the other side."[42] Since the new synagogue was not built until 1871, the congregation had time to reconsider this arrangement. In 1870 the board of directors expressed their "sincere wish . . . that the Pews [of the new synagogue] shall be family pews and the divine worship changed accordingly, thereby, securing to the congn its welfare and maintaining its strictest order and decorum." The board sought Jastrow's "sanction" for the proposed arrangement.[43]

Jastrow's well-considered response, written in German, explained that when family pews were first suggested, he had spoken against the proposal because he sensed that the motivation for the change grew out of a desire to shock and disturb the more conservative members of the community. Jastrow carefully distinguished between the possibility of family members sitting together and what he described as both sexes sitting together indiscriminately and the possible outrages that practice might lead to. In the present instance, Jastrow felt that the proposal for family pews came from men of whose religious earnestness he was sure and who could be trusted to guard against any possible abuse of the worship service. On the basis of this perception, he declared himself willing to sanction the change.[44]

Jastrow's account, if accurate, suggests that by 1870 it was the conservative and serious members of a traditional congregation who decided that the best interests of the congregation lay, not in the strictest *observance,* but in the "strictest order and decorum." In the 1870s numerous other holdouts against Reform, congregations that continued to be led by advocates of traditionalism (if not Orthodoxy) in America, adopted a range of practices, including family pews, that emerged in close association with the Reform tendency in Judaism.[45]

Even the staunchest champions of Jewish Orthodoxy at this time, Congregations Shearith Israel in New York and Mikveh Israel in Philadelphia, eventually had to fight off campaigns to bring mixed seating to their sanctuaries. Numerous traditional congregations went through protracted struggles and sometimes courtroom battles over mixed seating, but among acculturated Jews (as opposed to more recent immigrants), mixed seating became the accepted pattern for synagogue design.[46] In 1886 the *Jewish Reformer* observed that the "time was, when family pews were declared [by conservatives] to be a danger to the morals of Judaism. Preachers protested with little judgment and much zeal against their introduction. Now, among the conservatives there is scarce a recollection of a different state of things."[47]

The Decline of the Congregant

The impact of all these changes on women's place in the synagogue community was both obvious and subtle. The most apparent changes seemed to elevate female status in the public sphere of prayer. Reforming rabbis celebrated their belief that Reform had successfully emancipated women in the synagogue. Yet even though women found seats in sanctuaries where their equality was now proclaimed and their presence (at least in terms of attendance) was dominant, responsibility for and leadership of public worship had shifted entirely to the front of the auditorium.

One 1855 visitor to the new Temple Emanu-El, replete with family pews, described an atmosphere in which "one of the most prominent [impressions] is the absence of any participation in the religious ceremonies by the congregation." Responsibility for the prayer service itself had been invested in public functionaries declaiming from the front of the sanctuary: "The minister and reader do all the praying, the organ and choir perform the music." The congregants themselves had been transformed into spectators: "The visitors appear as mere dummies . . . the visitor acts no part, but that of *auditor* . . . [E]xcept for an occasional rising from the seat, the congregation does not participate in the worship."[48] A later observer noted that the worshiper had been "robbed" of "his own voice."[49]

The pattern observed by these visitors at Emanu-El was replicated in the many grand Reform temples built after the Civil War. Women became emancipated just in time to become part of an assembly that was rapidly losing its identity as a traditional *kahal* (community or congregation). In fact, the congregation was now often referred to as an "audience."[50] Women did gain a sort of equality with men as worshipers in the sanctuary, but it was a role that had already been greatly devalued. Women gained the right to join men in the shrinking role of congregant.[51]

Women and the Redefinition of Jewish Community

The changes wrought by the emerging Reform movement transformed the role of women in the American synagogue in other ways as well. One effect of bringing women down from the balcony was to undermine the identity of women as a distinct group within the congregation. In their 1853 petition, fourteen women in Cincinnati's Bene Israel congregation had forcibly expressed their sense of themselves as a presence within the congregation and demanded that attention be paid to maintaining the curtain that separated them from men during worship.[52] In succeeding years, even as congregational leaders celebrated female equality and as affluent Protestant women modeled activist public religious identities, acculturated Jewish women, in Cincinnati and elsewhere, came to seem strangely quiescent.

In 1855, two years after the petition demanding stricter separation of the sexes, another group of Bene Israel women sent a letter to the congregation's new rabbi, Max Lilienthal, accompanied by a rabbinical robe and hat. This time they placed themselves in the vanguard of Reform, encouraging their new rabbi to "proceed unflinchingly and fearlessly in the path you have chosen." The ladies offered their prayers and influence to assist him on his way. For although they acknowledged that "we have no voice in the council of our congregation yet is our influence considerable out of it, and this we cheerfully extend to you and your noble and praise worthy cause."[53] The help these women offered was in the traditional female mode of influence, which they promised to exert upon their male counterparts who actually controlled the congregation's affairs. The Bene Israel women's letter echoed one written a year earlier by the women of Cincinnati's B'nai Yeshurun, when they offered their new rabbi, Isaac M. Wise, "an elegant clerical suit" and a cap, as a "token of our esteem and regard for the worthy manner in which you uphold the dignity of our religion."[54]

These letters are noteworthy on two levels. First, they indicate the willingness and ability of the women in each of these communities to organize as a group, acting and identifying with each other for a common goal. In their letter to Lilienthal, the women of Bene Israel again identified their shared position within the congregation and indicated their recognition of the potential leverage and influence inherent in that position. These women felt sufficiently confident to commit the female component of the congregation to use their "prayers and influence" in support of Lilienthal's "noble undertaking," which, it was already clear in October 1855, would lead the congregation far from the traditional status quo that some of them had stalwartly defended only two years before.

These letters demonstrate the willingness of their writers to speak collectively as Jewish women, but they are also of special note in that they represent the last formalized expression of group identity and purpose to come from the women of these congregations for many decades. Although Cincinnati's Jewish women in 1855 appeared prepared to take an active role in the organizational life of their community, the succeeding decades actually saw a decline in their public activism.

One development that may help explain the relative inactivity of Cincinnati's mid-nineteenth-century Jewish women, a pattern also evident in other emerging centers of American Judaism, was the shifting definition of congregational life under the influence of the Reform movement. Pushed by Rabbis Wise and Lilienthal, the Cincinnati congregations expanded their long-standing concern with the maintenance of decorum and respectability within their synagogues into an unrelenting emphasis on impressive ceremonies and, ultimately, magnificent edifices. With their focus turned inward, both congregations became increasingly centered on worship.

In 1859 Bene Israel's Joseph Abraham privately claimed that despite Max Lilienthal's efforts, "with the exception of having the choir with female singers we have no change in the service."[55] Notwithstanding Abraham's apparent pride that he and his fellow traditionalists were maintaining the orthodox character of their congregation, however, the Jewish community of Bene Israel and of Cincinnati generally had already been transformed. Issues at the core of congregational concerns for years had quickly and quietly disappeared.

Congregational leaders allowed their roles in providing Jewish Cincinnatians with the means to a traditionally observant Jewish life to lapse. Shortly after the arrival of Wise and Lilienthal, both congregations abandoned the responsibility of providing and overseeing kosher slaughtering for their communities. Similarly, Bene Israel withdrew its sponsorship for the ritual bath that it had overseen for many years; B'nai Yeshurun members no longer gathered at ritually specified times twice a year for the traditional purpose of all-night "Learning" sessions.[56] The attention of the congregations' boards of trustees, like that of their rabbis, turned almost exclusively to the form of worship in the synagogue.

With congregational concerns in most American cities increasingly narrowed to the limited focus of worship, burial, and (sometimes) education, and without other local sources of religious authority, support for the pursuit of traditional domestic observance weakened even further. As a result, the experience of Judaism became increasingly concentrated in the synagogue, where concern focused increasingly on aesthetics and on achieving a decorous style of worship. All of these shifts had a profound effect on women's relationship to Jewish identity and the synagogue.

The eventual introduction of family pews in most acculturated congregations emphasized the growing importance of synagogue attendance to the religious identity of acculturated Jewish women. The accompanying changes in the nature of congregational participation, however, limited the ways in which women, finally "emancipated" from the gallery, could be integrated into the worship experience. As the ambit of the synagogue narrowed into the worship-centered sphere of the sanctuary, the possibilities for women to participate meaningfully in Jewish communal life actually seem to have constricted even further. As religious leadership became increasingly assumed by paid male professionals standing at the front of the sanctuary, the governance of the congregation remained in the hands of male lay leaders. Only men could serve as congregational officers or on congregational boards and committees, not least because women were still not officially members of their congregations. Adjustments in synagogue structures that accompanied the ascendance of the American Reform movement offered women different seats from which to worship but did not afford them access to synagogue leadership or influence.

Jewish Women's Organizational Life after the Civil War

The exclusion of women from congregational leadership did not differentiate American synagogues from American Protestant churches of the same era. A general pattern of apparent organizational inactivity in the major centers of Jewish population in the East, Midwest, and West, however, contrasts intriguingly with the developing organizational life of Protestant women, who otherwise appear to have provided influential models for the religious life of acculturating Jewish women. For middle-class Protestant women across the country in the post–Civil War period, women's numerical dominance of the pews was reinforced by their central role in general church-related activities. The chance to forge public identities through church-related work focused especially upon missionary efforts abroad and the fight for temperance at home. Historians have described the years after the Civil War as an era when the expansion of Christian women's work for benevolence and social reform was incorporated locally and nationally into organizations that "seemed to spring up everywhere."[57] Religiously defined activists elaborated complex regional and national networks engaging the energies of hundreds of thousands of devoted female workers.

Anne Firor Scott, in her history of American women's associations observes that "one thing is certain" of the decades after the Civil War: "women in unprecedented numbers created or joined organizations."[58] In missionary societies, the Woman's Christian Temperance Union (founded in 1874), and the Young Women's Christian Association (which began its work under this name in Boston in 1866), Scott identifies three major clusters of women's activism. These movements bred rich associational networks that engaged women both in local issues and in concerns beyond their own communities.

The restructuring of American synagogues to incorporate family pews and women's continued domination of regular worship attendance during this period seem to demonstrate a general embrace of American Protestant models of female religious identity. The integration of women into the synagogue might have thus been expected to galvanize women's energies to serve the needs of the synagogue and community, in a manner akin to that demonstrated by activist Protestant women. Yet instead of expanding in the postwar era, female Jewish organizational life in the 1860s, 1870s, and early 1880s seems to have contracted precisely in those decades that Anne Firor Scott identifies as so "pivotal" for the growth and emergence of women's associational life.[59]

Ironically, the growing success of an American Reform movement, even with its emphasis on equality for women within Judaism, contributed to subduing the public voice that many American Jewish women had begun to express in the 1850s. As congregations focused increasingly on synagogue ritual and decorum, many of the extrasynagogal activities affiliated with the congregations, such as the Ladies' Benevolent Societies, became increasingly marginalized. Jewish men, who may have felt a decline in status in their role as congregants, could still take prominent roles in congregational governance or find a place in the Jewish fraternal orders, which were greatly expanding at this time. Women found fewer venues for public participation. The women's gallery may have disappeared, but the male-oriented structure of Jewish public life left women with few options for engagement beyond the synagogue school or sanctuary.

In addition, the Christian orientation and goals of Protestant women's movements prevented Jewish women from participating in their work or attempting to create parallel groups. The missionary activity that engaged so many thousands of Christian women could not easily be copied by a religious group that hardly wanted to be seen as proselytizing to non-Jews and that resented being themselves the target of missionary efforts.[60] Similarly, temperance was not an issue that spoke to Jewish hearts, whether because certain aspects of Jewish ritual revolved around wine or because of Jewish concerns about protecting the boundary between church and state.[61] Some temperance workers may have believed that their work transcended religious denominationalism. But when members of the Ladies Temperance Association in Leavenworth, Kansas, invited women of the local synagogue to join in their work, the Jewish women had to explain that they could not join in the Christian religious services that were often an integral part of temperance activism.[62]

Whatever the reasons, Jewish women, unlike their Protestant counterparts, did not create significant national organizations in the 1860s, 1870s, and 1880s. The United Order of True Sisters (Unabhängiger Orden Treuer Schwestern), founded in 1845 at Temple Emanu-El in New York as a counterpart to the men's fraternal order B'nai B'rith, counted a number of branches in different cities, and its 1864 constitution provided for a Grand Lodge in which regional representatives met to establish national policies for the group. Archival evidence on the order's activities through much of the nineteenth century, however, is limited. It would appear that local chapters served principally as mutual aid societies, in which members, in accord with traditional Jewish practice, watched over their sick sisters, helped to prepare the dead for burial, and provided some death benefits. Although the 1864 constitution specifically pointed beyond mutual aid to call for public activism from its members, reports of True Sisters' activities rarely appeared in the public record. Its association with B'nai B'rith clearly did not translate into equal importance or influence.[63]

Most of Jewish women's activism in the post–Civil War period focused on fund-raising for community projects that were often initiated and directed by men. American Jewish women had begun to cultivate a talent for fund-raising in the antebellum period. During the Civil War, Jewish women took full part, along with their Christian neighbors, in efforts to support soldiers in the field. Jewish women in many communities formed organizations like Philadelphia's Ladies' Hebrew Relief Association for Sick and Wounded Union Soldiers, or, like the Jewish women of Mobile, Alabama, "contributed with a liberal hand to wounded soldiers and soldiers' needy families."[64] Jewish participation in the great Sanitary Fairs across the North, which raised hundreds of thousands of dollars to aid soldiers at the front, created awareness of the potential of women's organizations to raise sums that could make a difference.[65]

The ability to collect funds for focused purposes continued to afford women a vital role in postwar Jewish life, yet even this function was undermined by the growing institutionalization of Jewish community work in numerous cities. At the same time that American synagogues were narrowing their focus upon worship, a number of the larger American Jewish communities also attempted to rationalize the charitable work that went on outside of the synagogue. The creation of unified Jewish relief agencies often weakened existing women's groups. Male leaders seeking to institutionalize cooperation between local charities always sought the inclusion of women's groups and their funds. Inevitably, however, women's participation in such collective efforts undermined their independent status in the community. New midcentury federations never included female leaders on the directing boards of the new organizations.

This dynamic was exemplified in Chicago, where two women's groups participated in the creation of the United Hebrew Relief Association (UHRA) in 1860. Representatives of all the constituent groups appeared among the trustees and officers of the new organization, with the exception of the two women's groups and the Young Men's Fraternity. Frequent acknowledgments by the association's officers of the work done by the Ladies' Sewing Society, which was formed in 1861 in association with the UHRA's work, indicate that although they were not represented in the leadership, women carried much of the burden of the practical work, supplying thousands of garments for an association that preferred to assist the poor with provisions rather than money.[66]

In 1859 a Cincinnati correspondent to the *Jewish Messenger* reported that the city had formerly hosted "a great number of societies for benevolent purposes." Then, "about a year back several were merged into one." The resulting "Relief Society" supplied "alms and support to the needy and afflicted." The author went on to describe a number of remaining women's organizations and their contributions, including $150 from the Ladies' Hebrew Benevolent Society, to the new federated charity.[67] After this, however, the city's long-established ladies' societies appear to have receded from public view. An 1861 notice published in Wise's German language newspaper *Die Deborah* called upon the women of Cincinnati to join the society of the women of Congregation Bene Israel (for a "contribution of only three dollars for an entire year") in responding to the needs of the growing numbers of poor Jewish women in the city. Such an invitation seems more an effort to revive a dormant organization than the act of an ongoing concern. Similarly, a published call to the "honored mothers and daughters" of B'nai Yeshurun to join in organizing a Fair Society, so that they might give a fair to benefit the congregation, sounds like a request by male congregational leaders for a one-time effort to support the building fund, rather than a call upon an established women's organization already affiliated with the congregation.[68]

In Philadelphia the Society of the United Hebrew Charities (UHC) was created in 1869 through a merger of existing societies, including the German Hebrew Ladies' Benevolent Society and the Ladies' Hebrew Sewing Society. Revenues of the Hebrew Charity Ball Association, which at one time had gone chiefly to support the work of the city's Jewish women's associations, were transferred to the unified society. So too, an early historian reported, were the "duties" of the former societies "transferred . . . to one institution." As in Chicago, although all the male former presidents of the founding societies were included on the new society's board of managers, no women appeared among the leaders of the new Philadelphia organization. Women's participation in the work of the new society appears to have been limited until the 1890s to the work of "a Ladies' Committee of seventeen members, in charge of the Clothing Department," which was considered a continuation of the work of the old Sewing Society.[69]

Leaders of Philadelphia's still active Female Hebrew Benevolent Society, despite the expectation that they too would join the UHC, opted to remain autonomous, continuing their work and their independent leadership. Members of the Hebrew Sunday School Society likewise sustained their devoted work. Yet, as suggested by the organization of the city's United Hebrew Charities, even in Philadelphia the benevolent work of women clearly had lost some of its salience. Evelyn Bodeck notes that the Jewish Foster Home established in 1855 was, with the exception of organized relief for sick and wounded soldiers of the Civil War, the last major independent effort of Philadelphia's German Jewish women.[70] But even this organization was ceded to male leadership in 1874, when the Foster Home's female board of directors was replaced by a male board of managers, to be assisted by the "Ladies of the Associate Board."[71]

Attempts in 1858 and 1859 to unite New York's Jewish philanthropic activities failed. A similar consolidating impulse, however, can be seen in the absorption in 1870 of Congregation Shearith Israel's Hebrew Female Benevolent Society into its male counterpart, the Hebrew Relief Society, at which point the female society "ceased to function as an independent organization."[72]

One particular aspect of the Civil War's destructiveness that did encourage activism among charitable Jewish women was the intensified need of war widows and orphans. In 1863 Isaac M. Wise addressed his female readership, calling upon them to organize support for a widows and orphan asylum that would serve the entire "West," from "Milwaukee to Memphis and Leavenworth to Pittsburgh."[73] The proposed asylum, a project sponsored by the national Jewish men's organization B'nai B'rith, drew interest from women throughout the Midwest and, after the war's conclusion, from the South as well.

In Cincinnati, Wise's appeal brought forth an initial membership of 300 women, who committed themselves to contribute $4 a year to the creation of the proposed asylum. Although Wise's report of this society in *Die Deborah* and, presumably, the society itself bore the stamp of his vision, it took committed women to sustain the society from year to year and to accumulate $4,000 within the first two years of its existence. Wise went to great lengths in *Die Deborah* to explain why this sort of project—caring for "grieving sisters and helpless orphans"—was eminently suited to appeal to the tender female heart and, at the same time, to help realize his own dream of a united "American Israel."[74]

Proud as he was of the effort put forth by Cincinnati's Jewish women, Wise chided the women of other cities throughout the West and South for their apparent lack of interest in the project. Still, when the doors of the new Cleveland orphan asylum opened in 1868, its male leaders readily acknowledged that all their "labors and endeavors would have been futile without the assistance of the ladies." Wise noted that, after the B'nai B'rith members who had initiated the project in 1863, "the first persons . . . to take hold of the idea were the ladies of Cincinnati, Cleveland, Detroit, St. Louis, and afterward of Louisville, Memphis, Nashville, Evansville, and Milwaukee." Thirty-three Orphan Asylum Auxiliary Associations and Hebrew Ladies' Benevolent Societies and Associations throughout the Midwest and South sent in sums ranging from $7.25 to $1,000 for a total of $7,688. This sum was supplemented with proceeds from fairs, raffles, balls, concerts, "pic-nics," and lectures held for the benefit of the asylum. A Memphis picnic raised $872 and a Milwaukee fair, $1,644.[75]

The extent of female support for the asylum was reflected in its directors, which counted six women and three men, elected by those who paid membership dues. Even though the asylum's board of trustees was all male, and though, apart from one local committee which looked after supplies and dry goods, all asylum governance was left to men, it was clear that Jewish women of the Midwest and South had embraced this project as their own. Rather quickly, however, the asylum's male officers began to worry that their female support was less than reliable. The secretary's third annual report noted that many of the local benevolent associations which had "heretofore contribut[ed] have lately ceased to exist for want of a thorough organization." Still, when a special call was made in the fourth year to hold festivals and entertainments to support the asylum, it "was nobly responded to." One fair in "Generous Cincinnati" actually raised $31,000. The substantial funds raised by women for the orphan asylum and for other institutions, such as Chicago's United Hebrew Relief Association, demonstrated women's power to raise impressive sums. The want of "thorough organization," however, limited their ability to sustain these efforts.[76]

In Detroit, Wise's 1863 call prompted the assembly of fifty-three women "as well as a goodly number of gentlemen" to found the Ladies Society for the Support of Hebrew Widows and Orphans.[77] This group decided that rather than participate in "gathering Widows and orphans indiscriminately from all parts of the country to one home; thus . . . taking bereaved women from their friends, their homes and family and even their dead," they would form a society to support widows and orphans within their own city and state. In the "days succeeding the war . . . when money seemed to lie loose about the country," the women held a series of balls and entertainments and quickly attained their $3,000 endowment goal. Accordingly, they began to pay out pensions to local "needy widows and orphans." The women found, however, that it was difficult for many men in the community to take their efforts seriously. As the society's president recalled twenty years later, "In the first years of our society's existence we did not have overmuch cause to be encouraged by the confidence which many of the gentlemen had in the success of our society." There was "no doubt that we could collect moneys and do good charitable work," but many, even among the men connected with the society, did not really believe that "they were associated with the administration of an earnest, every day matter of fact, business-principled society."

Those who had little sense of the society, like the men from the local B'nai B'rith who came to "solicit a portion of our arduously acquired endowment" when the Cleveland orphan asylum opened in 1868, "looked upon it as perhaps nothing more than a pretext for occasional afternoon tea-parties."[78]

In fact, it took some time before the women of the society felt confident enough to maintain their revenue for their own purposes. Contrary to the laws of their society, which mandated that all funds must remain within Michigan, the women did send $500 to the Cleveland asylum. Much of the proceeds from their earliest balls were donated to the local Jewish relief society, which received $1,200, and to three local non-Jewish charities, which received a total of $150. Eventually, the society stopped giving balls, gathering its funds from investment income and yearly dues, and concentrated its assets and attention on the relief of its own pensioners. But this was possible only after they had overcome the condescension of the community's male leaders and societies and won the right to determine the direction of their own efforts.[79]

In cities where Jewish community was more established, the very success of the community's claims to stability and respectability often crowded women out of opportunities to shape and oversee independent initiatives in significant areas of community interest. The greatest energy in fund-raising and institution-building among Jewish women seems to have emerged where organized Jewish community was weakest. It may have been in the South, where numerous communities first organized themselves and built synagogues in the decades after the Civil War, that Jewish women were able to have the greatest communal impact. Archival evidence suggests that in a number of communities women were strikingly successful in bringing communities to life through their fund-raising efforts. In fact the conspicuous activity of women in a number of southern communities contrasts starkly with the absence of women's initiative and leadership elsewhere.

In Natchez, Mississippi, for instance, one of the temple's early presidents gave Jeanette Mayer "the credit for the building of our temple more so than any other," for she was the one to whom "fell the lot and duty to organize our women." By raising $6,266 with two fairs held in 1868 and 1870 and informing "the Gentlemen of the Hebra Keducha congregation" that the proceeds would be "at their disposal at any time, that said sum will be needed, for the purpose of erecting a house of Worship," the Jewish women of Natchez gave walls to their synagogue and life to their community.[80] A similar dynamic prevailed in Baton Rouge, Louisiana, where the city's Jewish women "associated [them]selves together" in 1871 "for the purpose of building in the City of Baton Rouge, a Synagogue for Jewish worship." Over a number of years the Baton Rouge women raised the funds to buy a lot for the synagogue, to initiate its construction, and eventually to pay off its debt.[81] This same pattern prevailed in Anniston, Alabama, where the synagogue's 1893 cornerstone reads, "Erected by Ladies' Hebrew Benevolent Society."[82]

Given the obvious importance and success of these groups, it is surprising to see how hard it was for them to sustain themselves as organizations. In both Natchez and Baton Rouge, the groups formed, held a fair or other fund-raising event, handed the proceeds over to the congregation, and then quickly ran out of steam. Months or years later when the synagogue leaders needed something from them again, they would reorganize. The only time these groups seem to have been able to sustain a sense of purpose was when they were able to focus on a discrete fund-raising goal.

In Natchez, existing records show the community's Jewish women first organizing themselves on March 22, 1865, for the "purpose of mutual benefit," focusing on the traditional Jewish activity of nursing each other through sickness. This first communal effort, however, appears to have gone defunct within a few months. An organization using the same minute book reemerged three years later as the Hebrew Ladies Aid Association, with the same ostensible purposes. Its first substantial activity, however, undertaken within two months of its refounding, was a fair for the benefit of "the building of the Temple in contemplation." Having made the proceeds of $3,675 from the fair available to the congregation, the association appeared to lose all momentum and purpose. The society moved from monthly to quarterly meetings, where business was limited to the collection of dues or which were canceled entirely due to lack of a quorum. Discussions in 1868 and 1869 focused on whether to hold another fair, but "members not agreeing there was no action taken." Eventually, in December 1870, two years after the first fair, a second was held to benefit "the Temple now in the course of erection." Once the temple was completed in 1872, women of the society found employment in planning a dedication ball and then, over succeeding years, in continuing to raise money for payments on the synagogue's debt.[83]

The case of Baton Rouge's Ladies Hebrew Association is striking both for the impact that women had in building the community and for the group's inability to maintain a meaningful existence apart from the need to raise discrete sums of money for the congregation. Founded January 29, 1871, for the express purpose of building a synagogue, the association conducted little business for more than a year, until on September 23, 1872, its members determined to "give a ball," which raised $671. In June 1874 the group informed the congregation that the association's donations should not be used to pay rent but rather "that the said money only be used for the purposes of the Building Fund." In October the ladies determined that if the "Gentleman's Congregation" purchased a particular property for use as a synagogue, they would contribute $1,200 toward its purchase price. Eventually the women donated a $500 bond to the congregation, directed their attention to "any inside improvements" in the synagogue, and determined in March 1877 "to discontinue the Association," paying any money still on hand to the president of the congregation.[84]

A year later, the society reemerged with the same constitution and, over the course of a year and a half, contributed $643, realized from donations, raffles, and a ball, to the congregational cause. After disbanding again in 1879, the association was once again reorganized in January 1882 "at the earnest solicitation of the members of the Congregation Chari-Chesed." Still, the organization seemed to drift and meetings lapsed as the members seemed unable to sustain the group's activity when there was no particular congregational or fund-raising event upon which to focus. The records show a brief flurry of activity in 1885, when the women determined to shift their focus from "the purpose of aiding the Synagogue" and decided that in the future, their funds would be "used for the best and most available purposes in whatever Charity etc its services be needed." With this motivation, the women gathered in full force to arrange a "Moonlight Festival," raising $323.30, which, in the end, the women agreed to give over to the congregation anyway. After the successful festival, the society again disappeared from view, reemerging once again two years later, in 1887.[85]

Manuscript records from a number of small southern and midwestern communities show that many groups did succeed in maintaining a continuous existence. The Female Hebrew Benevolent Society of Norfolk, Virginia, founded in 1867, lasted through the century as a mutual aid society and a source of small-town charity. At times the Norfolk women found the same inspiration that galvanized the women of Baton Rouge and Natchez in appeals from desperate male synagogue officials for vital financial assistance. In 1869 the congregation's president sought assistance with the synagogue's debt to avert "the total destruction of God's House" and avoid bringing "shame to all Israelites." The women offered $75 as long as the congregation would guarantee that the rest of the debt would be paid. Subsequently, the society held two balls "for the Benefit of the synagogue," raising $76 in June and $131 in September. In 1878 the society again granted a congregational request by offering a $600 loan to the synagogue at 7 percent interest. Congregational records of the time indicate the board's effort to "devise means of raising sufficient funds" to cover expenditures. The minutes reflect that resolutions to hold a ball were ultimately judged to be "inexpedient" but fail to mention that help did come from the Female Hebrew Benevolent Society.[86]

For the most part, however, the women of Norfolk were content to occupy themselves with the business of watching over each other's illnesses and burials, offering charity to indigent members of their community, and sending financial assistance to those stricken with yellow fever in Memphis and Shreveport or to the "Savannah sufferers." Although for fifteen years of their existence they were run under male leadership, the organization appears to have sustained both its energy and its dues collections, reporting a balance of over $1,000 in 1882. The fact that many of the group's members returned the sick aid assistance they received from the society as a matter of course may suggest that the group was more important to its members as a social club than as a practical society.[87]

Mutual aid societies continued to provide Jewish women with a framework for community in many cities and towns. The charitable contributions and even the practical need for such societies, however, were limited by the generally rising prosperity of the nation's Jewish population. Although organizations like Detroit's Ladies Society for the Support of Hebrew Widows and Orphans and Philadelphia's Female Hebrew Benevolent Society managed to stay busy with their relatively limited rosters of clients, there was little call for new charitable endeavors. Cincinnati's Ladies' Aid Society for the Cleveland Orphan

Asylum continued to collect $4 a year from its members to support the Cleveland asylum, although in 1877 the society called upon its members to add $1 to their annual dues. Interestingly, this increment was added in response to Isaac M. Wise's nationwide call for the Jewish women of America to create Hebrew Ladies' Educational Aid Societies, which would commit members to $1 annual contributions "for the support of the indigent students of Hebrew Union College." Wise found widespread support from hundreds of women who signaled their commitment by signing their names to "scrolls of honor" that were then sent to the Hebrew Union College.[88] It seems noteworthy that in Cincinnati, where the college was founded in 1875 with substantial support from the local Jewish community, the officers of the society for the support of the orphans' asylum thought it best to integrate their Ladies' Educational Aid Society into the city's one preexisting and vital ladies' aid organization. The fact that this organization had clearly become centered chiefly upon the collection of yearly dues again testifies to the weakness of women's organizational life among Cincinnati's acculturated Jewish women.

A final instructive example of the public contributions of Jewish women to the institutional life of Jewish communities in the post–Civil War era is found in the West. In Portland, Oregon, Congregation Beth Israel, founded in 1868, fell upon difficult financial times in the 1870s. Having unsuccessfully tested a number of options to deal with their crisis, the congregation's board finally called upon the women of the congregation to hold a fair. As the fair committee later reported, they entered upon their assignment with little expectation of success. In the event however, the 1875 fair raised $3,683, suddenly enabling the congregation not only to attend to all its long-deferred renovation projects, but also to buy and clear a burial ground and to lower its monthly dues from $5.00 to $2.50. In turning the money over to the congregational board, the fair committee submitted only one deferential request, asking that the board grant the congregation's often frustrated and often controversial rabbi a one-time bonus of $300. Although the women left the continuing governance of the congregation to their husbands, one indication that they might have learned from the opportunity to work together is that the First Portland Hebrew Ladies' Benevolent Association was organized that same year.[89]

This limited exploration of women's collective contributions to their communities in the decades following the Civil War yields a complicated picture. Viewed from a perspective that assumes public

Jewish life was an exclusively male province, American Jewish women in this period appear in numerous localities and particularly across the South as the surprisingly energetic initiators and supporters of vital community-building projects. Viewed against the backdrop of Jewish women's emerging organizational life in the antebellum period, however, and in the context of the blossoming world of Protestant women's organizations, American Jewish women in this period seem strangely quiescent.

Definitive statements about the significance of nineteenth-century Jewish women's organizations must await further study. A few central patterns do emerge, however, from the material surveyed here. In the decades succeeding the Civil War, women's voluntary associations contributed vitally to creating and sustaining community in a number of locations, and across the country, Jewish women proved themselves adept at raising money. But apart from small mutual aid and charitable societies, they rarely maintained consistent movements or pursued autonomous power within their own communities. In general, local women seemed ever ready to respond to the requests of male synagogue leaders to come to the rescue of synagogues that seemed forever in debt. What seems clear in many communities is that despite their evident skill at raising money, Jewish women during this era were not connecting this ability to their own larger purposes. Their commitment to building and sustaining synagogues for the most part seemed limited to raising money and handing it over to men for dispensation. In many cities Jewish women's efforts were irregular and their energies were offered in response to particular requests. Women lacked the context of sustained, organized groups pursuing a systematic plan of work or a continuing purpose. Even where women's groups did sustain themselves through this period, it was only toward the end of the century that women in places like Baton Rouge, Norfolk, and Portland began to tell synagogue boards what to do with the money they provided.

Women had little authority over any aspect of synagogue activity, even in those activities that late twentieth-century observers have assumed had been given over to women. Records indicate that many responsibilities that might have been assigned to women were assumed by men, whether or not the actual work was done by women. The board of trustees of Cleveland's Tifereth Israel in the 1870s and 1880s, for example, regularly formed all-male committees to decorate the synagogue for special events and to organize picnics for the school children.[90] And a vote of thanks to a Mr. H. Sontage for his "valuable assistance" in decorating the temple in 1877 suggests that this was not a situation in which the men were simply delegating these tasks to their wives.[91] This situation becomes more understandable given that during this period the congregation actually took responsibility for very few matters besides those relating to the synagogue building, worship services, and school.

Although women continued to play important roles, particularly in congregational religious schools, their benevolent and educational work was often subsumed under male supervision. The situation was summarized by the school director of San Francisco's Sherith Israel congregation in the early 1870s when he responded to a recommendation that the congregation employ a woman as principal: "We do not approve it," the director reported to the congregation. "Without venturing upon an argument on the question we unhesitatingly affirm that only under the leadership of qualified men can the School prosper. Ladies however can assist in the work."[92]

The American Jewish attempt to prove that the American synagogue could be seen as a parallel to the churches of respectable Christian denominations created a truncated religious community. Jewish men found fuller communal expression through the elaboration of a network of secular Jewish clubs and societies. Women's access to such organizations was much more limited. The groups and activities that had formed around the synagogue were undermined when Jewish leaders intensified their focus on the practice and space of worship. A presumably unintentional by-product of the resulting compartmentalization of Jewish religious life was to leave women with few outlets for the expression of religious identity. Paradoxically, a series of reforms, including mixed choirs and mixed seating, intended to emancipate woman in the synagogue left her with a redefined religious space but little to do.

Reform's initial solution to the problem of woman's marginalization in the synagogue in a society that honored women as religious exemplars proved insufficient. Like the traditionalists before them, Reformers still struggled with the dichotomy between American expectations of female religiosity and the religious roles available to Jewish women in America. Having taken over the pews of the synagogue, Jewish women were poised to work out their own construction of American female Jewish identity.

CHAPTER SIX

Kaufmann Kohler and the Ideal Jewish Woman

At the beginning of the nineteenth century women began to find a place in the American synagogue. By the end of the century, they would begin to transform their public identity as Jewish women. The elaboration of public religious roles for women emerged as one part of a broad effort, joined by Jewish community leaders and individual female congregants, to legitimize Judaism and Jewish identity within the American religious landscape. But the successful effort of American Jews to create a recognizably American religion was complicated by an accompanying need to sustain Jewish distinctiveness.

Judaism could not merit the accolades of respectability without elevating women above the marginal status accorded to them within the traditional synagogue. At a symbolic level, however, American Jewish leaders needed women to be more than just a dedicated presence in the synagogue. After all, if Jewish women were not creating Jewish homes, what difference would it make that they attended synagogue? American Jews were unable to embrace a wholly synagogue-centered religion as a satisfying expression of the full range of Jewish religiosity. If American Judaism was only to be a somewhat Hebraized version of bourgeois American worship, why not simply adopt Felix Adler's de-ethnicized creed of Ethical Culture or follow through on the efforts of some prominent Reform rabbis to work out a modus vivendi with American Unitarianism?[1] American Jews may have chosen to distance themselves from the dense domestic and communal fabric that defined traditional Jewish life. Still, they needed meaningful connections to that world to justify their continued distinctive existence within a society that seemed to invite them to dispense with those practices that separated them from the respectable mainstream. The symbolic role ascribed to Jewish women, past and present, stood at the center of attempts by American Jewish leaders to exist in this tension between assimilation and tradition.

As much as the religious identities of American Jewish women had been transformed by their creation as nineteenth-century synagogue-goers, rhetorical descriptions of female Jewish religiosity remained grounded in traditional frameworks. Celebration of the qualities of Sarah, Esther, and Rebecca and evocations of the traditional Jewish home guided by a saintly and wise mother appeared constantly in Jewish sermons and newspapers. Though acculturated American Jews strove mightily to leave behind an isolated Jewish world of kashrut and Shabbat (Sabbath), nostalgic memories of a purer world continued to speak powerfully from and to Jewish hearts. A close look at the thought of Kaufmann Kohler, one leading Jewish Reformer caught between his profound commitments to both a rational Jewish future and a nostalgic Jewish past, illuminates the fundamental ambivalence about women's religious roles that persisted even among those who pressed for the principle of women's religious equality.

Together with his rabbinical colleagues, Kohler believed that the emancipation of women within the synagogue was an intrinsic part of the Reform project. Kohler affirmed that from the start, "all innovations in the Synagog and school were made with the view of securing perfect equality between woman and man before God."[2] As ghetto walls had been torn down for the Jew, so religious reformers tore down internal synagogue walls and legalistic strictures that had long isolated women and stifled their religious expression. Just as emancipation brought the Jew freedom and membership in society, so the founders and proponents of Reform Judaism in the United States believed they had emancipated the Jewish woman within her own religion. In Kohler's words, "Reform Judaism has pulled down the screen from the gallery behind which alone the Jewish Woman of old was allowed to take part in divine service."[3]

In his time Kaufmann Kohler was respected by both radical and conservative Jews as one of the most influential and articulate shapers of American Jewish thought. A recent historian of the Reform movement has noted that "in the last decades of the nineteenth century and the first of the twentieth, it was especially Kaufmann Kohler who spoke for American Reform Judaism."[4] Yet although devoted to the effort to redefine an old religion for a new age, Kohler was also deeply troubled throughout his career by the religious state of America's Jews and by the very nature of the Reform project in which he was so integrally involved.

Kohler's struggle to place women within his conception of an ideal modern Judaism reflected the profound conflicts underlying his attempts to define Judaism for the modern world. In his effort to define a Judaism that would appeal to individuals who lived in a society shaped by customs and ideas far removed from the assumptions of traditional Judaism, Kohler attempted to retain Jewish distinctiveness by imbuing new, unfamiliar forms with a spiritual essence that he identified with the Jewish past. It is not surprising, then, that he looked to the past to understand the religious essence of the lives of American Jewish women. It may be more surprising to find that despite Reform's redefinitions of woman's role and of Judaism, Kohler was unable to distinguish contemporary Jewish women from an ideal grounded in the past.

The Ideal Jewish Woman, Past and Present

Examination of the past treatment of Jewish women seemed to provide some of the best arguments for the Reform project. Kohler's starkest presentation, which echoed the readings offered by German Reformers like Abraham Geiger, described a Mosaic-Talmudic legal system that reduced the Jewish woman to a creature without will— bought and sold on the marriage market, subject to the sexual and mercenary whims of husband or father, and treated by the same religious and civil laws that governed children and slaves, her value equated with her ability to bear children.[5] To Kohler it seemed that the absurdity of this traditional position in modern times must be obvious to all. "In one word," he asked, "do our orthodox rabbis dare acknowledge the talmudical rules as binding in regard to *woman?*"[6]

Yet Kohler, again like Geiger and many other earlier Jewish writers on women, also praised the Jewish tradition for recognizing the merits of women in an age when other cultures had excluded them from all participation in community concerns. It was "only the Jewish religion," Kohler claimed, which "assigned woman a worthier place" and recognized that woman was of the same "flesh and the same ethical nature" as man. "Beginning with Biblical times," he wrote, "we find the Hebrew woman at once occupies a far more dignified position than do the women of other nations."[7] Kohler recognized that many believed that the Jewish woman "like any other Oriental woman [had been] pushed into the background and forced into inactivity." In response, he endeavored "to show that in many respects woman lent Judaism the character it has, and that her influence deep and silent like the warmth of the sun, has ever been in the ascendant."[8]

Thus, in speaking of the Jewish woman's historical position, Kohler set out with two seemingly inconsistent goals. On the one hand, the injustice women suffered under the authority of traditional religious law seemed to highlight the progressive and transformative nature of Reform's achievement. On the other hand, Kohler wanted to use the past to validate the empowerment of women as religious actors. The tension suffusing Kohler's thought emerges starkly. If the narrow-minded Talmudists had truly squashed the religious soul of woman, how was it that she had remained such a pure spiritual figure? And if the modern age had granted her spiritual freedom for the first time, why were her traditional virtues now so sorely missed? Kohler rejected the narrow pieties of the past, but he celebrated the virtues and values that he admitted were created in an ethos shaped by those very pieties.

Kohler insisted on crediting Jewish women with a virtue, an involvement, and a place in Jewish history that he believed had not been sufficiently recognized by earlier observers. "What gave the Sabbath and festivals, the home life, the table, the entire private and social life of the Jew their peculiar character?" he asked. "It seems to me that these points have never been carefully considered in connection with my theme: Woman."[9] Much of Jewish history was lived in difficult, often oppressive circumstances, and Kohler quite readily assigned credit for both the survival of the Jewish people and the greatness of their history to the piety and faithfulness of Jewish women. Women had preserved what was truly special about Jewish existence. Even in the darkest times, "true, chaste, and noble" family ethics had provided an inexhaustible source of refreshment to the Jewish soul.[10]

The Israelite women of Egypt embodied piety, sacrifice, and loyalty as they taught their children the religion of their ancestors. They brought hope, belief, and courage to the bleak lives of their enslaved husbands. Not only in slavery but "through the times and lands of history," Israel's women had provided a miraculous well from which "the water of life bubbled freely from the dry earth." By offering incomparable love and motherly sacrifice, Jewish women had been able to raise children who aspired to religious learning and good deeds even in the grimmest of environments.[11] Kohler described "the Jewess of the Talmudical age" as "a model wife, guardian of home, promoter of piety and of religious education and ministering angel of charity."[12] And so throughout history the self-sacrificing, pious, nurturing feminine ideal that Kohler found in the Jewish past approximated idealized descriptions of nineteenth-century female virtue.

Kohler transferred the specific ideals that he derived from the past and from contemporary culture into a model for every Jewish woman, ancient and modern. In 1888 he described Esther as the "savior of her race." He then went on to ask, "Is not every woman on earth destined by Divine Providence to redeem, to elevate, and improve her race, to win man and ennoble him by the sweet and sympathetic qualities of her soul?"[13] By extolling the role of women in Jewish history and by equating the ideal with the typical, Kohler superimposed age-old virtues on Jewish women of his own day. His exhortatory goal in focusing on past women's lives was to alert contemporary women to their own duties and responsibilities. For despite his flowery prose, Kohler was far from happy with the state of the modern Jewish woman or of the Jewish home, woman's privileged domain.

Woman's traditional role as redeemer of her environment should, in Kohler's opinion, only be strengthened in the modern era, which granted her greater "privileges and opportunities, and therewith" greater "duties and responsibilities."[14] Social advances had broadened woman's sphere and the scale of her influence. Under the aegis of Reform, women's rights in the temple had finally been acknowledged within Judaism. The stunting effects of Talmudism had been wiped away, and women were free to bring the uplifting influence of their pure spirits and the inspiration of their exemplary lives to their people. In an 1875 article on "woman's calling," Kohler noted that woman's harsh experience, "her heavy sufferings" as servant to the more brutal male, had "developed the finer strings of the woman's soul."[15] How much more so the Jewish woman, subject to degradation as both woman and Jew, must have refined a particularly sensitive soul and noble spirit, which in an enlightened world could now help shape both society and the narrower sphere of her religion. As Kohler often observed, "Jewish woman has it within her power today more than ever before to restore to our home, to our heart, to our entire social life, the blessings, the spirituality, the happiness and peace that we so sorely miss."[16]

Yet shortly after his arrival in America in 1869, Kohler challenged his German-reading audience to consider what had become of the wellspring of female devotion that sustained the Jewish people through so many centuries of trial. So long as Israel was still in the wilderness, still in the school of suffering, women had worked to sustain the soul and spirit of their people. But now, "in this promised land of freedom," Kohler inquired, "is it all forgotten, has the water gone back?" "Israel's women," he observed, were no longer concerned with illuminating their homes with a spiritual light or with pursuing the special honor attached to the educational achievements of their sons. Rather than taking advantage of the freedom they had been granted in the synagogue in order to exercise their redemptive influence upon society, women seemed to be abandoning their traditional roles altogether. As a direct result of the Jewish woman's negligence, the Jewish family sense, domestic virtue, and traditional manners seemed to have disappeared from Israel.[17]

In his often repeated lament for the fading of "the pristine Jewish purity and household virtue,"[18] Kohler's indictment of women was implicit. Women, after all, held the "magic wand" that could restore the blessings of Jewish customs, ethics, and education that the "unrest of the new era had covered with ashes."[19] If women were not directly responsible for the current crisis, it was one in which they were intimately involved. The malaise in American Jewish life that Kohler sought to confront was not only of the synagogue; it manifested itself specifically and most disturbingly in the very homes that one might suppose ideal Jewish women would have made strong.

Women's failure to preserve the character of Jewish life was, of course, no more than a reflection of the experience of Jews in the United States in the decades after 1850. In the modern era, Jews, like women, had been offered unprecedented opportunities. New worlds of culture, education, and occupation had opened for Jews in America. European advocates of Jewish emancipation had argued that once the legal barriers and social prejudices that stunted Jewish life were removed, the Jew's spiritual deformities would disappear and he would be freed to take a proper and exemplary place in society. Indeed, German Jews in the United States did advance into new avenues in business, culture, and politics.

Kohler and his colleagues believed that Reform Judaism had preserved Judaism as a viable option for Jews who had moved far beyond the ghetto walls. "Replacing a dead language by a living one, and Oriental customs by modern ones," Kohler declared in 1875, Reform Judaism had "tuned the hearts to new strains of devotion, and filled the houses of worship with the music of new aspirations . . . [It had] lightened the burden of the Mosaic law and reconciled modern life with religion."[20] Yet despite Kohler's insistence that "Reform lifted [Judaism] from the dust, made the synagogue a source of pride and self-respect to the Jew and lent the religion of the despised race a power it never had before,"[21] he also recognized the profound failure of Reform. Synagogues stood empty, and Jews lived lives devoid of Jewish content. Instead of enriching the Jewish religion, acculturation only seemed to enfeeble Judaism. In this new era Kohler, for one, perceived a bleak time of irreligion and apathy.

There was nothing modest about Kohler's ideas of what women could and should do to mend the situation. Having assigned women so much credit for sustaining the Jewish family spirit and devotion through bleak millennia, Kohler felt justified in investing contemporary women with the responsibility of redeeming his own spiritually bleak age. In 1888, with no lack of hyperbole, Kohler insisted that woman's "lofty idealism, . . . her innate religious inspiration and piety . . . [and] her angelic grace, purity and love" invested her with the "glorious privilege" of "rescu[ing] modern society from the mire and mud of sin and wretched guilt, and lift[ing] it to loftier aims and standards, to make the Jewish star of household virtue and chastity shine again in its pristine glory." By saving the Jewish home and providing an inspirational model for the rest of society, Jewish women could "thus redeem not only the Jewish, but the human race, to make all worthy of the shrine of the God of holiness and virtue."[22]

Generally, when Kohler addressed the role of women in Judaism, he was speaking or writing mainly *for* women. Not surprisingly, he often took "woman" as his theme when he addressed women's groups. In the 1870s and 1880s, Kohler wrote often for newspapers expressing Reform points of view. Although much of his work was published in English in these newspapers, all of his articles focusing on women were published in German in an attempt to reach an immigrant female audience.[23] But it would be a mistake to conclude that his beliefs concerning the roles of women and of the home within Judaism were irrelevant to the rest of his thought. In fact, the development of Kohler's understanding of Judaism in the United States makes more sense if his ideas are considered in relation to his views on the place of women in Judaism.

Testing the Ideal: Kohler's Reform Efforts in 1885

The role of Kohler's concerns about the Jewish domestic sphere in his efforts to create a modern, credible Jewish-American identity can best be illuminated through an examination of his thought during the most active and critical period of his career. In 1885 Kohler gave a prominent series of lectures in which he defended Reform against a traditional rabbi's challenge. He also convened an American rabbinical conference, calling upon its representatives to set out the principles by which Judaism could maintain its vitality in a modern world. Following the conference, Kohler assumed the chief editorship of the *Jewish Reformer,* a newspaper intended to represent the Reform viewpoint. By assuming the role of spokesman for the reform tendency within Judaism, he helped to give shape and substance to the American Jewish Reform movement. In that busy year, as he articulated his hopes for the triumph of Judaism as the ultimate realization of rational religion, Kohler also expressed his uneasiness about the current state of Judaism.

In the early years of Kohler's career in the United States, American Judaism was dominated, both numerically and organizationally, by Jews who, like Kohler, came from Germany. In the early 1880s Reform Judaism seemed to be triumphing among America's approximately 250,000 Jews. The only national organization for congregations was the Union of American Hebrew Congregations (UAHC), founded in 1873; its affiliates were increasingly being identified as allied with the Reform cause. In 1879 the UAHC claimed 118 member congregations.[24]

It was also in 1879 that Kohler consolidated his position as a leader within American Judaism by becoming rabbi of Temple Beth-El in New York City. After ten years in America, having served congregations in Detroit and Chicago, Kohler had established himself as one of the best-educated, most serious, and most radical rabbis in the land. He heartily endorsed the Reform cause and called for the abandonment of customs that disturbed modern sensibilities. He dismissed Hebrew as a "dry oriental language."[25] He condemned unedited presentations of the Bible because of the book's "impure and offensive chapters," which lent "words to matters which ought not to be mentioned before the youth or before a mixed assembly."[26] He advocated the celebration of a Sunday Sabbath for Jews who were unable to observe the traditional Sabbath on Saturday.

But Kohler also condemned those who would practice a Reform Judaism motivated only by convenience. It had not proven very difficult to wean American Jews away from the fundamentalist beliefs and practices of their ancestors. The real challenge for Reform Judaism, as embraced by Kohler, was to see that those who abandoned orthodoxy did not abandon Judaism altogether. Kohler advocated change in the interest of creating a Judaism that could provide a meaningful and substantive religious framework for modern Jews.

By his presence in New York, Kohler was inevitably exposed to the changing face of American Jewry. At the very moment when the idea of an American Reform Judaism seemed on its way to institutional triumph, the early 1880s brought the first massive waves of immigrants from Russia and eastern Europe, who would come to dominate American Judaism numerically and, eventually, institutionally. East European Jewish immigrants took little interest in the efforts of Reformers and their decorous, ornate, respectable religion, which the newcomers barely recognized as Judaism. As Kohler saw it, the increasing numbers of east Europeans and their indifference to the benefits of religious reform meant that Reform leaders, despite "thirty-five years" of work "in this country . . . for the emancipation from . . . Mosaico-Talmudical Judaism," had to defend their position against the claims of traditional Jews who seemed intent upon forcing Jews to "again bend our neck" to the yoke of religious law.[27] Thus, when Rabbi Alexander Kohut arrived from Hungary in 1885 to serve as the rabbi of the Ahavath Chesed congregation in New York and embraced the role of spokesman against the further growth of Reform Judaism, Kohler's response was particularly important.

When Kohut commenced a series of lectures blasting Reform Judaism as a sham religion, Kohler stepped forward as Reform's defender. In responding to Kohut, Kohler attempted to define a space for Jewish existence and identity between what he saw as the inflexible, obsolete rule of orthodoxy and a bland humanism that abandoned all grounding in spiritual and historical experience. Kohler answered Kohut's lecture series with one of his own, entitled "Backwards or Forwards?"

In these lectures Kohler emphasized that he forfeited his commitment to the forms of the past with regret. "It may be," he acknowledged, "and I doubt it not for a moment, that those who yet sincerely cling to the old views and practices are much happier and more satisfied with their fixed standard of religion than we are today in our transitory state." But despite their attractive simplicity, traditional beliefs and observances were no longer an option for those who, like Kohler and most other inhabitants of the modern world, "having once eaten from the forbidden fruits of universal knowledge, see . . . the golden gates of Paradisiacal childhood irrevocably shut behind us." There was no choice but to move forward, recognizing that "we cannot restore the past except at the sacrifice of our future."[28]

From this perspective, the traditional laws and practices followed by Jewish women to create religious homes had clearly outlived their usefulness. Domestic ritual and observance had become "obsolete and meaningless practices of the past," which Kohler insisted must be "discard[ed] on principle" and replaced with "better and more adequate forms of religious devotion and life." Again, Kohler insisted on his sentimental attachment to the practices of the past. "I shall always remember with longing the deep impressions of my childhood," he admitted, as he recalled a time when "not the synagogue only, but the house, not the Sabbath only, but each day" was filled with "holy thought." But despite his nostalgia, Kohler did not believe that this life could be "conjured back."[29]

At one time, rigid Talmudic dicta had been able to deepen Jewish piety and invest "each step of life with the character of religious sanctity and purity." To Jews whose ghetto-bound lives were otherwise so bleak, traditional practice had offered "elevating and inspiring forms of devotion, apt to remind the mistress of the household or the other members of the family of their sacred duties within the domestic sphere." Now "all the rules and ordinances offered by the Mosaico-Rabbinical law concerning *domestic life*" had become "[v]oid of all moral lessons and suggestive thought." They had become a dry, arbitrary list of restrictions, "legal forms and usages" offering nothing "that ennobles and refines the soul."[30]

Kohler argued that the ancient forms of Jewish observance that had once sanctified Jewish lives now seemed so bizarrely archaic that they could only choke any true devotional spirit. Kohler did not deem domestic piety obsolete, but he did believe that it needed to be revitalized. He faulted Reform efforts for not addressing this challenge. In his response to Kohut, as throughout his career, Kohler emphasized his view that one of Reform's greatest "shortcomings consist[ed] in its neglect of domestic devotion."[31] He could not dismiss his own childhood memories of a world suffused with an order and beauty derived from the forms imposed by Judaism. A life untouched by any ceremony or devotion would also be devoid of vibrancy and certainly could not be Jewish.

Kohler believed that Reform thinkers had indeed identified the vital step that must be taken to sustain and redeem Judaism. Advocates of Reform hoped to focus on the "inner truth" that lay beneath Judaism's stagnant forms. The tradition could flourish in a modern age only by "bringing out all that is humane and everlastingly good and true in the ancient laws." New forms had to be discovered so that these truths could be found not only in the synagogue but, as of old, in every breath that the Jew took. Thus, for Kohler the greatest task of Reform became that of finding new and appropriate forms "adequate to the age." "The great mistake which we have been making all along," Kohler would insist in 1906, "is that in the attempt at reforming the Synagog, we overlooked the greater need of a reconsecrated homelife."[32]

In November 1885, following his exchange with Kohut, Kohler called together in Pittsburgh the most notable assemblage of American rabbis of the nineteenth century. Kohut's conservative challenge was one factor motivating this gathering. But Kohler's initial response to Kohut, together with his address to the delegates at the Pittsburgh Conference, indicated that what really frightened Kohler about the state of American Judaism was the "appalling religious indifference and lethargy among the masses."[33] His concerns were not limited simply to declining synagogue attendance: "The pristine Jewish purity and household virtue is no less fading. We are visibly losing our prerogative as a holy nation."[34]

The Pittsburgh Platform, promulgated at this conference—largely

Kohler's work—has been considered the definitive statement of classical Reform Judaism. The platform represented the crystallization of Reform as a distinct movement, and it remained the central expression of Reform principles until the Columbus Platform appeared in 1937. Kohler believed that the Pittsburgh document would offer a positive program to those Jews for whom unquestioning belief and practice had become impossible.

Kohler hoped that the disappearance of orthodoxy from the lives of modern Jews would become more than just a function of "laxity and indifference." He acknowledged that "the overwhelming majority of Jews within the domain of modern culture disregard altogether the Mosaic-Rabbinical laws regarding diet or dress, concerning work or the kindling of lights on Sabbath, or any other ancient rite." He believed that Jewish leaders must accept that "law and tradition [had] irrevocably lost its hold upon the modern Jew." Only then could they go on to create a meaningful religion in a modern context. Reform leaders needed to affirm that their rejection of traditional practices were not the whims of frivolous "rebels and traitors" seeking their own convenience. Rather, they needed to make clear that they "transgress these laws on principle." As the platform itself went on to make clear, these Reformers believed that for modern Jews the traditional religious laws were "apt rather to obstruct than to further modern spiritual elevation."[35]

Kohler also declared the centrality of Jewish women to his efforts, identifying Jewish women "as the best and most welcome element to further this reform measure." Kohler proudly described Reform Judaism's recognition of "the high dignity of woman as the co-partner and helpmate of man." He argued for even further advances, maintaining that "Reform Judaism will never reach its higher goal without having first accorded in the congregational council and in the entire religious and moral sphere of life, equal voice to woman with man." Addressing his Reform colleagues, Kohler insisted, "Our religious life in America demands woman's help and participation," and he acknowledged that Reform efforts were dependent on women, with their "broader and more tender" sympathies, mainly because so little could be expected of men, "few of whom find even the time for our Sabbath School work on Sundays." Thus Kohler celebrated women's emancipation within Reform Judaism and expressed gratitude for their present and potential contributions to the congregation.[36]

Yet it is clear that the deep malaise Kohler perceived within American Judaism would be little affected by women's "self-denying devotion and enthusiastic zeal" if its only effect was regular synagogue attendance. Kohler's deep longing for an all-encompassing Judaism expressed itself in his lament for the dimming of "religion's fire," which "has almost burned out on the domestic altar." Kohler knew that no matter what Reformers achieved in the synagogue, Judaism could have no future as long as the "ice of indifference" remained "gathered around the Jewish hearth." Even as Kohler advocated discarding old ways and rituals and making Judaism more responsive to the times, he pointed out to his colleagues that it may have been a serious mistake for "Our Reform" to confine "its work of improving the mode of worship to the Synagog, leaving the home unprovided with impressive and solemn forms and symbols." Kohler's pain is apparent when he notes that "of all the incentives to Sabbath and holiday joy and cheerfulness at home, little is left except perhaps now and then the Seder on Passover Eve, and even this is growing stale and unattractive."[37]

The Pittsburgh Platform addressed issues of theology, doctrine, and law, areas in which the Reform movement needed to define its position and in which Kohler, as a congregational rabbi, worked. Yet as his 1885 oratory made clear, Kohler was also seeking something that had nothing to do with the Pittsburgh Platform's rational universalism or its rejection of ceremonial law. Not even a flood of emancipated female synagogue-goers would have consoled him. Essentially, Kohler had not given up on the ideal of a Jewish home that would evoke a distinctive Jewish virtue. His call for "new striking and stirring, attractive and beautiful forms adapted to the needs and the taste of our age and people" was a plea for the re-creation of the Jewish home, so that "as of yore," it would be "the bright focus of a cheering faith and a hallowed life full of inspiration, comfort and sacred reminiscences."[38]

Defining the Limits of Identity: Judaism, Women, and the Sabbath

Although Kohler appreciated the noble presence and service of women in the synagogue as they filled the pews (often to the exclusion of men), piloted Sunday schools, and, by the end of the century, participated in expanding congregational activities, he was not satisfied. The coming of women to the public space of the synagogue had redeemed neither the synagogue nor Judaism. "Dare we give expression to disappointment," he asked in 1906, "because the fruitage is slow to ripen, the anticipated change has not come about? . . . As yet the great revival of the Synagog, so eagerly looked for, has not come, nor has the religious ardor anywhere perceptibly increased."[39]

The hopes generated by emancipation—of both women and Jews—had not been fully realized. To the contrary, some of the implications of emancipation had proven quite threatening. Having recognized woman's spiritual and moral equality and her claim upon a seat next to her husband in the sanctuary, having argued for her full membership in the congregation and its councils, Kohler was extremely careful to show that the logic of this emancipation did not imply a complete blurring of the distinctions between women and men. He advocated a particular rendering of the character of women's virtue. The biblical Miriam, for instance, merited Kohler's praise precisely because she recognized her own limits: "Only in the circle of her sex did she spread the seeds of living God consciousness and in quiet modesty and noble reticence as fits woman's calling." It was only when she felt that her spiritual equality had been questioned that she was willing to challenge Moses: "Does God only speak through Moses, does he not also speak through us?"[40]

Kohler felt that woman's greatest power was and is as persuader, as he pointed to examples like Deborah and Miriam who served as inspirations to the male leaders and generals who advanced their people's destiny. "Behold Miriam," he declared, "at the side of Moses the leader! Or Deborah, the prophetess, at the side of Barak, the general!"[41] As for those women who put themselves at the center, who chose to lead rather than persuade, Kohler asked, "Would you have her in front of an army? Joan d'Arc is no true woman. Would you have her preside over a court of justice? Portia's verdict is far from impartial justice. Would you see her at the helm of a State? Her nature is too delicate to brave the fierce storms of public life."[42] Kohler dismissed such women as no women at all. Judith (who saved her people by first enticing an enemy general and then beheading him with his own sword) lacked "the sweetness and delicate grace of a woman." Esther, in contrast, chose to "plead" rather than "strike." Of Esther,

Kohler declared, "She might have proudly disowned her despised race in the critical hour, but then she would not have been a true woman."[43]

Kohler was unable to countenance the idea of a woman who might not fit his definition. The new era's threat of disorder was exemplified in the figure of a woman refusing to play her proper role. In fact, the possibility of such a creature seemed monstrous to Kohler: "A woman without tenderness, without gentleness, without the power of self-suppression to an almost infinite degree is a creature so anomalous that she cannot fail to do enormous harm, both to her own sex and the other . . . She . . . becomes a devil in disguise."[44]

Kohler's effort to put such narrow bounds on female identity reflected the difficulties involved in attempting to embrace emancipation while excluding the implications of its logic. In an 1875 article he asked, "Is it woman's calling to become a man?"[45] Kohler presented this question to show its absurdity, but he recognized that it was a question—he recognized the difficulty of imposing limits on equality once granted. The question of how to emancipate women but preserve their essence as women suggested a parallel question: how do you emancipate Jews and not end up with gentiles? The dangers of blurring distinctions were as great in constructing Jewish practice as they were in constructing gender roles.

Kohler would have preferred a Judaism without ambiguity. The goal of Reform had been to discriminate "between the essentials and non-essentials."[46] Indeed, Kohler often pointed out the basic institutions and components without which Judaism could not exist. In his discourse Kohler tended to equate women, the home, and the Sabbath with each other, and he equated each with Judaism itself. In some sense, Sabbath, domestic devotion, and the virtuous woman were one; no one entity could exist without the others. The purity of each of these symbols depended on the purity of the others. A discussion of any one of these symbols easily became a discussion of them all, as Kohler demonstrated in 1898: "Not the synagogue but the home as [Judaism's] main factor and safeguard, the wife and the mother decide the destiny of the Jew . . . Not the synagogue but the home must see Judaism regenerated, the Sabbath peace and joy restored and the spirit of devotion and prayer revived."[47] Kohler's equation of woman, home, and Sabbath with the essence of Judaism was not just glib rhetoric. In his struggle to delineate a coherent American Jewish identity, Kohler ultimately drew the same sharp lines around Judaism that he drew around Jewish women.

In 1874 Kohler was the first rabbi to introduce successful Jewish Sunday worship in America. In 1891, however, to the dismay of his fellow radicals, he rejected Sunday observance of the Jewish Sabbath in any form. Kohler's changing views on a proper Jewish Sabbath for America reveal the depth of both his commitment and his ambivalence toward the effort to balance the demands of contemporary society with what he believed to be the irreducible essence of Judaism. At all times he insisted on the centrality of the Sabbath to Jewish practice, belief, and identity, and to the survival of Judaism.

"Alas for the Jewish day of Sabbath," Kohler lamented in 1873, "Its brightness and splendor are gone; its blossoms withered. It is no day of holy rest any more, no day of recreation and elevation and sanctification, but a day of noise, of labor, and business." At the beginning of his American career it was clear to Kohler that the Jewish people could not "close their business for two days in the week and compete with their fellow citizens with any success."[48] The demands of business had permanently undermined the sanctity of the Jewish Sabbath. As Kohler observed in 1876, "There [is no] hope of seeing it restored unless new walls were to shut the Jewish people off from intercourse with their fellow-citizens."[49] He had no interest in rebuilding walls that would isolate the Jewish community in America, and he realized that there was no place for such walls in the framework of American society or in the lives of Americanized Jews. Walls were what Jews had been trying to escape.

Kohler's solution was to transfer the Jewish day of Sabbath from its traditional Saturday observance to Sunday. "The truth is," he observed, "that Sunday is the actual day of rest for the majority of Jews in this country as well as for Christians."[50] Although the idea of a Sunday Sabbath had been suggested and in some cases enacted by Reformers in Germany earlier in the century, it continued to represent a radical break with one of the basic components of Jewish tradition.

For Kohler this radical break reflected not indifference to the Jewish Sabbath but rather recognition of its profound importance. In the progressive enervation of the Saturday Sabbath he perceived the destruction of meaningful Jewish life. "Mark well," he said, "the issue is not between Saturday and Sunday, but between Judaism saved and

Judaism lost!"[51] Kohler was willing to sacrifice the form of an inconvenient day and substitute another so that the true substance of the Sabbath could be realized. Such a day would not be the Sabbath of historical memory, but at least it would not be a sham, a day of business pretending to be a true Sabbath.

In speaking of the "beautiful Sabbath lamp of household piety and devotion," Kohler clearly associated the Sabbath (and "the glow it brought to the domestic table") with the ethos of the Jewish home. It was, after all, the heart "chiefly of the Jewish woman, who best represents the heart of the household," which clung most "fervently to the old historical Sabbath with its manifold dear remembrances." Kohler believed that the Sabbath's role in sustaining and nurturing Jewish life was similar to the role that women should play. At different times he described both women and the Sabbath as providing "a fountain of living waters," which had sustained the Jewish people through the harsh centuries of their existence. When Kohler deplored the loss of a Sabbath that once had been the center of the Jewish week, he could easily have been talking about women: "Ever since the crown of glory was torn from the head of our Sabbath queen, the priceless jewels of Jewish life, deep devotion and piety, filial reverence and domestic purity have lost much of their pristine lustre," resulting in an "awful lethargy" among Jews left with only the "dying embers of their former religious fervor."[52]

At first Kohler had believed that the spirit of the blissful Sabbath day of the past, while it could not be wholly resuscitated, could survive in a form adjusted to the needs of the age. At that time he clearly believed that the boundaries of Jewish identity were subject to manipulation: "If we cannot have the Sabbath, we take the Sunday as the rallying day."[53] Before he changed his mind on the Sabbath, Kohler had argued for cosmopolitanism and the "dropping one by one [of] the rites and forms of nationality and exclusive sect." Kohler celebrated the "advocates of reform" who were rendering "our religion as broad and comprehensive as to admit all that is sacred, ennobling and inspiring in the field of literature, art, science, and law," enabling the Reformer to "remodel his festivals, his ceremonies and rituals so as to imbue them with universal interest and make them expressive of universal truth." He did not worry that the celebration of Sabbath on Sunday would threaten Judaism with absorption by the surrounding world. Rather, he chose to believe that a Sunday Sabbath "would regenerate the ancient faith" and enable modern Jews to connect with their ancient religion, giving Judaism a voice that others would hear, respect, and perhaps emulate.[54]

In 1891, when Kohler reversed his position on which day to call the Sabbath, he expressed disillusionment with his former cosmopolitan creed. He admitted that he once looked forward to the day when "Reformed Judaism should infuse its New Year's day's earnestness into the First day of January, have its Passover and Pentecost ideas and symbols transferred to Easter and the Christian Pentecost . . . and its Festival of Lights to the 25th of December." It was "this last logical conclusion," Kohler acknowledged, "which drove a big nail into" his radicalism. He finally realized that "radicalism to its very last consequences" meant not the preservation of Judaism but its destruction.[55] Distressed by growing European anti-Semitism and the murderous pogroms against Russia's Jews, Kohler felt he must change his own attitude in response to "THE CHANGED ATTITUDE OF THE WORLD TOWARDS THE JEW . . . What a mockery this so-called Christian civilization turned out to be!" Kohler exclaimed. "What a sham and a fraud has this era of tolerance and enlightenment become! . . . The world still hates the Jew." To Kohler the implications were clear: "Dare we . . . recognize the predominance of Christian culture by accepting the Christian Sunday as our day of rest?"[56]

Kohler once observed that "the large majority of Jews at least in Western countries no longer observe these commandments, and the question is, are these nonobservant Jews identical with the non-Jews. Are we liberal Jews who have assimilated non-Jewish culture really Jews no longer?"[57] Again, the parallel question suggested itself: "Is it woman's calling to become a man?" Although he once argued that particular rituals were irrelevant to Jewishness, it is clear that by 1891 Kohler had come to believe that the Jewish essence could only be preserved if contained within specifically Jewish forms. Thrust into what turned out to be the harsh world of "enlightened" Christian civilization, Judaism, like the tender female thrust into the "whirlpool of life's raging struggle" could not survive.[58] This was the outcome of pushing the logic of emancipation to its furthest extent.

Having reembraced the Saturday Sabbath, Kohler still needed to draw lines that would mark the distinctiveness of Jewish life. He bemoaned the "colorless cosmopolitanism" and "the monotony of prosperity" in which so many American Jews lived and in which, without a meaningful Sabbath day, "one day passes with us like another."[59] It is perhaps not surprising, "since most of our business and professional men are of necessity kept away from the divine service on" Saturday, that Kohler assigned the responsibility of Sabbath maintenance to women. Holding to his belief that the Sabbath and the home needed to be restored in Jewish lives, he candidly observed, "Of course, this great duty devolves first of all on the mother."[60]

Preserving the Past

Although Kohler changed his mind about central issues regarding the place of Judaism in American society, his ideas about the role of women in Judaism remained generally constant. Interestingly, the evolution of his ideas about other issues makes more sense when viewed in relation to his position on women. Kohler's consistency on this question suggests that early in his career he felt a profound discomfort with the Reform project. In lamenting the decline of the Jewish domestic sphere, he identified one area in which these conflicts could be expressed.

In 1879 Kohler celebrated the great work of Reform Judaism but cautioned that "its work is but half done and would be futile, should it not be pursued in the domestic circles." Reformers had succeeded in the public realm by "beautif[ying] our houses of worship, filling them with new light, and life, and song. It has now to offer us new attractive forms of domestic devotion, too. It must give us, in place of obsolete orthodox customs, a sweet home religion."[61] In a sort of valedictory address delivered to the Central Conference of American Rabbis forty-five years later, Kohler reiterated this point: "After all, our Reform must not be confined to the Synagog. Our home must again be made what it was, the sanctuary of piety."[62] Along the way, Kohler never ceased to demand new forms so that old values could be perpetuated. Presumably, Kohler had envisioned the Sunday Sabbath as the very sort of new form that would answer the devotional needs of modern Jews who were forced to respond to the demands of the market. His subsequent disillusionment with the Sunday Sabbath seemed to teach him that whatever new forms were found had to resemble old forms. In 1924 he asked the Jewish mother to "again teach her child to recite its morning and evening prayer and say the grace at every meal . . . What lent the Jewish home at all times its beauty of holiness was the ceremonial system so rich in elevating power, and since these old traditional forms have lost their appealing force, Reform has to step in and replace them by more attractive ones."[63]

At the end of the nineteenth century, Kohler and his Reform colleagues sought a ritual aesthetic and a degree of participation in the larger society that precluded the observance of practices that had long defined the Jewish community and home. Many Reformers disparaged the traditional practices and strictures that had shaped women's lives and the Jewish way of life. They embraced equality for women and insisted on places for women in the synagogue. In practice, Reformers were successful in creating a Judaism that answered the aesthetic and social needs of their acculturating constituency. They were satisfied that their innovations enabled nonghettoized Jews to continue to affiliate with their faith. But in grieving over homes and lives that to him seemed empty of religion, Kohler came to recognize the cost of the conveniences of equal citizenship and participation in modern life. He could see that the knowledge and piety of Jewish men would be sacrificed to the demands of a materially driven world. Kohler knew that he and his colleagues had succeeded in "reforming Judaism, but not the Jew."[64]

Although the Reform project was driven by the force of reason, Kohler longed for a Judaism that touched the soul and heart. The problem with modern society, Kohler argued in 1891, was that "the blood has all rushed up to the brain and the heart emptied of its vital fluid has its chills and fevers." The solution, he said in 1899, would not come from "the intellectual woman," whose circulation also sent "blood rushing to the head and away from the heart." Rather, it would be "the hearty, the whole-souled tender-hearted Rebecca-like woman" who would finally bring "the lost paradise back to man."[65]

Nineteenth-century ideas about the inherently religious nature of women reinforced Kohler's wish and belief that women did not have to be a part of the advanced age that necessitated Reform Judaism. "The new era" had diminished the virtue and merit of Jewish women. When Kohler talked about women and the home, he spoke of the ideal home as he envisioned it, and, as he put it most tellingly, that home would ideally be "what it was."[66]

Ultimately, Kohler wanted to preserve the traditional values of the Jewish home but exclude the narrow piety that had created them. He took refuge in a prevailing middle-class ideology about women that tirelessly celebrated their devotion to an idealized domesticity. In calling for a renewal of the Jewish home through new ceremonies that spoke to modern sensibilities, Kohler was secure enough about the Jewish place in American society to believe that religion could encompass more than just the moment of formal worship. And he knew from his youth that it took distinctively Jewish forms to create a meaningful Judaism. But he was not bold enough to suppose that such differences could impinge upon the realm of business or intercourse with the outside world. Such admissions of difference were possible only for those whose lives could still be imagined back into the past. In expecting women to maintain distinctive roles as ideal Jewish women, Kohler assigned them the responsibility for maintaining the distinctiveness of Judaism.

The American Jewish Reform movement sought to harmonize Judaism with the expectations of a modern era. As a prominent Reform rabbi, Kaufmann Kohler took a leading role in this effort to transform a way of life into a way of being American. But the effort to realize the emancipation of Jews while preserving Judaism was fraught with ambiguity, an ambiguity exemplified by the struggle to find a place for women in the reformed religion. Although Reform Judaism sought to meet the modern needs of both men and women, the only vital future Kaufmann Kohler could envision for Judaism was one in which women would continue to embody and sustain the Jewish past.

CHAPTER SEVEN

Beyond the Gallery: American Jewish Women in the 1890s

Despite the limitations imposed by leaders like Kohler and by the practical constraints of synagogue traditions and structure, acculturated Jewish women toward the end of the nineteenth century did begin to forge a path toward a more conspicuous public religious identity. The 1890s brought a distinct shift in both the pattern of women's synagogue involvement and the shape of the Jewish Reform temple in the United States. These developments were not unrelated. The last decade of the nineteenth century saw the establishment of sisterhood-type auxiliaries on a local level and the organization of Jewish women on a national scale in the founding of the National Council of Jewish Women. These new organizations unleashed the energies of thousands of women, creating dynamic public identities for participants *as* Jewish women. Their efforts transformed notions about the place and purpose of the synagogue in the lives of American Jews.

By the 1880s the Reform tendency in American Judaism was well established, as its style and innovations distinguished the Judaism of acculturated Jews from that of recent immigrants. Supported largely by Jews whose primarily central European families had arrived in the United States earlier in the century, the dominance of this movement was about to be tested by the impact of the burgeoning numbers of new immigrants arriving from eastern Europe.[1] But in the 1880s, Reformers could look around and see that even synagogues that defined themselves as traditional had adopted many of the practices characteristic of Reform.[2] As Jeffrey Gurock has summarized the situation, although Orthodox congregations numbered about 200 in 1860, by 1880 they "were reduced to a mere handful of the some 275 synagogues serving this country's acculturated Jews."[3]

Although questions about choirs, mixed seating, and observing the second day of holidays continued to trouble more traditional congregations, these issues had apparently been laid to rest in Reform communities. Despite continued debate over the observance of a Sunday Sabbath, the American Reform temple of the 1890s was not a site of extensive debate over ritual reform. As Isaac M. Wise announced to his assembled disciples at the 1897 meeting of the Central Conference of American Rabbis, "We are done with the synagogical reforms."[4] Reform practice had settled into a consistent pattern of decorous worship conducted mainly in English, accompanied by organ, choir, and sermon, and attended by (a few) men without prayer shawls or head coverings, seated together with women in cushioned family pews.[5] As one of Chicago's Reform rabbis observed in 1896, the work of Reform to "modernize the synagogue and to abolish ceremonies . . . has been done, and for us is as dead an issue as the abolition of slavery."[6]

Reform leaders believed that broad acceptance of mixed seating in the synagogue sanctuary manifested their community's firm commitment to American conceptions of women's religious equality. Meanwhile, the absence of family pews increasingly became the distinguishing marker of congregations that wished to affirm their Orthodoxy. Whether in progressive or traditional congregational settings, however, active participation by women in worship and general synagogue activity was extremely limited. Despite a professed concern with religious equality for women on the part of acculturating male Jewish leaders, Jewish women remained largely disenfranchised within their religious communities. Although the 1890s did not bring any significant change in the nature of women's role in the worship service, the decade did see a reconceptualization of women's relationship to the synagogue and of what it meant to express one's religious (and perhaps ethnic) identity as a Jewish woman.

As the end of the nineteenth century approached, Protestant women, continuing to build engaged public roles for themselves in religiously oriented work, began to demand greater recognition for their contributions to their churches and denominations. As the question of women's rights and responsibilities percolated through the surrounding society, Jewish women began to seek out ways to expand the limited pathways available to them for the creation of activist female identities within a Jewish context. Having accepted the principle that Jewish women merited the same respect accorded their Christian counterparts, the acculturated American Jewish community had to work to create roles for Jewish women that did not contrast too glaringly with the example of non-Jewish women.

Throughout the second half of the nineteenth century, Jewish women's involvement in activities identified with Judaism had been a pale reflection of Christian women's involvement in church work. By the early 1890s female Christian activism had become a powerful cultural force, as women of various Protestant denominations found themselves at the center of influential mass movements, working for temperance and supporting missionary endeavors in the United States and abroad.[7] There were also women fighting for recognition as lay representatives and ministers at various denominational congresses.[8] This ferment did eventually carry over into the nation's synagogues, where as the last decade of the century approached, most women were still affiliated only by virtue of their male relatives.

Jewish women rarely filled the role of religiously identified activist. This lack began to appear as a deficiency when measured against the achievements of Christian women. In 1896, Rosa Sonneschein, editor of the *American Jewess,* noted the frequent observation "that among Jewish young women there is a lack of that individual sense of responsibility for the performance of higher duties which is so commonly present in the case of their Christian sisters." Among young Christian women, Sonneschein pointed out, "it is the rule rather than the exception to belong to one or more organizations whose aims are ethical or philanthropic . . . [T]he young ladies among the Christian denominations are frequently found visiting the poor." Sonneschein drew her readers' attention to Jewish women's absence in the area of "this ideal personal administration of charity so frequently to be witnessed among the better class of Christian women of a similar age."[9]

Those who wanted to call upon the communal energies of the "better class" of Jewish women saw this situation as an embarrassment and a challenge. In 1893 Rebekah Kohut, the founder of the Ahavath Chesed congregation's sisterhood in New York and the wife of its rabbi, recalled an encounter with Josephine Shaw Lowell, whom she described as "one of our most estimable women, and a member of the Charity Organization Society of New York City." Lowell had confronted Kohut with a troubling question, which she passed on to her coreligionists: "'Have you no missionaries, no King's Daughters among your people? I visit your poor constantly, and have never yet met any of the better class Jewesses in the lower quarter of the city!' The dart," Kohut reported, "went straight home. I knew too well the truth of her statement."[10]

If Jewish women had lagged behind their Christian sisters, Sonneschein pointed out that "until a comparatively recent period there was little or no demand for such service among the Jews in this country. The poor among them were comparatively few, and the regularly organized channels of relief sufficed to supply all demands." According to Sonneschein, "the hordes of ignorant and degraded Jews that of late years settled down upon our cities presented a new condition of affairs." Their need for "instruction and elevation as much as material relief" created an imperative demand upon the women of the nation's more settled and acculturated Jewish population.[11] Flora Schwab of Cleveland noted that Jewish women had long been inactive, not because of any lack of ability or empathy, but because they lacked "a field of operations in which to act."[12]

Sisterhoods of Personal Service

As these comments suggest, the influx of eastern European Jews was a primary catalyst among the various related developments that pushed Jewish women toward a closer approximation of the Christian model of women's associations and responsibilities. This migration, which began in earnest in the 1880s and surged during the 1890s, rapidly transformed the situation and population of Jews in the United States, creating a demand upon the established Jewish community that had to be met in new ways. In New York City, the point of arrival for hundreds of thousands of new immigrants, the need was particularly pressing.

As the immigrant population grew, existing benevolent and relief societies continued to try to provide for the poor in their midst. Meanwhile, long-standing beliefs that women were possessed of inherently charitable natures continued to be expressed. The November 9, 1888, issue of the *Jewish Exponent* described the noble work of "the most representative men of the Philadelphia Jewish community" in addressing the problem of immigrant poverty. The editors advocated a plan to send poor immigrants out "into the vast districts of our broad country yet needing inhabitants," rather than into crowded city slums. On the same page another editorial called upon the "Jewish young ladies of Philadelphia" to enter into the work of teaching young immigrant girls: "What nobler work than that of uplifting the lowly?" The same page also contained notice of the annual meeting of the Female Hebrew Benevolent Society ("the oldest of our charitable institutions"), praising the organization for performing its "considerable amount of good work in a quiet, modest way."[13]

All the pieces that would come together in the 1890s were present on that page: the mounting problem of immigrant deprivation and how best to organize for its relief, the expectation that young native Jewish women "can well afford to give a small part of their time" to the work of "uplifting the lowly," and a continuing tradition of women's benevolent organizations. The traditional strategies of the benevolent societies, however, would be rendered obsolete by the scope of an immigrant problem that was not going to be solved by rural transfers. The "quiet, modest" ways of the established societies would have to yield to a more activist model of charitable organization. The "startling increase of distress" demanded some new kind of organization of female benevolence.[14]

In 1888 Gustav Gottheil, the minister of New York's Temple Emanu-El, took the significant step of assembling the women of his congregation to organize them into a "sisterhood of personal service." The purpose of the organization was "to aid the better class of the poor, to foster a nobler charity and cultivate a higher religious ideal within the fold of Israel." Starting "with a few workers and very meagre means," within a few years, under the authority of their president, Dr. Gottheil, the women of Emanu-El, 150 workers strong, had organized a complex range of philanthropic activities and built an extensive and efficient governing structure. The services they provided to immigrants included personal visits and limited cash relief for the sick and needy, an employment bureau, schools, classes and clubs for working girls, an industrial and religious school for immigrant youth, child day care, and kindergartens.[15]

According to one involved observer, the new organization found its inspiration in a Christian women's group, the Society of King's Daughters. The director of the United Hebrew Charities also reported that "some of our congregations have been endeavoring to emulate the good done by the King's Daughter's—a society of Christian ladies to whom we owe many acts of kindness to our poor."[16] The Society of King's Daughters was founded in New York in 1886 by the wife of a Methodist minister to encourage "Christian activity" among all denominations of Protestant women. The growth of this organization was phenomenal. Within two years, it claimed 75,000 members and by 1906, 500,000. The women across the country who took up its work established hundreds of institutions ranging from settlement houses and industrial schools to libraries and homes for working girls, incurables, and discharged convicts.[17]

The King's Daughters offered Protestant women the opportunity for intensive religiously oriented work in addressing social issues beyond their own churches. The level of response to the King's Daughters, as well as the numerous societies supporting missionary work and temperance, suggests that Christian women too were seeking ways to channel their energies into religious outlets. Some denominations toward the end of the century began to establish orders of deaconesses that enabled Protestant women to devote the kind of energy to church work that Catholic women had long been able to invest in the Church as nuns.[18] Although not as prevalent as the King's Daughters, the establishment of deaconess institutions "was significant," argues Aaron Abell, "in the sense that it pointed the way to the fuller utilization of women in all fields of religious and social service."[19]

The successful model presented by the King's Daughters, described by a Jewish observer as having "spread over the globe, having branches almost everywhere," encouraged Jewish women to respond to "a similar Order."[20] According to this source, the timing of the introduction of the sisterhood at Emanu-El as a new organization for Jewish women "was so opportune that already [one and a half years later] four more congregations in this city have established their Sisterhoods, all doing active service."[21] The other large New York congregations quickly founded their own Sisterhoods of Personal Service and entered the ranks of workers for immigrant relief. Eventually, under the aegis of New York's United Hebrew Charities, these different groups formed a network to cover the needs of the immigrant districts by dividing up responsibilities for different geographical areas among the different sisterhoods.[22] Although these organizations were outward-directed, they introduced a measure of shared purpose and community to the women of these congregations. As the vice president of Temple Emanu-El's sisterhood observed in 1895, "We, ourselves, have found how blessed it is for sisters to dwell together in the unity of humane endeavors."[23]

The formulation "Sisterhood of Personal Service" used to describe these groups replaced the old "Benevolent Society" formula. Although Jewish women's groups of the 1890s should be seen in the tradition of Jewish societies, the change of names indicates that sisterhood organizers intended a self-conscious departure from old traditions of female benevolence. Likewise, the surge of energy that accompanied their introduction suggests that the new organizations were able to tap a latent energy that eluded the old organizational forms and causes.

The significance of the new model of female organization around the synagogue may be measured by the appearance of a special weekly column in the *American Hebrew* entitled "Personal Service," introduced in March 1891. The magazine's editors observed that "the Field which it represents is peculiarly theirs [the ladies'], and though the time is brief since they have entered upon it, they may feel proud of the good work already done."[24] In its accounts of work underway and of sisterhoods in the process of formation, the column covered the growth of a burgeoning movement.[25]

One detail that emerges clearly from these reports is the influence of male rabbis in the organization of these women's groups. Gottheil served as president of Emanu-El's sisterhood, Rudolph Grossman as president of Temple Beth-El's group, and the *American Hebrew* column recorded that "Rabbi Stolz, of Chicago, is endeavoring to start a Personal Service Society in connection with his congregation."[26] In March 1891 a meeting of one hundred women at Rodeph Shalom in New York, organized by two women of the congregation, was addressed by Reverend Dr. Aaron Wise, who "explained the necessity which had arisen from the performance of some charitable work by the ladies of the congregation in a systematic manner." Wise made it clear that no congregation that aspired to eminence could now afford to neglect this emerging movement: "Congregation Rodeph Sholom among the foremost in all other matters, should not be backward in this."[27]

Also in 1891, the Chicago rabbi Emil G. Hirsch testified to the significance of this innovation when he praised Gustav Gottheil for having the "happy thought . . . to organize a long latent force of his congregation" into Emanu-El's Sisterhood of Personal Service. "Too long," Hirsch observed, had Jewish congregations "neglected this promising field," this "opportunity awaiting." Hirsch recognized that Emanu-El's new organization was reminiscent of the older style of synagogue community with its many societies and groups. Hirsch maintained his allegiance to the synagogue of narrow ambit, noting, "We did a wise thing" in "taking the charities out of the hands of the congregation," yet he recognized that "as a result, we allowed to lie fallow a mighty promise of moral power . . . The [sisterhood] work is a revival of the old Jewish Chebrah adapted to the new surrounding and with this difference, that the women are those who are enrolled in the service."[28] For Hirsch and for others, the establishment of Sisterhoods of Personal Service provided an important avenue through which to channel women's energy for work associated with the congregation.

Expansion of the Reform Temple

Hirsch's comments reflected his belief that Reform temples like his own had consciously and "wisely" acted to remove extraneous activities like charities from congregational concerns. Yet his acceptance of the need to cultivate a field within the congregation that had been "allowed to lie fallow" resonated with a growing frustration at the excessive emphasis on worship and sanctuary that marked the late nineteenth-century Reform temple. Although acculturated American Jews were well pleased with the substantial and impressive edifices that added their distinctive silhouettes to the skylines of many American cities, many worried that these impressive facades had little behind them. "What is there more senseless," one critic asked, "than to invest from $100,000 to $500,000 in a pile of stone, standing empty all the year round with the exception of two or three days, open but one day in the week and then, in most congregations, not visited?"[29]

Despite a generally successful effort to present solemn ceremonies in magnificent edifices, the American Reform temple seemed to be in crisis. In 1879 the president of Chicago's Sinai Congregation reported that despite an impressive temple, and "a minister [Kaufmann Kohler] of whom we are justly proud . . . we have brought religious matters to a standstill and have transformed our grand temple in[to] a vacuum."[30] The rabbis at the 1885 Pittsburgh Conference commiserated over an outlook for "Judaism in this country [that] looks gloomy in the extreme." Most seemed to agree with the rabbi who noted sparse attendance, dominated on Friday nights by gentiles and on Saturday mornings by women.[31] The *American Hebrew* commented on Jewish congregations generally, "There are no colors gloomy enough to paint too morbidly the conditions that are at present sustained. The real majority of our people come into actual contact with the organized religious forces but once a year—on the high holidays."[32]

In Chicago, Hirsch believed he had found a solution to the crisis in the Sunday service, whose virtues and success he tirelessly trumpeted in the pages of his weekly newspaper, the *Reform Advocate*. Others claimed that new buildings and engaging lectures could fill the benches: "Our temple, which has been recently rebuilt and which represents a most beautiful edifice, is filled with worshippers both Friday evenings and Sabbath mornings. The English lectures . . . recently introduced by our rabbi, are highly appreciated and largely attended by young and old, men and women."[33] Others hoped that late Friday night services would bring the congregations to the synagogue. Kaufmann Kohler convened the 1885 Pittsburgh Rabbinical Conference with the intention of addressing "the appalling indifference which has taken hold of the masses."[34]

Some of those who perceived a crisis in the American synagogue began to call for an effort to involve the congregant both inside and outside the sanctuary. In 1885, addressing his rabbinical colleagues in New York, Henry Pereira Mendes of Shearith Israel called for the transformation of congregants from "listeners into participants." In addition, Mendes suggested that authentic participation would jolt listeners out of their seats and into service beyond the synagogue. "Congregational work," Mendes claimed, "includes whatever will humanize the members." Here Mendes indicated his recognition that Jewish women were awaiting cultivation: "In this, as in the last [rejuvenation of the worship service], the co-operation of the ladies must be secured. On the sunshine of ladies' smiles the fruits of success depend for their ripening. Let their aid be invoked for school committee work, for any department where tact, gentleness, and thoughtfulness are required." Mendes asked that "all the young ladies" of the congregation be attached to a sewing society to benefit some special charity and advised, as well, that "such young as can be induced" should also be encouraged to participate in charity work. Although he observed that "there would doubtless be very few" young men willing to join in the effort, still, "the example of one might influence a second."[35]

In the face of male indifference, Mendes, an Orthodox rabbi, recognized the need for female energies if he wished to expand the "sphere of congregational work." Isaac M. Wise had also been arguing for years that a change in female congregational status would change the congregation. "You must enfranchise woman," he declared. "She must be a member, she must have a voice and a vote in your assemblies . . . We must have women among the Boards for the sake of principle . . . We must have woman's influence in every department of the congregation, in order to infuse life into the dead bones."[36] As early as 1871, the *Jewish Times* had used the same metaphor from Ezekiel to call for woman's suffrage within the congregation: "The old bones require a shaking, the infusion of a new element, of fresh uncontaminated life-blood is needed to give vigor, energy and spirit to our modern congregations. Indifference eats away our marrow and sinew; and the sentiment of piety, the religious inclination, the enthusiastic and magnetic influence of woman may bring us that element so sorely needed."[37] The same point was echoed in an 1881 *Jewish Messenger* editorial, which observed that "assuredly [the American Jewish woman] does not need the synagogue so much as it needs her in its present apathetic state."[38]

Despite these calls, some by influential ministers of important congregations, the status of Jewish women within congregations did not begin to change until the turn of the century. But women's contributions to the congregation and the infusion of life that they could bring were felt sooner. As Gottheil and his fellow New York rabbis began to direct the energy of their female congregants to the needs of immigrants, other male Jewish leaders began to involve women in an attempt to revive the synagogue.

In April 1887 the *Jewish Exponent* called attention to "a movement . . . noticeable for some time in most of the leading Jewish congregations to invite a more general co-operation in congregational affairs."[39] In their explanation of how young men could be incorporated into this vital project, the *Exponent*'s editors revealed the logic that would help to bring women into the endeavor. The *Exponent*'s call for greater inclusion focused on the young men of the community but recognized that to build the synagogue into the real "centre of religious activity . . . the energies of all who desire to aid in the development of the Jewish cause" must be called into service. "It is with this view," the *Exponent* reported, "that the narrow laws have been broadened, and all, both men and women who belong to a congregation," should be made "capable of taking part in congregational affairs."[40]

The *Exponent*'s editors realized "that in order to attach persons permanently to a congregation, you must interest them in its work and give them a share in the management and direction of its affairs." The congregation must open "its doors widely to welcome all who would join its ranks, and lend their efforts towards advancing its interests." The editors added that "in order to maintain the interest of the members in congregational affairs, their powers must be more than merely nominal."[41] This philosophy was echoed by Henry Berkowitz in an 1889 pamphlet, "How to Organize a Hebrew Sabbath-School." Berkowitz advocated harnessing the energies of one's community through empowerment and inclusion. "Make it your business," Berkowitz instructed, "to personally speak to ALL (be careful to slight no one of the Jewish people, young and old), in your community and elicit their interest in your project. After that bring them all together . . . soliciting the women, as well as the men to express their views."[42]

This advice from Berkowitz became particularly significant in light of the role he played in the effort to expand the ambit of the synagogue. Berkowitz, a member of the first graduating class of Hebrew Union College (HUC) in 1883, led the way in attempting to make the synagogue a center of cultural activity that would draw Jews back to the sanctuary.[43] The movement toward synagogue expansion, pioneered by the first generation of Hebrew Union College graduates, intersected with a striking resurgence of women's participation and involvement in synagogue activities.

In October 1888, shortly after taking a pulpit in Kansas City, Berkowitz introduced an auxiliary society at Congregation B'nai Jehudah to work with the congregation in its "various educational, charitable, and religious purposes."[44] In its November 2, 1888, issue, the *Jewish Exponent* seemed, without specifically mentioning Berkowitz's efforts, to be enthusiastically endorsing his work. The newspaper called for "a remoulding and popularization of the synagogue," so that, from "nothing more than a lecture-hall," it could return to its former status as "the centre of Jewish life."[45]

Much of Berkowitz's campaign to make the synagogue again into a "living, acting, working element in the life of American Jews" was to be staffed by women.[46] The organization that Berkowitz started was open to everyone in the community and drew unashamedly upon the energies of the congregation's women, including them in its governance as second vice president, corresponding secretary, and treasurer, as well as trustees. The assignment to women of these positions of public leadership was unprecedented in any organization connected with an American synagogue, except for those explicitly constituted as ladies' groups. The Kansas City L.A.C.E. Society organized literary meetings, lectures, a temple library, charity work, a Purim entertainment, a picnic for Sunday school children, and floral decorations for the pulpit.[47]

When Berkowitz moved on to Philadelphia in 1892, his Kansas City society faded, but the expansion of the synagogal sphere that he pioneered was carried on, with various combinations of the activities introduced in Kansas City displayed in congregations around the country. Rabbi Joseph Krauskopf, an HUC classmate and brother-in-law of Berkowitz, had himself moved to Philadelphia from Kansas City in 1887. Krauskopf introduced a number of innovations that expanded the congregational work of Keneseth Israel, his new pulpit, starting with a young people's literary society called the Knowledge Seekers.[48] Taking note of his friend's work back at B'nai Jehudah, Krauskopf facilitated the continuing expansion of congregationally sponsored groups at Keneseth Israel, which came to include, among others, a choral society, a postconfirmation class, and a Personal Interest Society. By 1893 the temple's records reported that "fifteen distinct educational, religious and charitable institutions are enumerated that have been created by, or that have emanated from the Congregation."[49] In 1892 Keneseth Israel celebrated the dedication of a new synagogue building, which had become necessary, in part, to accommodate the new congregational activities.[50]

Within five years, the type of programs introduced by Berkowitz had changed the nature of the American synagogue. Congregations documented their own expansion in temple yearbooks, which began to appear in the 1890s. These yearbooks suddenly began to seem necessary to recount the doings of the disparate organizations that now fell under the congregational umbrella. These developments were especially prevalent in congregations guided by recent graduates of the still young Hebrew Union College and were certainly not universal. David Kaufman argues that the development of the Reform temple as a self-consciously constructed "synagogue-center" did not emerge until after 1900.[51]

An extensive description of the congregational activities at New York's Shearith Israel published in the *American Hebrew* in 1897 questioned the popular supposition "that a congregation is simply a means to provide a suitable place of worship . . . and to secure a last resting place." In its consideration "of the activities of a congregation as illustrated by the Spanish and Portuguese community," the newspaper remarked upon a general transformation taking place at acculturated American synagogues, whether they were Reform or Orthodox. The portrayal of this Orthodox congregation as "a center of activity for intellectual, social and philanthropic work" suggests the growing appeal of the synagogue as a sponsor of many different kinds of services. If, as the article presumed, some family might produce a son or grandson to whom "no ritual [could] appeal," would it be "right to cut them off from all share in congregational work? Is it not better and wiser to find even for these some field of activity more congenial?"[52]

In addition to worship services, the article detailed the congregation's offerings of a Sunday school (organized in 1808), an alumni association (organized in 1887), a teachers' association, a burial society, a relief society, ladies' societies, ladies' classes, mission schools, and charity work. While many of these activities stemmed from the early history of the congregation, the most active groups were of recent vintage. Thus, along with a description of the early origins of the congregation's women's groups, the article reported that "last year, the Ladies' Aid, the Kindergarten and the Envelope Society were united and called the Shearith Israel Sisterhood." The activities of this sisterhood paralleled those of New York's other congregations. The observation that the group had "reached a stage which warrants its own building" provides a measure of the new organization's vitality.[53]

The trend toward expansion was more prominent in some places than others, yet it apparently was pervasive enough in 1896 for Emil G. Hirsch to make competition over synagogue expansion a subject of satire. He described the rabbi who suddenly had to worry "lest his neighbor across the way be credited by the congregational advertising agencies with a larger number of wheels successfully driven by the dynamo in the basement of the temple." Hirsch mocked the range of activities emanating from contemporary synagogues: "If one dishes out soup, the other must sell coal and ice; if one has a library, the other must at least run a music festival; if one is a farmer, the other must build in town an Eden; if one has a class in Hottentot, the other must open a rival shop for the distilling of Sanscrit roots."[54] As the vital space of the congregation expanded beyond the physical space of the sanctuary, women found room to define themselves in public roles within the congregation. Before examining these roles, however, one additional factor in the activation of a public identity for Jewish women must be considered.

The Jewish Women's Congress and the National Council of Jewish Women

Along with the sisterhoods, and the new idea of the temple as an expanded center of Jewish life, the third factor critical to the creation of a prominent public identity for Jewish women was the formation of the National Council of Jewish Women (NCJW). The Jewish Women's Congress, part of the World's Parliament of Religion held at Chicago's Columbian Exposition and World's Fair in September 1893, and the National Council of Jewish Women, which emerged out of it, established the ground for American Jewish women to enter the field of communal and philanthropic work.

Calls for a national federation of women's organizations had arisen quite early in the sisterhood movement, emphasizing the importance of a national platform for "broader views and broader aims, and if need be, for concerted action."[55] This desire found expression around the country. Organizers in Buffalo called for a "national organization of Jewish Women" under the name "Daughters of the Star."[56] In Baltimore, activists convened "the first annual convention of the Daughters of Israel" with a view to forming "a general organization of women." At this meeting, it was noted that "the movement has spread to Sumter, S.C." Further, "letters of inquiry as to the general character of the organization and the method of joining, have been received from Chicago, Savannah, New York, Buffalo and Petersburg." "These facts," the *American Hebrew*'s correspondent reported, "prove that the need for such an order has long existed and go to show that our women are not slow to see the advantages of union."[57] Those who anticipated the coalescence of a unified movement looked forward to the time when "annual meetings of the 'Daughters of Israel' might become the occasions for national conventions of the most intellectual of our Jewish women" to join in grappling "with the problem of poverty and pauperism."[58]

As it happened, the impulse toward a truly national convention of Jewish women was not realized until 1893, when the men responsible for the proposed Jewish Congress refused to find a place for women in their plans. According to Hannah Solomon, who organized the Jewish Women's Congress and became president of the NCJW, "although they invited us to assist in arranging their congress . . . the only part of the program they wished us to fill was the chairs."[59] The refusal of the men to make room for even "two twenty-minute papers" by prominent Jewish women, "whose utterances ever find place in journals of the first rank," spurred Solomon and her coworkers to assemble an entire conference of their own.[60]

The impact on the organizational energy of Jewish women was tremendous; women across the country responded to the initial call for a congress with apparent fervor. Four hundred women showed up for a planning session held in Chicago.[61] Meetings were also held in other cities in anticipation of the congress. A new Cincinnati group calling itself the Cincinnati Branch of the Jewish Congress of Women met in May 1893 to hear addresses by both the Reverend Dr. Wise and the president of the organization, Louise Mannheimer, an author of books on Jewish subjects. Similarly, "pursuant to a call from Chicago, an Auxiliary Woman's Association was permanently established" in Vicksburg, Mississippi, which met to appoint two representatives and two alternates to serve as "representatives of the Jewish ladies of Vicksburg."[62]

The enthusiasm of these preconvention meetings was only intensified following the success of the congress and the decision to establish a permanent national organization, even though it was not certain yet what the purpose of the organization would be. One commentator noted that "even the women most prominent in the movement are not able to speak with clearness as to the end which they propose to attain."[63] The early council workers were certainly not immune to criticism, but the energy that their activities generated was suddenly front and center.[64] Even the often cynical Emil G. Hirsch welcomed the council's influence: "In recent years, no movement within Judaism has asserted itself which is freighted with greater possibilities for good than this." Hirsch noted that the NCJW was "one of the very rare and few symptoms making the prognosis of the lethargic state of Judaism other than utterly hopeless."[65]

By gathering to do communal work, the women of the congress and the NCJW explicitly aspired to a standard set by Christian women's benevolent activities. By matching this religious and spiritual ideal, they hoped to establish their own parallel identity and, not incidentally, their own merit. Flora Schwab noted, "The National Council of Jewish Women stands to us in the same relation as the organization of our Christian sisters, who builded well indeed, when they formed organizations extending like a network over the land . . . carrying their lessons even to dark Africa. Our Jewish council," she declared, "is the organization which will represent the modern Jewish woman side by side with her non-Jewish sisters."[66]

New York educator Julia Richman, however, objected to the implication that Jewish women needed to "rise to an equal plane with our non-Jewish sisters," questioning in what way "we do not equal them." Solomon, the NCJW president, also insisted that such comparisons were "entirely out of place."[67] Yet others affirmed that, indeed, Jewish women did need to rise "to a higher level. We are in some respects not on a level with our Christian sisters," observed Laura Jacobson of St. Louis. Christian women had recognized the need "to enter into a broader sphere." The damning result, according to Jacobson, was "that if you go into a Christian church upon a Sabbath morning, their Sabbath morning, you will find many more than you find in attendance in a Jewish synagogue."[68] In a society where spirituality was considered an essential attribute of femininity, Julia Richman's question about why "so few of our own young people" are fitted to teach in religious schools prompted a damning indictment: "Is it because we are less spiritual, than our friends of alien faiths?"[69]

The feeling that Jewish women were legitimating their moral and spiritual claims by coming together with educational and benevolent intent was confirmed by the leaders of non-Jewish women's groups, who reached out to them with sisterly feelings. Ellen M. Henrotin, president of the National Federation of Women's Clubs, told the NCJW assembly in 1896 that "Jew and Gentile no longer exist. We stand hand to hand, heart to heart . . . We ask no longer of any woman, what do you believe, what is your sect, . . . but are you a clubable woman, are you willing to go to work with us. And if she says yes, she is of us."[70] The women of the NCJW relished the feeling that they were being accepted as equals and thrilled at the great interest that organized Christian women seemed to take in their doings.[71] To gain this respect, Jewish women needed to participate openly and actively in the world. Absence from benevolent and reform movements would never redound to their credit. As Flora Schwab noted, "We cannot afford to be considered only well dressed women; we cannot afford to be only housekeepers."[72]

The actual impact of these organizations varied from city to city. From a small western town without a synagogue, it was reported that the women of the local section, twelve in number, had organized a Sabbath school for the Jewish children of the community, had been instrumental in forming a congregation for Sabbath evening services, met on Saturday morning to read a service presided over by the president of the section, gathered for a study circle, and cooperated in works of philanthropy. Larger sections incorporated all of these activities and, in addition, reported study circles led by rabbis and presentations of scholarly papers by women themselves. They also had some success in placing female representatives on congregational Sabbath school boards, in addition to extensive involvement in philanthropic work.[73]

The Impact on Congregational Life

In her 1925 memoir, Rebekah Kohut described her role as the first president of the New York section of the NCJW in a chapter entitled "Emergence of the Jewess," a phrase that referred not only to her personal experience but also to the general impact that the formation of the council had upon many who joined her in its work.[74] The introduction of a formal national organization energized acculturated Jewish women across the country, offering them a structure to facilitate and validate their activism as public "Jewesses." The NCJW gave Jewish women a reason to come together and inspired the reorganization and rethinking of preexisting Jewish women's groups. As the officers of the NCJW asserted, the "indirect influence of the council" had created "an active and increasing interest in our religion," and "a desire to work has been awakened where before was only lethargy. Energies only waiting for a channel into which to throw themselves have been properly directed."[75] In many communities, whatever (often moribund) women's organizations had existed were reenergized, often renaming themselves as sections of the National Council of Jewish Women.[76] When this dynamic combined with the mobilization of women in immigrant charity work and in the expansion of the congregational world, the potential for women's participation in synagogue-related activities finally began to be realized.

Congregational records show the gradual elaboration of new roles for women within the synagogal sphere during the 1890s. In 1887 the president of Tifereth Israel in Cleveland appointed a committee of "8 ladies to secure a new sett of Curtains before the shrine and [to] cover the Pulpit."[77] Adolf Guttmacher, rabbi and historian of the Baltimore Hebrew Congregation, recorded in 1905 that when the congregation dedicated a new synagogue in 1891, the newly formed Ladies' Auxiliary donated curtains for the ark and covers for the reading desk. They also placed pictures in the school rooms, offered entertainments for the students, and furnished the rooms assigned to the minister and choir. Guttmacher observed that "though in former years the ladies of the congregation were not organized, yet they made many gifts to the synagogue." He noted that when the original synagogue was renovated in 1860, women had also donated curtains *(p'ro'hes)* to hang before the ark.[78] Here, as elsewhere, the more organized participation of women in the synagogue began with responsibilities that women had traditionally undertaken on a more informal basis.

An important transitional point came when, instead of gathering ad hoc groups of women to attend to particular needs, congregations began to organize women to undertake these same kinds of responsibilities on a permanent and organized basis. Thus, at Baltimore's Har Sinai an 1894 meeting of the congregation's members and seat holders was called by the president of the congregation to address the "immediate need" of furnishing the new temple with carpets and draperies. In response, a Ladies' Auxiliary was founded, which bought the drapes but then determined to remain in existence "to assist the temple financially and to promote sociability among all connected with the temple."[79]

The Hebrew Benevolent Congregation in Atlanta resolved in 1894 that "3 ladies be appointed each month to see that those whose duty it is to keep the Temple in good condition perform their duty properly."[80] Also in 1894, three women of Cleveland's Tifereth Israel were appointed as a "house committee" to "oversee the cleaning and general arrangement of things at the Temple." Allowing women to exercise their influence over the choice of coverings for the radiator hardly seems a monumental innovation, yet inclusion of the House Committee among the temple's other committees represented the first time that women were officially listed as representatives or officers of the congregation in any capacity. The congregational president hastened to thank the committee members for fulfilling their "arduous duties."[81]

The reorganization of existing women's societies and the formation of new congregational auxiliaries where none had existed resulted in new opportunities for women in many American synagogues during the 1890s. Motivation for all this activity seemed to come from both men's and women's initiatives. After a new graduate of Hebrew Union College arrived at Denver's Temple Emanuel in 1889, the congregation's Sewing Society was reconstituted in 1890 as the Ladies' Auxiliary.[82] The congregation in Bellaire, Ohio, reported in 1896 that their ladies had "established an organization auxiliary to the congregation," which had contributed to "the furnishing of the synagogue."[83] An 1896 report from Syracuse recorded that a Ladies' Auxiliary Society "was organized about a month ago for the purpose of better developing the social and educational side of its congregational life."[84]

The Woman's Temple Association founded at Tifereth Israel in Cleveland in 1897 "aimed to do some of the work of the Congregation for which they as women were especially adapted."[85] Members anticipated "generally to have the women do women's work; interest themselves in the service, Sabbath school and such other activities whereby they will be of material help to the men, women and children of the congregation."[86] With Rabbi Moses Gries as presiding officer, the association quickly undertook the establishment of nine committees, ranging from responsibility (with the men of the Public Worship Committee) for choir auditions to providing the temple with flowers.[87]

In other congregations, the establishment of general congregational auxiliary societies provided interested women with a platform for congregational activism. At Philadelphia's Rodeph Shalom, under the leadership of Henry Berkowitz, the Auxiliary Society (established in

1894) brought women into prominent leadership positions. They served as "chairmen" of the literary and school sections of the auxiliary and as members of committees that oversaw a variety of synagogue activities.[88] Representation on these committees was especially important, as the committees serving parallel functions at the congregational level excluded women entirely. Eventually, involvement in what were constituted as auxiliary groups brought women increased recognition, providing an important, if limited, first forum for women's voices within the congregation. A list of the officers and committees at Rodeph Shalom for 1897–1898 shows women on congregational subcommittees (for the library and floral decorations) and, perhaps more significantly, as members of the committees that oversaw education within the congregation.[89]

A campaign by the National Council of Jewish Women to include women on synagogue school and choir committees included sending letters to congregational boards. In May 1896 the NCJW reported that "the request to put women in the Sabbath School Boards of the congregations has been met by almost universal acquiescence. Women will be appointed for the ensuing year. Several congregations have amended their By-laws to allow this. We regret that several of our leading congregations have seen fit to ignore or refuse our request."[90] In Cleveland the Sabbath School Committee of Tifereth Israel reported, after the appointment of two women to their board, "The co-operation of the ladies with your committee is still in the experimental stage. The necessity for the same is as obvious now as in the past."[91] In Philadelphia, at least, the synagogues that responded to this call ranged from Reform to Orthodox.[92]

This kind of progress was by no means universal. Many congregations stalwartly maintained their all-male mastheads. Bene Israel in Cincinnati did establish a ladies' auxiliary to the school board in 1903 ("there are many things in connection with the school that ladies are particularly apt in doing, such as beautifying the school rooms, the arranging of entertainments for the school and the like"), and in 1906 a three-woman Ladies' Auxiliary Committee was established to "attend to . . . details in the care and supervision of the interior of the Temple and Sabbath school buildings."[93] Yet the temple's male leadership was obviously not prepared to place women on any governing committee. As late as 1906, the board politely informed the secretary of Cincinnati's NCJW section that, in regard to the council's request that the board appoint a woman to the synagogue's choir committee, "the Board of Trustees does not deem it advisable at this time to grant the request."[94] It is striking that neither Bene Israel nor its sister Reform congregation in Cincinnati, B'nai Yeshurun, established any congregational women's associations until 1913. In that year the National Federation of Temple Sisterhoods was founded in Cincinnati at a meeting of the Union of American Hebrew Congregations. Thus, both congregations founded sisterhoods in time to become founding members of the national organization.

The Question and Meaning of Membership

Where women began to make a tangible impact on congregation life, their emerging public identities challenged the existing structural definitions of synagogue life. In Cleveland, for instance, Moses Gries oversaw both a vast expansion of congregational activity and the gradual integration of women leaders into synagogue governance. In 1895 Gries's congregation took what it believed was an unprecedented step, as the congregation's president greeted "for the first time in the history I believe of any Jewish Congregation . . . the Ladies as visitors and Members at an Annual Congregational meeting."[95] This special annual meeting, cum social gathering, was organized by the Public Worship Committee with the aid of the Ladies House Committee.[96] The congregation's president explained that this welcome was only what justice required: "She certainly who takes the most active interest in religious and human affairs should be a part and parcel of the recognized membership."[97] In Cleveland and elsewhere, the issue of synagogue membership for women was suddenly a real and insistent question. To many, membership seemed but a well-deserved reward to women for their faithful service and presence. The injection of women's energies into the communal and religious spheres of acculturated Jewish life during the 1890s placed new demands on the categories of inclusion within the synagogue community. Calls to grant membership to women, voiced more and more forcibly from 1895 on, made it clear that the emergence of new public identities for Jewish women required new ways to acknowledge their changing status.

The question of synagogue membership for women arose as a number of Christian denominations debated whether to allow women to take part in the deliberations of their movements. Despite the respect for female religiosity professed by church leaders and despite the centrality of women's presence in denominational work, late-nineteenth-century fights about the proper place of women in church affairs revealed that church leaders were still willing to use traditional Christian limitations on women's voices in the church to exclude women from denominational leadership.

This tension came to a head at the end of the century when women, who had established powerful public religious institutions and identities in their own right, sought to represent themselves in church deliberations. In 1888 Frances Willard, leader of the Woman's Christian Temperance Union and thus one of the most powerful Methodists in America, was one of five women elected to serve as lay representatives to the General Conference of the Methodist Episcopal Church, which met every four years. When Willard and her colleagues arrived at the General Conference, however, they were refused seats because they were women.[98]

Controversies like these in the Methodist, Episcopal, and Presbyterian churches revolved around Pauline injunctions against woman's voice in teaching religion and questions of religious authority that went back to the disciples of Jesus. Despite the Christian context of the debate, however, this agitation over the recognition of women in leading Protestant denominations helped to sharpen questions about the place of Jewish women in their own congregational communities.[99] Questions about women's position in the synagogue, which many in the Reform community thought they had adequately addressed with the introduction of family pews, mixed choirs, and confirmations, arose again as women's increased involvement in congregational activities raised expectations for congregational validation and recognition.

Some commentators during the period of Reform ascendancy had questioned the continued exclusion of women from the governing bodies of American synagogues. Isaac M. Wise, for instance, had long called, at least rhetorically, for the complete emancipation of women in the synagogue. In 1876 Wise had celebrated Reform's achievement in giving woman "her place in the temple." Yet he cautioned, "We can not stop here, the reform is not complete yet. You must enfranchise woman in your congregations, she must be a member, must have a voice and a vote in your assemblies." Women, he claimed, would bring "heart, soul, piety, and mutual respect" to congregational meetings. "We must have women among the Boards for the sake of the principle, and to rouse in them an interest for congregational affairs," he concluded.[100] "Give to your ladies a more active part in the management of your congregations and congregational affairs," the *American Israelite* urged in 1885. "Ladies should be members of the Board . . . The ladies have more time and more influence, let them do part of the work."[101] A female contributor to the *Jewish South* in the early 1880s also called for women's emancipation within the synagogue: "Let the women speak out in their churches. Let us vote; let us work; let us influence and organize until we see a congress of all the Jewish congregations in America in session."[102]

The editors of the *Jewish Messenger* put the question quite starkly in 1881: "Our progressive leaders may have reformed away the lattice work to the ladies' gallery, and the gallery itself," but they have "committed the more heinous wrong of retaining the lattice-work in the constitution of their synagogues . . . Why has the educated American Jewess no voice in the synagogue?" The editors noted that "other sects, mere striplings compared with ours are utilizing grandly the powers and influence of their women, and accord them a respectful place in their councils. Can we afford to neglect so vital a measure, and expect to continue a healthy, vigorous denomination?"[103]

In 1886 Leopold Wintner, who served as rabbi for a congregation in Brooklyn, broached the topic with his colleagues at a meeting of the Jewish Minister's Association in New York. Wintner recounted the progress that American Jews had made in their treatment of women, but he declared, "We must not stop half way. We must give woman a place in the congregation." Wintner advanced a number of practical arguments: "If the wife had the right to become a member independently of her husband, we would have, from that family at least one person taking active interest in congregational matters."[104]

Although the Jewish Minister's Association approved Wintner's resolution, such calls for the enfranchisement of women generally drew little practical response. Wise's congregation did not take up his plea. The only congregation that acted on this sort of suggestion in the 1880s seems to have been Philadelphia's Mikveh Israel, where women gained access to membership in 1882.[105] Perhaps this isolated innovation was the Orthodox congregation's way of showing that even though they maintained separate seating, they were not deficient in their respect for women. Although Mikveh Israel's policy is interesting in itself, no other congregation followed their lead. The general lack of movement on this issue suggests that the inspiration for the proposed reform was drawn, not from within Jewish communities, but from the model of Christian congregations.

In the 1890s, however, as women's involvement began to redefine the American synagogue, the question of synagogue membership for women was also redefined. Mounting pressure for formal recognition of women's presence and voice in the synagogue became more effective as proponents of female inclusion began to equate religious identity with the ability to participate in synagogue governance. "Nobody in America," Rabbi Max Landsberg of Rochester declared, "would still think of subscribing to the preposterous idea that woman is inferior to man in a religious sense, . . . nobody would think of denying that she is the most powerful factor in the promotion of religious life and sentiment." Calling for "perfect religious equality," Landsberg asserted that "there is no conceivable reason why our women should not have a voice in the management of our congregations, why they should not enjoy all the privileges of active membership."[106]

Others also turned the quest for essentially political recognition into a validation of spiritual equality. "The women of Israel are thirsting for the word of God," Rosa Sonneschein declared, as she reviewed congregational membership lists that carried "altogether more than 20,000 names." Yet "no matter where the list came from, no matter how the name sounded, it was prefaced by the simple *Mr.* Not even the most radical congregation on record put before its members' names *Mr. and Mrs.*" Sonneschein defined "religious liberty" as the granting of "equal rights in the Synagogue" and described the struggle to gain membership and positions on congregational boards as a spiritual quest. "Let them drink directly from the fountain of religion," she declared.[107] Fair access to religious identity had become a function of one's place in the governance of the congregation, rather than in the worship of the congregation. To many, it was clear that only membership conveyed "perfect religious equality."[108]

By the end of the nineteenth century, some Jewish congregations began to make provisions for associate female membership and to appoint women to the committees that governed synagogue religious schools. A full acceptance of women's participation and suffrage in congregational governance, however, did not come until after 1920, when the Nineteenth Amendment to the U.S. Constitution established female suffrage as the way of the land.

Women Rabbis?

At the turn of the century, as at the beginning of the century, synagogue communities were seeking to foster and honor public expressions of female religiosity. Contemporaries were quite aware that behind the question of equal membership and participation in the governance of the congregation lurked the potentially more troubling question of spiritual leadership. Arguments for the ordination of women played an explicit and important part in Christian denominational debates of this period. Among acculturated Jews, the question was generally treated more theoretically and whimsically than seriously.

In their early call for woman's religious enfranchisement, editors of the *Jewish Messenger* had carefully limited their proposals to giving women a voice in congregational management that might extend as far as a seat on the school board: "What do we propose? To train women as rabbis or render the office of Parnass [congregational president] open to ladies? Certainly not."[109] Yet the debate over women's status in the synagogue, constructed as it was as a debate over female religious status, carried within it implicit claims upon access to leadership.

In 1893, Emil G. Hirsch alluded to the title of Frances Willard's popular book calling for the ordination of women in his own article, "Woman in the Pulpit." The increasing salience of Jewish women's organizational success seemed to press the question upon him. In fact, he declared that "the question whether woman should be admitted into the Jewish pulpit admits of no negative solution." His outlook was shaped not only by the recent success of the Jewish Women's Congress but also by the example of Ray Frank, a Jewish woman who (amid much notoriety) had made a small preaching career for herself and was seen by many as a woman rabbi.[110]

Yet Hirsch's endorsement was tempered by his usual cynicism. Having declared that women should have access to the rabbinate, as to any other position for which they might be qualified, he entered upon a long disquisition on what it took to prepare for this position. To excerpt just a few of the qualifications enumerated by Hirsch, a rabbi had to be a Jewish theologian, as well as "a man (or woman) of general culture." The rabbi's expertise must include general philosophy, the classics, psychology, history, ethics, study of the family and the state, and then, in addition, "a comprehensive knowledge of the literature and history of Judaism."[111] It was self-evident that no woman in the United States in the 1890s would have had access to the kind of education Hirsch was describing, and there was little prospect of such access in the near future. In fact, Hirsch may have believed that nobody enjoyed the kind of broad knowledge required for the job, except, perhaps, Emil G. Hirsch, himself.

Nevertheless, Jewish women in the 1890s did begin to approach the *bimah*. In 1886, when the Reverend Dr. Guttman was absent from his pulpit in Syracuse, Miss Ida E. Goldman had filled in by reading an essay on the Talmud "from his pulpit."[112] In Hirsch's own congregation, Hannah Solomon took the pulpit to deliver a sermon during one of the rabbi's absences. The spread of confirmation services also gave young women a taste of religious leadership and public expression.

One case (presumably rare) of an adult confirmation service illustrated the potentially radical implications of the religious opportunities offered to female confirmands. In 1896 Mrs. Ida Zenobia Frazer, after a three-year course of study, was confirmed in a synagogue in Richmond, Virginia. The *American Hebrew* described a "simple, yet impressive," ceremony: "After the scroll of the law had been read . . . the lady entered from the centre aisle and was met at the foot of the steps of the altar by the Rabbi." The newspaper's account may have been hinting that what was termed a "confirmation" was in fact a conversion: "The candidate advanced to the pulpit, where the Rabbi . . . questioned her as to the principles of Judaism, . . . and the promise to abide by their teachings." Even if this testimony did represent a conversion rather than a confirmation, the public and declamatory role that Frazer took in the ceremony was quite striking: "The ten commandments were read in original Hebrew by the candidate . . . After the hymn [which she wrote] was sung, she advanced to the pulpit and read her confirmation sermon, entitled, 'The song of a soul.'"[113] Young girls often offered prayers and Hebrew recitals in confirmation services, but when these acts were reproduced by an adult woman, they must have appeared as a challenge to the otherwise rigid assignment of public religious roles to men.[114] Ida Frazer's extraordinary confirmation, akin to a present-day adult bat mitzvah, afforded this one woman unusual access to the religious space and leadership of the American synagogue. Clearly she would not have had this opportunity if the definitions of religious space and leadership were not themselves being challenged and redefined.

As women responded to new opportunities to make themselves an active force in American Judaism, they helped to change the shape of the synagogue and shifted the terms of the debate. In 1889 Mary M. Cohen, in a story entitled "A Problem for Purim," described a Purim conversation in which one character timidly confronts a group of young peers: "'I would like to make a suggestion,' said Dora Ulman . . . but it will shock you all considerably." After some encouragement from the group, Dora "blushed a little, than made a desperate plunge into her subject. 'Could not—our *women*—be—ministers?' All but Lionel were struck dumb."[115] Cohen presented Dora's position with great seriousness and armed her female characters with powerful retorts to the doubts raised by the men in the ensuing fictional debate. Still, it should be remembered, Purim is the one day in the Jewish year when many of the stringent requirements of Jewish law are suspended. On Purim, for instance, men are permitted to dress as women, and women as men. Cohen's decision to place this discussion in the context of this holiday indicates her awareness that Dora's diffident suggestion, for all its merit, was hardly likely to be taken seriously. The author understood that for the time being, the radical idea of women becoming rabbis would have to remain "a problem for Purim," a subject for hypothetical speculation and the imagination.

By the late 1890s, the presence of women had again transformed the American synagogue. After decades of quiescence, American Jewish women succeeded in claiming a dynamic and influential religious identity of their own. As Max Landsberg observed, "Well is the fact appreciated, that the flourishing condition of our Jewish congregations in America . . . could not exist without the noble and active cooperation of our women. Their work in the department of active and especially organized charity is . . . zealous . . . [W]omen render the most valuable services as teachers . . . and it is well known that they furnish the largest contingent in the attendance at religious services."[116]

As women took advantage of the opportunities available to make themselves into an active force in American Judaism, they helped to shift the terms of the debate. In 1897 when Hirsch asked a number of prominent women to take part in his symposium "Woman in the Synagogue," it was revealing that the question he posed did not actually revolve around current issues faced by congregations as they incorporated women's work and presence into their spiritual and institutional structures. Instead, he repeated the question suggested by Mary M. Cohen in 1889: "Should she occupy the pulpit?"[117] Many of his respondents said no, some said yes; no one seemed to consider it a terribly realistic question. Yet they were prepared to answer it seriously. This time, no one was struck dumb. Through their presence and their activism, Jewish women at the end of the nineteenth century had succeeded in redefining what it could mean to be a Jewish woman.

Epilogue:
Twentieth-Century Resonances

I have a framed photograph in my dining room that used to rest on my grandmother's polished baby grand piano. In this photo, probably taken in the early 1950s, my grandmother sits in the front row of a small group of middle-aged women. The row of women standing behind beam with a restrained but palpable sense of the momentousness of the occasion. Expressions of pride, pleasure, and confidence mark their faces. A few seem a bit stunned. Those seated in the front row alongside the guest of honor, meanwhile, seem to be nearly bursting with pride and excitement. It may be the quality of the print that makes many of their dresses appear so shiny, but they all effect a restrained elegance clearly meant to honor the occasion. At the center of the picture, looking charmed by the enthusiasm of those surrounding her, sits Eleanor Roosevelt. She seems to understand their desire to be as close to her as they can. Her demeanor is comfortable and gracious, despite the way my grandmother is leaning into her left arm.

I have often marveled at the image of these women, most of them presumably, like my grandmother, born in different lands, raised in immigrant families, and shaped by Jewish Orthodoxy, coming to find themselves as members and leaders of the New Haven chapter of Hadassah, gathered around the patrician former first lady of the United States. Somehow my grandmother, along with the others in the photograph, attained enough of a public identity *as a Jewish woman* to find herself, with all the pride that the American dream could inspire, with the opportunity to push her generous upper arm firmly into Mrs. Roosevelt's side.

To me this photograph speaks volumes about the potential power of public identities created through access to organizational life. For my grandmother, a lifelong commitment to Zionism and participation in Zionist organizations brought her, if only for a photographic moment, to the first lady's side. On another occasion she personally witnessed the United Nations' approval of the creation of the State of Israel. My grandmother and her compatriots in the photograph were hardly among American Zionism's prominent leaders. Yet association with this cause gave them a firm identity within their community and access to public identities and concerns well beyond the limits of New Haven.

The personal and public experiences of my grandmother, who lived through most of the twentieth century, bear no direct connection to the communities and issues at the core of this study. As a child caught up in the great wave of eastern European immigration that overwhelmed America's small native-born Jewish population at the end of the nineteenth century, she had little contact with those acculturated Jews who had arrived in an earlier era. The American Orthodoxy of her parents evolved in a context far removed from the assimilation experiences of earlier immigrants. But the nineteenth-century struggle to elaborate meaningful public identities for American Jewish women, which I have documented in this study, bore fruit in my grandmother's ability to shape much of her life around her commitment to the Jewish people and homeland.[1] Just as assuredly, nineteenth-century tensions over proper roles for American Jewish women continue to play out in my own current occupation as a teacher of rabbis (both male and female).

My grandmother and I have formulated our Jewish identities on the basis of disparate personal circumstances and radically transformed social contexts. Although our specific interests and opportunities differ, my own commitment to Jewish life grows out of the strength and surety of my grandmother's convictions. She and I, and the many other twentieth-century American Jewish women who have invested some part of their personal and public identities in the Jewish community, have continued a process of reconciling the changing and sometimes divergent expectations for women's lives presented by Jewish and American cultures.[2]

Eastern European Jewish immigrants to the United States, the progenitors of most of today's American Jewish population, experienced their own particular demographic, residential, organizational, and social realities. Yet the much smaller mid-nineteenth-century Jewish population offered turn-of-the-century newcomers the most influential models of what constituted American Judaism and Jewish life. Twentieth-century Jewish women have thus encountered a terrain contoured not only by the circumstances of our own historical moments but also by the work of the women who came before us and, particularly, by those women who chose to situate part of their religious identities in the synagogues of eighteenth- and nineteenth-century America. Although most of us share no direct familial relation with these women, we have certainly inherited their legacy.

Nineteenth-Century Precedents

As this study has shown, every major transformation of the American synagogue through the end of the nineteenth century was integrally associated with major redefinitions of the place that women were to take within and beyond its walls. The results of these transformations defined the American synagogue and American Jewish public life. From the beginning, the middle-class American emphasis on church piety as an essential aspect of women's lives made the synagogue into a central arena for the contest between Jewish and American models of appropriately gendered religiosity. Nudged by often irreverent young women looking for good seats in synagogue galleries, male synagogue proprietors began to adjust the space assigned to women. The earliest American synagogues distinguished themselves from their European antecedents and contemporaries by opening up the women's gallery, breaking down the barrier that had concretized the ritual marginalization of women in public Jewish worship.

The emergence of women as a dominant, if passive, presence in public worship and the growing desire of congregational leaders to position their costly synagogues as monuments to their own prosperity and refinement demanded a further restructuring of the physical space of Jewish worship. The resulting introduction of family pews in the synagogues of America's acculturating Jews shortly after midcentury signaled a reform effort that situated institutional constructions of Judaism squarely within the realm of public worship. The opulent synagogues that appeared in America's urban centers in the years after the Civil War were home to a self-conscious and focused effort to create a public Judaism that would satisfy the needs of an acculturated American Jewish population. These temples, governed by male rabbis and male congregational officers and focused intently upon public worship, left little room for women to find active public identities as Jewish women.

Toward the end of the nineteenth century, however, American rabbinical and lay leaders began to see that their great success in creating decorous and refined worship settings left them with synagogue communities that felt dry and lifeless. The reinvigoration of women's individual and organizational contributions to synagogue life during the 1890s fueled efforts to redress this situation. Women again played a central role in transforming synagogue structure and emphasis. Women's energies and skills, channeled into the work of congregationally affiliated groups, allowed synagogues to expand beyond the sanctuary into a broadened expression of Jewish religious and institutional life.

By the end of this period, American Jewish women had established a powerful female presence in the synagogue sanctuary and a powerful organizational presence in the many expanding areas of communal Jewish life. Their achievement defined the opportunities for public Jewish identity and activity that would be available to the coming generations of twentieth-century American Jewish women.

Lessons for New Immigrants

As eastern European Jews created their own versions of American Judaism, they, like earlier immigrants, looked both to traditional structures and to available models of American religion and Judaism. Men determined the initial patterns of organized immigrant Judaism in America's larger cities. They responded to the strangeness of the New World by establishing settings for familiar religious and social interaction with their own *landslayt,* those who emigrated from the same locale or region. They created myriad improvised *landsmanshaft* shuls, which often provided no space or structures to accommodate women. As immigrants grew more prosperous and better organized, they banded together across narrow lines of regional origin to create better-endowed assemblies, constructing new buildings or acquiring old churches or synagogues for their congregations.

These first large immigrant synagogues excluded the strange, formalized style of worship that newer immigrants perceived in the temples of their more Americanized brethren.[3] They preserved the traditional liturgy, some of the traditional informality of the *landsmanshaft* shul, and the women's gallery. Yet even in the earliest of these larger, more elaborate synagogues, it is easy to see expectations calibrated to the American setting beginning to inflect Old World models of Judaism. Despite their traditionalism, these new settings for religious Jewish community in many ways emulated established models of what it meant to be Jewish in the United States. Exterior architecture often imitated or incorporated designs from synagogues whose communities embraced ritual reform.[4] Intense rivalry to import the most celebrated cantorial voices from Europe, referred to as the "hazan craze" by later historians, helped to introduce some of the formality and elegance that organs and choirs brought to less Orthodox settings.[5]

Finally, the women's galleries in these synagogues, although observant of the gender separation mandated by Jewish tradition, generally reflected the expectation that in the United States, religion, even regular public worship, was also women's business. Jumping from storefront shuls (referred to as *shtibls*) that included no women's space, these more elaborate edifices often included outsized gallery areas endowed with clear views of the services. The establishment of youth congregations, intended to draw Americanizing young people into the organized Orthodox community, had to appeal to both women and men to offer a sufficiently attractive mode of American religious life. As a result, the earliest models of a distinctively American style of Orthodoxy among eastern European immigrants responded to the religious and social needs of both men and women, even while retaining the traditional convention of separate seating.[6]

The expansion of what Jenna Weissman Joselit has termed a "determinedly modern Orthodoxy" among New York Jews in the interwar years featured a commitment to traditional liturgy and observance, along with an emphasis on aesthetics, decorum, and Americanization.[7] Not surprisingly, these communities learned that one central way to demonstrate that their Orthodoxy was neither backward nor un-American was to "cultivat[e] the synagogue attendance habit" among women. Spacious women's galleries or women's sections placed on the same floor with the men but separated by a partition *(mechitzah)*, like the open balconies of America's early synagogues, conveyed the message that in the United States female worshipers were considered a part of the congregation. The normative regular presence of women in the "bigger and better" synagogues of New York's prosperous Jewish community offered a sure sign that these communities should not be associated with the narrow-minded traditionalism of the ghetto.[8]

The density and increasing affluence of New York's Jewish population provided a reassuring environment for those acculturating Jews who hoped to maintain distinctively Orthodox modes of worship and observance.[9] Many more Jews, both inside and outside of New York, sought more mediated versions of religious expression. The American Judaism preached by graduates of New York's Jewish Theological Seminary, the core of an emerging Conservative movement during the interwar years, promised the advantages of Americanization while maintaining the substance of tradition. Founders of many proto-Conservative congregations hoped to create traditional settings in which acculturating immigrants and their children could feel Jewish and American at the same time. Their grand sanctuaries seemed ill suited to traditional versions of gender separation.[10] Some communities compromised among the varying degrees of attachment to tradition held by their members by maintaining separate sections for men and women on opposite sides of the sanctuary, while allowing those who wished to sit together to occupy the center section.[11] Many communities actually continued to profess allegiance to Orthodox Judaism while adopting mixed seating in their synagogues. By the 1950s, however, the presence of family seating became a firm dividing line between progressive and traditional Judaism.[12] For many, the seating of men and women together in worship services came to seem less a transgression of Jewish law than a requirement of American religion.

Twentieth-Century Women's Organizations

The great wave of eastern European Jewish immigrants thus relatively quickly adopted the norm of female synagogue presence, a pattern pioneered in the nation's earliest Jewish religious communities that still made sense in the religious and social environment of the early twentieth century. Prevailing models of synagogue community and Jewish life were not lost upon newer Jewish immigrants as they went about establishing their own versions of American Jewish life. They soon learned that the contributions of women's organizations were a vital part of American Jewish community. In this they benefited from the previous century of negotiation over the public identities of Jewish women. The expansion of public activities for acculturated women in the 1890s created a platform for the work of their immigrant successors and counterparts.

The activist sisterhoods created by women in the acculturated congregations of the late nineteenth century transcended denominational lines from the start and soon spread to the communities of more recent immigrants. The organized participation of women's groups often became a marker of modernity for Jewish communities and congregations, and women's synagogue work came to touch every expression of American Judaism. As Joselit has noted of synagogue sisterhoods during the interwar years, "no modern American synagogue—Reform, Conservative, or Orthodox—was without one."[13]

As the twentieth century dawned, acculturated women continued to negotiate and refine their public roles. The immigrant aid work that propelled New York's Sisterhoods of Personal Service into existence in the late 1880s gradually disappeared from sisterhood efforts, but the pattern of increasing engagement in congregational life continued to advance. In 1913, 156 representatives from the women's organizations of fifty-two congregations met in Cincinnati in conjunction with the convention of the Union of American Hebrew Congregations (UAHC) "for the purpose of organizing a Federation of Temple Sisterhoods."[14] The leaders behind the creation of the National Federation of Temple Sisterhoods (NFTS) were Rabbi George Zepin, an executive of the UAHC, and Carrie Simon, the wife of a Washington, D.C., rabbi. Simon served as the organization's founding president, and Zepin as its executive secretary.

The creation of a national federation prompted many Reform congregations without women's membership organizations to found synagogue sisterhoods of their own. In Cincinnati, once the call for the national convention had gone out, the city's two leading Reform synagogues quickly created sisterhood organizations so that their congregations might become founding members of the new federation. The new local organizations, tapping long-dormant energies awaiting an outlet, quickly went to work on matters both prosaic and spiritual. Within months of its founding, B'nai Yeshurun's sisterhood introduced "paper roller towels and waste baskets" at the congregation's religious schools, as well as a regular children's service, and attempted to create a social center for congregational youth. Invited for the first time to the congregation's annual meeting in 1913, women of the congregation heard the congregation's president acknowledge the sisterhood and his belief that "no single instrumentality of the Temple has ever been instituted which promises more for the expansion of its aims."[15]

In communities where synagogue women's groups already existed, identification with a national movement brought added impetus and stature to the work of local organizations. At both Philadelphia's Rodeph Shalom and Cleveland's Tifereth Israel, for instance, existing women's societies were reformulated in 1913. Within weeks of their return from the Cincinnati organizing convention, the Cleveland women who had been sent as representatives (wives of the male UAHC delegates) called a meeting for the "reorganization of women's work of the Temple." Within three weeks of the reorganization of the Woman's Auxiliary into the Temple Women's Association, 528 members had been enrolled, the women had organized the congregation's communal Passover seder, and an extensive committee structure had been put into place. A year later, the association reported 760 members and twenty-six working committees.[16] At Rodeph Shalom, the old Women's Auxiliary Committee, the main function of which had been "the conduct of our joyous Succoth Festival" responded to the call from the NFTS "to expand its scope of activities" and created the Rodeph Shalom Sisterhood, along with fifteen working committees. At the congregation's next annual meeting, Rabbi Henry Berkowitz pointed to the organization of the sisterhood as "the most notable event of the year" and observed as one result that for the first time ("after many years of pleading"), "we see the women here with the men, in full force attending the Annual Meeting."[17]

Not surprisingly, Conservative and Orthodox Jewish women soon adopted the model pioneered by the Reform movement for the national coordination of local sisterhoods. The National Women's League of the United Synagogue was founded in 1918 under the leadership of Mathilde Schechter, widow of Solomon Schechter, the former president of the Jewish Theological Seminary. A Women's Branch of the Union of Orthodox Jewish Congregations of America was established in 1926.[18]

In their many different communities, synagogue-oriented sisterhoods served common purposes. Sisterhood women worked to foster sociability and religious engagement within their congregations. They provided entertainments for religious school children and food for congregational events. They sought out new members among the parents of Sunday school students and encouraged existing members to attend worship services. They selected synagogue decor and raised funds to provide congregational furnishings. During World War I, sisterhoods provided an organizational framework for Jewish women's contributions to the war effort, thus identifying their work with the Jewish community.[19] Eventually, sisterhood women took on responsibility for synagogue kitchens, libraries, and gift shops.

They also arranged classes for themselves on Jewish subjects and sought to educate their members on how to be good Jewish women. All of the denominational organizations instructed members on the conduct of Jewish home rituals, with the Conservative and Orthodox organizations focused especially on providing resources to guide their members in maintaining traditional Jewish homes.[20] In Reform congregations, sisterhoods organized community seders and summer services. At annual Sisterhood Sabbaths, women took public pulpit roles, delivering sermons and often conducting the services themselves.[21] On a national level, sisterhood women took a leading role in supporting the work of the rabbinical schools of their movements. Both Reform's NFTS and the Conservative movement's Women's League raised funds for scholarships and the construction of dormitories for their respective rabbinical schools. In short, synagogue sisterhoods did much to define the life of their communities.

Outside of the synagogue, an activist, practical model of women's public work continued to animate the work of the National Council of Jewish Women and sparked the emergence of Hadassah, the Women's Zionist Organization of America, which was founded in 1912. Faith Rogow has pointed out that in every locale, NCJW members sought to address needs not being met by other agencies. Early efforts ranged broadly over areas of self-education, immigrant aid, and religious organization. As other women's groups emerged in the wave of Jewish women's activism pioneered at a national level by the NCJW, council women had to adjust their efforts to changing needs. Much of the NCJW's national efforts focused on immigrant aid work in New York, particularly at Ellis Island, where NCJW representatives received and looked after young Jewish women arriving alone. The systematic nature of the NCJW's Ellis Island and immigrant work helped the council to avoid being displaced, as New York's Sisterhoods of Personal Service had been, from the increasingly professionalized world of immigrant aid. Elsewhere, local NCJW sections maintained religious schools for children of immigrants and settlement houses to foster the cultural adjustment of immigrant youth.[22] In response to the great suffering and displacement of Jewish civilians during World War I, the NCJW developed an international agenda, sending Rebekah Kohut as head of a Reconstruction Committee to assist in rebuilding devastated communities and to assist those refugees seeking immigration into the United States. The NCJW's international efforts inspired women in many European cities to create council organizations of their own. In 1923, two hundred women from nineteen countries met in Vienna at the World Congress of Jewish Women, where Rebekah Kohut was elected president.[23]

Hadassah was founded as a national organization at the same time as the National Federation of Temple Sisterhoods and arose out of a similar social context. Henrietta Szold, an accomplished Jewish scholar and the daughter of a prominent rabbi in Baltimore, provided the vision and energy that led to the organization's creation. Szold's coworkers in Hadassah's creation were drawn from a women's Zionist study group that met at New York's Temple Emanu-El, and they included a diverse assortment of committed Jewish women from New York's prominent and acculturated Jewish community. The new group modeled its structure on that of the NCJW and by 1917 reported 2,710 members in thirty-three local chapters. Organized around the financial support of health initiatives in Palestine, Hadassah chose a more practical focus than the ideological Zionism advanced by male groups. Membership reached 38,000 in 1935, 142,000 in 1945, and 275,000 in 1952. Hadassah became the most successful Jewish organization in the United States, enrolling more women and raising more funds than any other American women's organization.[24] Although founded in large part by some of the same assimilated and privileged women who defined the new world of Jewish women's activism in the late nineteenth century, Hadassah's most active supporters emerged from the ranks of eastern European immigrants and their daughters. Offered a model of engagement and a national structure to encourage and support their Zionist proclivities, they did not have to wait decades to find a meaningful and effective way to express their public affinities as Jewish women.

Rising Expectations

Despite their pervasiveness and impact through much of the twentieth century, women's contributions to their congregations and community have often been a target for disparagement. Phrases like "sisterhood ladies" and "Hadassah arms" capture the frequently dismissive portrayals of Jewish women's public work as essentially trivial, staffed by middle-class women with bourgeois concerns. Indeed, historians have pointed to the many ways in which women were consistently displaced from substantive work in their communities. Male leaders often offered women flowery praise even as they worked to limit their participation and impact. Hadassah women in the 1920s struggled with the attempts of male Zionist leaders to subordinate their organization to a male-led hierarchy that sought control of their programs and their funds.[25] On countless occasions, women's organizations were asked to contribute their energies and resources to local charitable Jewish federations, only to be shut out of the newly formed leadership structures.[26] The creation of a world of professionalized social work displaced sisterhood women from engagement with the immigrant community. As Felicia Herman describes it, women found themselves removed from active engagement in shaping the lives of the broader Jewish community and "asked to perform only women's accepted household duties within the limited sphere of the synagogue." Rabbis and male leaders were pleased to have women take on the useful, but seemingly less-than-momentous task of making a synagogue a "home."[27]

Yet despite the limitations imposed by American culture and Jewish tradition, Jewish women did find public roles that made a difference both to themselves and to their communities.[28] Even within the limited, domesticated roles allowed to them, the presence, energy, and contributions of women to the American Jewish community continually challenged the settled and emerging patterns of twentieth-century

American Judaism. The sustained efforts of Jewish women, both nationally and locally, led many to expect greater recognition of women as full participants in the work of the community. With the passage of the Women's Suffrage Amendment to the U.S. Constitution in 1920, most Reform congregations finally moved to assign formal and full membership rights to women who were not widows or unmarried. This advance, in turn, led to regular female representation on congregational boards, as many sisterhood leaders in the early 1920s were invited to serve as trustees.[29] Through the sisterhood, then, women gained a voice both in local synagogue governance and in the national concerns addressed by NFTS.

The growth of a cadre of local and national sisterhood leaders, together with the logic implicit in the Women's Suffrage Amendment and in progressive Judaism, confronted Reform leaders especially with the question of female religious leadership. Discussions about the possibility of women rabbis had emerged in the 1890s, but when the same questions arose in the 1920s, their challenge was no longer largely theoretical. In 1920 Martha Neumark, a student enrolled in classes at Hebrew Union College (HUC) and the daughter of an HUC professor, asked to be assigned a High Holiday synagogue pulpit like her male classmates. Facing the very real possibility that Neumark might continue her studies and become a candidate for ordination, HUC's Board of Governors and faculty and the Reform movement's federation of rabbis, the Central Conference of American Rabbis (CCAR), all took up the question of whether to approve, in principle, the ordination of women rabbis. Some more traditional members of the HUC faculty expressed misgivings about whether the Reform movement, in ordaining women, would irreparably sunder itself from the other movements in Judaism. Nonetheless, the faculty unanimously agreed that this innovation was consistent with the inclusive and progressive tenets of the Reform movement and was equivalent to other major breaks with tradition accepted by the movement. Consideration of the issue at the 1922 CCAR convention was especially noteworthy for the delegates' decision to invite female members of the audience, mainly wives of the rabbis in attendance, to take part in the discussion. Although the faculty and the CCAR both voted to support the proposed change, HUC's Board of Governors, which had to make the final decision, ultimately rejected the proposal.[30]

Pamela S. Nadell has chronicled the unsuccessful efforts of a num-

ber of women who pursued rabbinical training and ordination at Hebrew Union College and Stephen S. Wise's Jewish Institute of Religion
in the 1920s and 1930s, and their continuing challenge to the barriers
that kept women out of the rabbinate.[31] For the most part, however,
the question of whether women should serve as rabbis lay dormant
during these decades, as the energy and creativity of women within
the movement provided their communities with a rich congregational
life. During World War II, as had been the case during World War
I, many women looked to the sisterhood to organize their contributions to the war effort. They entertained soldiers, knitted, crocheted,
baked cookies, organized blood banks, sold bonds, conducted first
aid classes, and resettled Jewish refugees, all under the auspices of
their congregational sisterhoods. Continued postwar growth in synagogue activity reflected a nationwide turn to religion that enlivened
both churches and synagogues through the 1950s. Sisterhoods were
critical to the flourishing of synagogue organizational life in the postwar era, sustaining community in older congregations and creating
new frameworks as old and new congregations found their way to the
suburbs.

The decade of the 1950s is popularly considered an era of limited
professional horizons for women, but the proportion of women
working outside the home, whether working-class or middle-class,
married or unmarried, increased throughout the decade.[32] Women
participated in a wide spectrum of voluntary organizations, and the
broadening of educational opportunities and a growing appreciation
of the public achievements of women made it more difficult to justify
blanket exclusions of women from any field. When the Reform congregation in Meridian, Mississippi, appointed Paula Ackerman, the
widow of their deceased rabbi, to serve as the community's interim
spiritual leader from 1951 to 1953, concerns among Reform leaders
about her lack of proper preparation and ordination were expressed
only privately.[33] In 1956 Rabbi Barnett Brickner, president of the Central Conference of American Rabbis, asked that body to declare a
commitment to the principle of female ordination. Although his proposal received general approval, the question was "laid on the table"
until those with opposing views could present their case—or, as it
turned out, indefinitely. One sign of discomfort with the tradition of
distinctive rituals to mark the religious obligations and duties of boys
and girls, or of men and women, was the growing popularity of the

bat mitzvah for girls, which emerged first in the Conservative movement and later gained popularity in the Reform movement, to complement the boy's bar mitzvah.

In the years following the publication of Betty Friedan's 1963 book *The Feminine Mystique,* the rhetoric of gender egalitarianism and equal opportunity became more familiar in the broader culture. Women of the National Federation of Temple Sisterhoods responded to these shifting cultural currents in their 1963 request that the governing (male) bodies of Reform Judaism again take up the question of women's ordination.

Ultimately, the issue was resolved without grand statements from the movement's institutional bodies. As Sally Priesand advanced through the course of study at the Hebrew Union College–Jewish Institute of Religion (HUC-JIR) in Cincinnati, the question was no longer one of abstract commitments but of practical realities. HUC-JIR president Nelson Glueck made clear that he would ordain a female candidate when the opportunity arose. Following Glueck's death in 1971, the responsibility fell to Glueck's successor, Alfred Gottschalk, who ordained Priesand as America's first female rabbi in 1972. The Reform movement's accomplishment was soon followed by the Reconstructionist Rabbinical College, which ordained its first female rabbi in 1973. The Conservative movement did not ordain a woman as rabbi until 1985.

Finding a Place in American Judaism

The nineteenth-century dynamic in which women's steady presence within the American synagogue ultimately helped to transform the communities of which they were a part was thus replicated in the twentieth century. For many years women in synagogue sisterhoods sustained much of the communal, social, and practical aspects of American Jewish congregational life. These decades of service established the legitimacy of the call for recognition of women's participation within their religious communities. The record of women's essential contributions to liberal American synagogues made it difficult to argue that women's rights in this sphere should be any less than those of men. In addition, as Pamela Nadell has shown, the publicity that gathered around Sally Priesand's aspiration to become a rabbi, reflecting social expectations for women's roles in Judaism, created widespread interest in and support for her quest.[34] Given women's accumulating contributions to public Jewish life and given the social ferment surrounding gender roles in the late 1960s, male leaders could no longer deny women access to the most prominent and symbolic role of Jewish religious leadership. The demand implicit in women's presence once again gathered enough momentum and weight to redraw the deeply inscribed boundaries of Jewish life. Like earlier innovations that redefined women's religious identity, the ordination of the first American woman rabbi in 1972 profoundly restructured the encounter of modern Jews with the traditions of Judaism, just as it signaled a major redefinition of synagogue leadership and life.

Sally Priesand's ordination seemed to remove the last symbolic remnant of the screens that once separated Jewish women in their galleries from the public religious life of their communities. Indeed, given the distance that has been traveled in regard to women's rights in American society, it might seem that the gender questions that troubled and shaped nineteenth-century American Judaism would by now have been laid to rest. After all, the Reform, Conservative, and Reconstructionist branches of Judaism all affirm the right and ability of women to serve as religious leaders. Among Jews of all denominations, women have gained access to the serious study of sacred texts. Women frequently take leading roles in congregational governance as well. Although the leadership of institutional Judaism in the United States remains overwhelmingly male, women in principle have access to positions of authority in all non-Orthodox institutions and worship settings. National and local Jewish women's organizations continue to encourage female leadership and activism.

Yet, as the nineteenth-century example of Kaufmann Kohler makes clear, a rhetorical commitment to gender equality does not guarantee realization of the fruits of equality. The attempt to delineate a meaningful public religious role for women still represents a confrontation, not just with traditional female roles, but also with the continuing pull and demands of Jewish tradition. For Kohler, the predominance of women in synagogue attendance was a visible reminder both of the American institution's distance from the traditional synagogue and of the threatening marginalization of Judaism in American life. The striking presence of women in public Jewish worship was a reminder of both the costs and the benefits of adapting a traditional culture to a modern society. Today, the desire by many for authentic Jewish worship and ritual experiences, together with heightened expectations for the full inclusion of women, exacerbates the difficulty of reconciling contemporary values with traditional Judaism. Many Jewish women continue to struggle with the implications of a deeply patriarchal religion and liturgy. They yearn to create a Judaism that will honor the past but no longer alienate their spirits or stifle their voices. Meanwhile, gay men and lesbians have taken up the demand for inclusion in Jewish community, consciousness, and ritual.[35] The leaders of American synagogues and American Judaism still confront issues of gender as they try to strike a balance between the Jewish past and present.

Beyond the controversies engendered by many of these questions, it is clear that the challenges and energy of those who push for change will shape the future course of the American synagogue and the Jewish community. Feminist critiques of worship and theology are generating some of the most creative and serious expressions of liturgical and communal innovation in contemporary Judaism.[36] As American Jews continue the struggle to fit the demands of a traditional religion and way of life into the competing framework of modern culture, it seems clear that the dilemmas of the nineteenth century will continue to resonate in twenty-first century Judaism.

Notes

In citing works in the notes, the following abbreviations have been used:

AJA   American Jewish Archives, Cincinnati, Ohio
LBIY   Leo Baeck Institute Yearbook
PAJHS Publications of the American Jewish Historical Society

Introduction: Women and the Synagogue

1. "The Antiquated Form of Synagogue Worship," *Asmonean* 11, no. 18 (February 16, 1855): 141.
2. "A Friend's Voice," *Israelite* 1, no. 6 (November 18, 1854): 46.
3. Henry Berkowitz, "Modern Esthers" (Rodeph Shalom Pulpit Message, March 15, 1919). Testimony to this pattern in acculturated synagogues can be found throughout the nineteenth century. An 1887 observer noted that "outside of the orthodox congregations, there are hardly a dozen young men who regularly attend divine services on the Sabbath . . . At a prominent Synagogue last Saturday, though the attendance was fair, there was not present a half dozen males above the age of 16!" "Our Baltimore Letter," *Jewish Exponent,* June 17, 1887, p. 9.
4. Ann Braude, "Women's History *Is* American Religious History," in Thomas A. Tweed, ed., *Retelling U.S. Religious History* (Berkeley: University of California Press, 1997). See also Ann Douglas, *The Feminization of American Culture* (New York: Anchor Press Doubleday, 1977), pp. 97–103; Barbara Welter, *Dimity Convictions: The American Woman in the Nineteenth Century* (Athens: Ohio University Press, 1976), pp. 84–86; Richard Shiels, "The Feminization of American Congregationalism, 1730–1835," *American Quarterly* 33 (Spring 1981): 48; and Terry D. Bilhartz, "Sex and

the Second Great Awakening: The Feminization of American Religion Reconsidered," in Philip R. Vandermeer and Robert P. Swierenga, eds., *Belief and Behavior: Essays in the New Religious History* (New Brunswick, N.J.: Rutgers University Press, 1991), pp. 117–127.

5. Colleen McDannell, *The Christian Home in Victorian America, 1840–1900* (Bloomington: Indiana University Press, 1986).

6. Paula Hyman, "The Other Half: Women in the Jewish Tradition," in Elizabeth Koltun, ed., *The Jewish Woman: New Perspectives* (New York: Schocken Books, 1976), p. 107.

7. Emily Taitz, "Women's Voices, Women's Prayers: The European Synagogues of the Middle Ages," in Susan Grossman and Rivka Haut, eds., *Daughters of the King: Women and the Synagogue* (Philadelphia: Jewish Publication Society, 1992), p. 66; Jenna Weissman Joselit, *New York's Jewish Jews: The Orthodox Community in the Interwar Years* (Bloomington: Indiana University Press, 1990). See also Rachel Wischnitzer, *The Architecture of the European Synagogue* (Philadelphia: Jewish Publication Society, 1964), p. 105. For more on the history of women's presence in the synagogue, see Chapter 2.

8. Recent arguments, especially within the Conservative movement, over the eligibility of women to serve as rabbis have revolved around this issue. See Beth S. Wenger, "The Politics of Women's Ordination: Jewish Law, Institutional Power, and the Debate over Women in the Rabbinate," in Jack Wertheimer, ed., *Tradition Renewed: A History of the Jewish Theological Seminary*, vol. 2 (New York: Jewish Theological Seminary of America, 1997), pp. 483–523.

9. Saul Berman, "The Status of Women in Halakhic Judaism," in Koltun, *Jewish Woman*, pp. 118–119, 127; Saul J. Berman, "Kol 'Isha," in Leo Landman, ed., *Rabbi Joseph H. Lookstein Memorial Volume* (New York: KTAV Publishing, 1980), pp. 45–66. See also Grossman and Haut, *Daughters of the King*, especially the essays in the section on halakhah, pp. 89–202. For a discussion of the impact of halakhah on women's lives beyond the synagogue, see Rachel Biale, *Women and Jewish Law: An Exploration of Women's Issues in Halakhic Sources* (New York: Schocken, 1984). Attempts to explain the relevance of halakhah to the lives of contemporary Jewish women include Michael Kaufman, *The Woman in Jewish Law and Tradition* (Northvale, N.J.: Jason Aronson, 1993) and Joel B. Wolowelsky, *Women, Jewish Law, and Modernity* (Hoboken, N.J.: KTAV Publishing, 1997).

10. Samuel Heilman, *Synagogue Life: A Study in Symbolic Interaction* (Chicago: University of Chicago Press, 1976), p. 73.

11. The standard explanation for the inclusion of this prayer in the morning liturgy is that it offers men a chance to express thanks for the additional obligations of prayer and observance incumbent upon them as men. Thus, they are not thanking God for their maleness per se, but for the extra opportunities afforded by that identity to express their devotion to God.

12. For influential work that takes this perspective, see Robert Anthony Orsi, *The Madonna of 115th Street: Faith and Community in Italian Harlem, 1880–1950* (New Haven: Yale University Press, 1985); Orsi, *Thank You, St. Jude: Women's Devotion to the Patron Saint of Hopeless Causes* (New Haven: Yale University Press, 1996); Keith Thomas, *Religion and the Decline of Magic* (London: Scribner, 1971); Carlo Ginzburg, *The Cheese and the Worms: The Cosmos of a Sixteenth-Century Miller,* trans. John Tedeschi and Anne Tedeschi (Baltimore: Johns Hopkins Press, 1980); David D. Hall, *Worlds of Wonder, Days of Judgment: Popular Religious Belief in Early New England* (New York: Knopf, 1989); and Charles E. Hambrick-Stowe, *The Practice of Piety: Puritan Devotional Disciplines in Seventeenth-Century New England* (Chapel Hill: University of North Carolina Press, 1982). For analysis of this trend, see Natalie Zemon Davis, "From 'Popular Religion' to Religious Cultures," in Steven Ozment, ed., *Reformation Europe: A Guide to Research* (St. Louis: Center for Reformation Research, 1982), pp. 322–341; Harry S. Stout and Catherine A. Brekus, "Declension, Gender, and the 'New Religious History,'" in Vandermeer and Swierenga, *Belief and Behavior,* pp. 15–37.

13. See, for example, the work of Chava Weissler on Yiddish devotional literature, *Voices of the Matriarchs: Listening to the Prayers of Early Modern Jewish Women* (Boston: Beacon Press, 1998); "The Traditional Piety of Ashkenazic Women," in Arthur Green, ed., *Jewish Spirituality,* vol. 2 (New York: Crossroad, 1987), pp. 245–275; and "Prayers in Yiddish and the Religious World of Ashkenazic Women," in Judith Baskin, ed., *Jewish Women in Historical Perspective* (Detroit: Wayne State University Press, 1991), pp. 159–181.

14. For instance, *Jewish Women in Historical Perspective,* edited by Judith Baskin, a valuable compendium of Jewish women's historical experience, devotes relatively little attention to the public expression of female religiosity. A few selections however, do emphasize women's involvement in synagogue life; see Ross S. Kraemer, "Jewish Women in the Diaspora World of Late Antiquity," in Baskin, *Historical Perspective,* pp. 48–49; Howard Adelman, "Italian Jewish Women," in Baskin, *Historical Perspective,* pp. 139–140.

15. See Rudolf Glanz, *The Jewish Woman in America: Two Female Immigrant Generations, 1820–1929,* vol. 2, *The German Jewish Woman* (New York: KTAV Publishing, 1976); Jacob R. Marcus, *The American Jewish Woman, 1654–1980* (New York: KTAV Publishing, 1981). As contemporary scholars start to take women's presence in the synagogue more seriously, this tendency to discount both the synagogue and the emergence of public identities for women who preceded late-nineteenth-century immigrants is beginning to change. Dianne Ashton's biography of Rebecca Gratz examines the creation of public identities for Philadelphia Jewish women through the educational and charitable organizations that framed Gratz's public life. Dianne Ashton, *Rebecca Gratz: Women and Judaism in Antebellum*

America (Detroit: Wayne State University Press, 1997). See also forthcoming works by Felicia Herman on the Sisterhoods of Personal Service, created in the 1890s, and Holly Snyder on women's religious lives in eighteenth-century British colonial America.

16. The most significant treatment of women's historical relationship to the synagogue, *Daughters of the King: Women and the Synagogue,* edited by Susan Grossman and Rivka Haut (see note 7), considers the historical dynamics of women's public worship in treatments of the Jerusalem Temple, the synagogue in ancient times, medieval Cairo, and medieval Europe. These essays offer a valuable reminder that attention to the place and role of women in the synagogue expands our understanding of both the history of Jewish women and the history of the synagogue. The collection's examination of the transformations of women's roles in the modern synagogue, however, is limited to the last decades of the twentieth century. The articles move directly from historical treatments of the premodern female experience of worship to consideration of present-day questions of religious law in a section entitled "Contemporary Realities." This formulation implies that the only frameworks relevant to women's experience of the synagogue are models from the distant past and the challenge of present-day social concerns, particularly feminism.

17. Jack Wertheimer, ed., *The American Synagogue: A Sanctuary Transformed* (Cambridge: Cambridge University Press, 1987), p. 68. See the essays by Jeffrey S. Gurock, "The Orthodox Synagogue," pp. 37–84; Leon A. Jick, "The Reform Synagogue," pp. 85–110; and Jack Wertheimer, "The Conservative Synagogue," pp. 111–149. In the same book, see also Abraham J. Karp, "Overview: The Synagogue in America—A Historical Typology," pp. 1–36. Karp's essay contains only a few references to women's presence in the synagogue.

18. Jonathan D. Sarna, "The Debate over Mixed Seating in the American Synagogue," in Wertheimer, *American Synagogue,* pp. 363–394. Jenna Weissman Joselit, "The Special Sphere of the Middle-Class American Jewish Woman: The Synagogue Sisterhood, 1890–1940," in Wertheimer, *American Synagogue,* pp. 206–230, also examines the role of women in the American synagogue, focusing mainly on the twentieth century.

19. Miriam Peskowitz, "Engendering Jewish Religious History," in Miriam Peskowitz and Laura Levitt, eds., *Judaism since Gender* (New York: Routledge, 1997), p. 33.

20. Linda Kerber, "Separate Sphere, Female Worlds, Woman's Place: The Rhetoric of Women's History," *Journal of American History* 75 (June 1988): 9–39; Nancy Hewitt, "Beyond the Search for Sisterhood: American Women's History in the 1980s," in Ellen Carol DuBois and Vicki L. Ruiz, eds., *Unequal Sisters: A Multi-Cultural Reader in U.S. Women's History* (New York: Routledge, 1990), pp. 1–14.

21. Braude, "Women's History," p. 99.

22. See Douglas, *Feminization of American Culture;* Welter, *Dimity Convictions;* Lori Ginzberg, *Women and the Work of Benevolence: Morality, Politics, and Class in the Nineteenth-Century United States* (New Haven: Yale University Press, 1990); Nancy A. Hewitt, *Women's Activism and Social Change: Rochester, New York, 1822–1872* (Ithaca: Cornell University Press, 1984); Carol Smith-Rosenberg, *Disorderly Conduct: Visions of Gender in Victorian America* (New York: Knopf, 1985); and Mary P. Ryan, *Cradle of the Middle Class: The Family in Oneida County, New York, 1790–1865* (Cambridge: Cambridge University Press, 1981). Beth S. Wenger's important article "Jewish Women and Voluntarism: Beyond the Myth of Enablers" applies this analysis to Jewish women's voluntarism; *American Jewish History* 79, no. 1 (Autumn 1989): 16–36.

23. See Richard L. Bushman, *The Refinement of America: Persons, Houses, Cities* (New York: Knopf, 1992); John F. Kasson, *Rudeness and Civility: Manners in Nineteenth-Century Urban America* (New York: Hill and Wang, 1990).

24. Karen Halttunen, *Confidence Men and Painted Women: A Study of Middle-Class Culture in America, 1830–1870* (New Haven: Yale University Press, 1982); Kevin Kelly Gaines, *Uplifting the Race: Black Leadership, Politics, and Culture in the Twentieth Century* (Chapel Hill: University of North Carolina Press, 1996); and Evelyn Brooks Higginbotham, *Righteous Discontent: The Women's Movement in the Black Baptist Church, 1880–1920* (Cambridge: Harvard University Press, 1993).

25. See, for instance, Ann Pellegrini, *Performance Anxieties: Staging Psychoanalysis, Staging Race* (New York: Routledge, 1997).

26. "More or Less," *American Hebrew* 8, no. 11 (October 28, 1881): 122.

1. Jewish Women: Acculturation in Old and New Worlds

1. David Philipson, *The Reform Movement in Judaism* (London, 1907), p. 355.

2. The most important works on women and acculturation in European Judaism, by Paula E. Hyman and Marion A. Kaplan, offer valuable explorations of the importance of the development of bourgeois domesticity in offering women a way to assimilate into the broader culture as they preserved Jewish homes. These works focus less on examining the extent to which women sought out public religious identities. See Paula E. Hyman, *Gender and Assimilation in Modern Jewish History: The Roles and Representation of Women* (Seattle: University of Washington Press, 1995); and Marion A. Kaplan, *The Making of the Jewish Middle Class: Women, Family, and Identity in Imperial Germany* (New York: Oxford University Press, 1991). The essays in *Paths of Emancipation: Jews, States, and Citizenship,* edited by Pierre Birnbaum and Ira Katznelson (Princeton: Princeton University Press, 1995), explore distinctive national experiences of emancipation but do

not address questions of gender. Maria Baader's forthcoming Ph.D. dissertation, "Inventing Bourgeois Judaism: Jewish Culture, Gender, and Religion in Germany, 1800–1870" (Columbia University), will shed important light on many of the questions considered here.

3. Paula E. Hyman suggests that "second- and third-generation Jewish families of Central European origin in America" experienced a "similar gender division in religious practice" to that experienced contemporaneously by acculturating central and western European Jews. In making this comparison, she connects the "'feminization' of the synagogue" seen in America with "the greater retention of Jewish ritual observance by middle-class Jewish women than by their male kin" that she discerns in European practice. Hyman, *Gender and Assimilation,* pp. 24–25. I argue here that the elaboration of domestic Judaism explored by Hyman and by Kaplan in *Jewish Middle Class* represents a much different response to the challenges of modern Jewish history than women's emergence in the synagogue-centered Judaism of the United States.

4. Rachel Biale, *Women and Jewish Law: An Exploration of Women's Issues in Halakhic Sources* (New York: Schocken Books, 1984), p. 40.

5. David Sorkin points out that "conversion and intermarriage were marginal phenomena," citing an "absolute total" of 11,000 conversions among German Jews from 1800 to 1870. Because they occurred in cycles, they "thus seemed more important than their actual numbers." See Sorkin, "The Impact of Emancipation on German Jewry: A Reconsideration," in Jonathan Frankel and Steven J. Zipperstein, eds., *Assimilation and Community: The Jews in Nineteenth-Century Europe* (Cambridge: Cambridge University Press, 1992), p. 181.

6. Abraham Geiger, "Die Stellung des weiblichen Geschlechtes in dem Judenthume unserer Zeit," *Wissenschaftliche Zeitschrift für jüdische Theologie* 3 (1837): 8.

7. Israel Jacobson, quoted in W. Gunther Plaut, ed., *The Rise of Reform Judaism: A Sourcebook of its European Origins* (New York: World Union for Progressive Judaism, 1963), p. 30.

8. Michael Creizenach, *Shulchan Aruch,* vol. 3 (Frankfurt am Main, 1839), p. 55, translated in Plaut, *Rise of Reform Judaism,* p. 226.

9. Michael A. Meyer, *Response to Modernity: A History of the Reform Movement in Judaism* (New York: Oxford University Press, 1988), p. 23.

10. Michael Meyer notes that the Reform rabbis in attendance at the 1845 rabbinical conference in Frankfurt responded to a query regarding what was permissible in the construction of a *mikveh.* See Meyer, *Response to Modernity,* p. 138. Their response, though not halakhic, indicates that they did not seek to abolish nonsynagogal institutions in the Jewish community; they accepted these institutions, but did not focus on them in their reform efforts.

11. Phyllis Cohen Albert, *The Modernization of French Jewry: Consistory and Community in the Nineteenth Century* (Hanover, N.H.: University Press of New England, 1977), pp. 385–386.

12. Paula E. Hyman, "The Social Contexts of Assimilation: Village Jews and City Jews in Alsace," in Frankel and Zipperstein, *Assimilation and Community,* p. 121.

13. Michael Galchinsky, *The Origin of the Modern Jewish Woman Writer: Romance and Reform in Victorian England* (Detroit: Wayne State University Press, 1996). Diane Lichtenstein identifies a "tradition" of nineteenth-century Jewish women writers in America, but these writers did not play the central role in theorizing Jewish emancipation that Galchinsky attributes to the British group. See Lichtenstein, *Writing Their Nations: The Tradition of Nineteenth-Century American Jewish Women Writers* (Bloomington: Indiana University Press, 1992).

14. Grace Aguilar, *The Women of Israel; or, Characters and Sketches from the Holy Scriptures and Jewish History Illustrative of the Past History, Present Duties, and Future Destiny of the Hebrew Females, as Based on the Word of God* (1844; reprint, London: n.d.), p. 10.

15. [David Einhorn], "Nachrichten," *Sinai* 3, no. 1 (February 1858): 824.

16. The following quotations are found in Geiger, "Stellung des weiblichen Geschlechtes," 1–14.

17. Plaut, *Rise of Reform Judaism,* p. 253.

18. Meyer, *Response to Modernity,* pp. 56–57.

19. From "Protocol of the First Rabbinic Assembly held in Braunschweig" (1844), quoted in Philipson, *Reform Movement,* p. 203.

20. David Einhorn, quoted in Plaut, *Rise of Reform Judaism,* p. 254.

21. Plaut, *Rise of Reform Judaism,* pp. 253–255.

22. Meyer, *Response to Modernity,* pp. 39–40, 50, 140; Plaut, *Rise of Reform Judaism,* pp. 172–173.

23. [Leopold] Zunz, *Die gottesdienstlichen Vorträge der Juden, historisch entwickelt* (Berlin, 1832), p. 457; "Initiation Religieuse," *Archives Israélites* 2 (1841) pp. 342–343; and West London Synagogue, dedication sermon, in Plaut, *Rise of Reform Judaism,* p. 48. The 1841 *Archives* article described a ceremony, borrowed from Germany, that one French father had used to celebrate the religious initiation of his daughter. The correspondent recommended the general introduction of such a ceremony into French synagogues based upon a uniform catechism and emphasized that such an innovation should be for *"the two sexes."* Emphasis in original.

24. Quoted in Paula E. Hyman, "The Modern Jewish Family: Image and Reality," in David Kraemer, ed., *The Jewish Family: Metaphor and Memory* (New York: Oxford University Press, 1989), p. 188.

25. See Mordechai Eliav, "Die Mädchenerziehung im Zeitalter der Aufklärung und der Emanzipation," in Julius Carlebach, ed., *Zur Geschichte der jüdischen Frau in Deutschland* (Berlin: Metropol-Verlag, 1993), pp. 97–111.

26. Michael Mitterauer and Reinhard Sieder, *The European Family: Patriarchy to Partnership from the Middle Ages to the Present,* trans. Karla Oosterveen and Manfred Horzinger (Chicago: University of Chicago Press, 1982),

pp. 131–132. For a fascinating discussion of some of these issues, see Julius Carlebach, "The Forgotten Connection. Women and Jews in the Conflict between Enlightenment and Romanticism," *Leo Baeck Institute Yearbook* (hereafter cited as *LBIY*) 24 (1979): 107–135.

27. Abraham Geiger, *Judaism and Its History*, trans. Charles Newburgh (1864; trans., New York: Bloch, 1911), p. 57.

28. Geiger, *Judaism and Its History*, p. 58. Michael Galchinsky points out a similar attempt by Grace Aguilar in *Women of Israel* to interpret "biblical heroines as positive or negative exemplars of Victorian respectability, grace, sympathy, and domesticity." Galchinsky, *Modern Jewish Woman Writer*, p. 148.

29. See Kaplan, *Jewish Middle Class*, pp. 64–84; Monika Richarz, *Jüdisches Leben in Deutschland: Selbstzeugnisse zur Sozialgeschichte im Kaiserreich*, 3 vols. (Stuttgart: Deutsche Verlags-Anstalt, 1976–1982).

30. Hyman, *Gender and Assimilation*, pp. 26–27; Kaplan, *Jewish Middle Class*, pp. 64–84; and Maria Baader, "Gender, Judaism, and Embourgeoisement in Early-Nineteenth-Century Germany" (Columbia University, 1994), pp. 20, 22.

31. *Protokolle der dritten Versammlung deutscher Rabbiner*, assembly held July 13–24, 1846 (Breslau, 1847), p. 254.

32. Kaplan, *Jewish Middle Class*, p. 79.

33. Shulamit S. Magnus, "Pauline Wengeroff and the Voice of Jewish Modernity," in T. M. Rudavsky, ed., *Gender and Judaism: The Transformation of Tradition* (New York: New York University Press, 1995), pp. 181–190; Shulamit S. Magnus, "Pauline Wengeroff and the Voice of Jewish Modernity" (paper presented at the conference "Gender and Judaism," Columbus, Ohio, April 26, 1993).

34. See Reinhard Rürup, "The Tortuous and Thorny Path to Legal Equality," *LBIY* 31 (1986): 9; Robert Liberles, "Was There a Jewish Movement for Emancipation in Germany?" *LBIY* 31 (1986): 35.

35. See Robert Liberles, "Emancipation and the Structure of the Jewish Community in the Nineteenth Century," *LBIY* 31 (1986): 61–65.

36. Meyer, *Response to Modernity*, p. 23; Steven M. Lowenstein, "The Pace of Modernization of German Jewry in the Nineteenth Century," *LBIY* 21 (1976): 41–56.

37. Jay R. Berkovitz, *The Shaping of Jewish Identity in Nineteenth-Century France* (Detroit: Wayne State University Press, 1989), p. 99; Hyman, "Social Contexts," pp. 111–114; and Paula E. Hyman, *The Emancipation of the Jews of Alsace: Acculturation and Tradition in the Nineteenth Century* (New Haven: Yale University Press, 1991), pp. 5, 11, 64–85.

38. Abraham Geiger, quoted in Max Wiener, *Abraham Geiger and Liberal Judaism: The Challenge of the Nineteenth Century*, (Cincinnati: Hebrew Union College Press, 1981), p. 89.

39. Robert Liberles, *Religious Conflict in Social Context: The Resurgence of*

Orthodox Judaism in Frankfurt Am Main, 1838–1877 (Westport, Conn.: Greenwood Press, 1985), pp. 165–172.

40. Michael Galchinsky points out that a number of Anglo-Jewish women writers offered a more literary critique of women's position in Jewish tradition. Galchinksy, *Modern Jewish Woman Writer.*

41. See Michael Meyer's discussion of the ways in which the United States, in contrast to European settings, was able to provide "an environment which could scarcely have been more conducive" to the growth of Jewish Reform; *Response to Modernity*, pp. 224–227.

42. Rosa Sonneschein, "The American Jewess," *American Jewess* 6, no. 5 (February 1898): 206.

2. Women's Emergence in the Early American Synagogue Community

1. Rachel Wischnitzer, *The Architecture of the European Synagogue* (Philadelphia: Jewish Publication Society, 1964), pp. 45, 53.

2. Ibid., p. 44.

3. Ibid., p. 76.

4. Carol Herselle Krinsky, *Synagogues of Europe: Architecture, History, Meaning* (Cambridge: MIT Press, 1985), p. 28; Richard Krautheimer, *Mittelalterliche Synagogen* (Berlin: Frankfurter Verlags-Anstalt, 1927), p. 132. Krautheimer cites a number of synagogues in which women's annexes were built onto existing synagogues, as well as a number of smaller synagogues where annexes were never added. He notes that the Regensburg synagogue destroyed in 1519 never had a women's section.

5. See picture in Wischnitzer, *European Synagogue*, pp. 108–109; or Krinsky, *Synagogues of Europe*, pp. 213–214.

6. Krinsky, *Synagogues of Europe*, pp. 28–29.

7. Israel Abrahams suggests this possibility: "The women had their own 'court' in the Temple, yet it is not impossible that they prayed together with the men in Talmudic times." *Jewish Life in the Middle Ages* (Philadelphia: Jewish Publication Society, 1896), p. 25.

8. Wischnitzer, *European Synagogue*, p. 51. Wischnitzer cites Eliezer ben Joel of Bonn and Cologne (d.1235), who reported that curtained-off areas enabled women to hear Sabbath sermons. She also presents a 1508 woodcut of the interior of a synagogue from a book satirizing Jewish customs, written by a convert from Judaism, Johannes Pfefferkorn, which shows a curtain at the back of a synagogue with women and their children standing behind it.

9. Wischnitzer, *European Synagogue*, pp. 71–72. Wischnitzer cites Hayyim Joseph David Azulai, who visited Carpentras in Provence in 1755 and 1777, and Thomas Platter, who visited Avignon in 1599.

10. Emily Taitz, "Women's Voices, Women's Prayers: The European Synagogues of the Middle Ages," in Susan Grossman and Rivka Haut, eds.,

Daughters of the King: Women and the Synagogue (Philadelphia: Jewish Publication Society, 1992), p. 66; Wischnitzer, *European Synagogue,* p. 105.

11. Abrahams, *Middle Ages,* p. 26. Further testimony to the existence of these female prayer leaders appears in the *American Hebrew,* which recalled "the days of the Alt-new Schul in Prague, famous for its woman-chazan, who every once in a while would open the door or curtain that separated male and female worshipers—just to make sure in what part of the service the former were." *American Hebrew* 59, no. 23 (October 9, 1896): 569.

12. Wischnitzer, *European Synagogue,* pp. 105–106; Krinsky, *Synagogues of Europe,* p. 387.

13. Krinsky, *Synagogues of Europe,* p. 29.

14. Krinsky, *Synagogues of Europe,* pp. 29, 52, 390; Helen Rosenau, "German Synagogues in the Early Period of Emancipation," *LBIY* 8 (1963): 216; Wischnitzer, *European Synagogue,* p. 89. See pictures in Krinsky, *Synagogues of Europe,* Wischnitzer, *European Synagogue,* and Harold Hammer-Schenk, *Synagogen in Deutschland: Geschichte Einer Baugattung im 19. und 20. Jahrhundert (1780–1933),* vol. 2 (Hamburg: H. Christians, 1981).

15. Krinsky, *Synagogues of Europe,* p. 52.

16. Holly Snyder's forthcoming work on Jewish life in British colonial America promises to yield a surprisingly rich portrait of Jewish women's lives during this era; see her recent paper "Queens of the Household: Jewish Women and Their 'Sphere' in Colonial British America" (paper delivered at the conference "Consultation on the Religious Lives of American Jewish Women," Temple University, March 22, 1998).

17. Lee M. Friedman, "The New York Synagogue in 1812," *Publications of the American Jewish Historical Society* (hereafter cited as *PAJHS*) 25 (1917): 132.

18. Peter Benes and Philip D. Zimmerman, *New England Meeting House and Church, 1630–1850* (Boston: Boston University, 1979), pp. 55–56; Robert J. Dinkin, "Seating the Meetinghouse in Early Massachusetts," in Robert Blair St. George, ed., *Material Life in America, 1600–1860* (Boston: Northeastern University Press, 1988), p. 412. See also Jonathan D. Sarna, "The Debate over Mixed Seating in the American Synagogue," in Jack Wertheimer, ed., *The American Synagogue: A Sanctuary Transformed,* (Cambridge: Cambridge University Press, 1987), pp. 365–366, 388 n. 10; Rachel Wischnitzer, *Synagogue Architecture in the United States: History and Interpretation* (Philadelphia: Jewish Publication Society, 1955), p. 12; Harry S. Stout and Catherine Brekus, "A New England Congregation: Center Church, New Haven, 1638–1989," in James P. Wind and James W. Lewis, eds., *American Congregations,* vol. 1, *Portraits of Twelve Religious Communities* (Chicago: University of Chicago Press, 1994), pp. 21–22.

19. Benes and Zimmerman, *New England,* pp. 55–56; Dinkin, *Seating the Meetinghouse,* p. 412; and Wischnitzer, *United States,* p. 12.

20. David de Sola Pool and Tamar de Sola Pool, *An Old Faith in a New World: Portrait of Shearith Israel, 1654–1954* (New York: Columbia University Press, 1955), p. 453. The description suggests that female worshipers could be glimpsed through openings in the gallery's front.

21. Stanley F. Chyet, "A Synagogue in Newport," *American Jewish Archives* 16, no. 1 (1964), p. 46.

22. Quoted in Morris A. Gutstein, *The Story of the Jews of Newport: Two and a Half Centuries of Judaism, 1658–1908* (New York: Bloch Publishing, 1936), pp. 100–101.

23. Wischnitzer, *United States*, p. 17.

24. Morris Jastrow Jr., "References to Jews in the Diary of Ezra Stiles," *PAJHS* 10 (1902): 9–10.

25. Jacob R. Marcus, *The Colonial American Jew, 1492–1776*, vol. 2 (Detroit: Wayne State University Press, 1970), p. 895.

26. See Wischnitzer, *European Synagogue*, p. 84.

27. See Hyman B. Grinstein, *The Rise of the Jewish Community of New York, 1654–1860* (Philadelphia: Jewish Publication Society, 1945), p. 68; Pool and Pool, *Old Faith*, pp. 42–43; Wischnitzer, *United States*, pp. 12, 15–16; and Nancy Halverson Schless, "Peter Harrison, the Touro Synagogue, and the Wren City Church," *Winterthur Portfolio* 8 (1973): 187–200. See also Brian de Breffny, *The Synagogue* (New York: Macmillan, 1978), p. 140; Edwin Wolf 2nd and Maxwell Whiteman, *The History of the Jews of Philadelphia from Colonial Times to the Age of Jackson* (Philadelphia: Jewish Publication Society, 1957), Wolf and Whiteman note that when plans for a Philadelphia synagogue were underway in 1782, Mordecai M. Mordecai "was assigned the important task of preparing letters in Hebrew to secure the approval of the London and Amsterdam synagogues for the design of the building" (p. 116).

28. Wischnitzer, *European Synagogue*, p. 105.

29. Marvin Lowenthal, *A World Passed By: Scenes and Memories of Jewish Civilization in Europe and North Africa* (New York: Harper and Brothers, 1933), p. 193. The present-day configuration of Amsterdam's Sephardic synagogue reflects various renovations conducted over the years, including some alteration of the women's gallery, but "none substantial enough to change [the synagogue's] basic appearance." Krinsky, *Synagogues of Europe*, p. 394.

30. There were some eighteenth- and early-nineteenth-century German synagogues that dispensed with the additional lattices and grillworks over the women's galleries. These examples, however, did not define an overall pattern. By the second half of the nineteenth century, open women's galleries became a common feature of the many grand synagogues being built by growing Jewish communities in European cities, as they tried to assert their successful acculturation through synagogue architecture. By this time, of course, the American counterparts to these impressive edifices had intro-

duced family pews in which men and women sat together; Krinsky, *Synagogues of Europe*, p. 63; Hammer-Schenck, *Synagogen in Deutschland*, vol. 1, p. 265. See illustrations in Hammer-Schenck, *Synagogen in Deutschland*, vol. 2, figs. 21 (Mühringen), 57 (München), 85 (Kassel), 144 (Hamburg), 153 (Hannover), 195 (Leipzig), 210 (Frankfurt a. M.); Hans-Peter Schwarz, ed., *Die Architektur der Synagoge* (Stuttgart: Klett-Cotta, 1988), pp. 120, 216; Krinsky, *Synagogues of Europe*, pp. 279, 284, 299, 416.

31. See the reproduction of the painting by S. N. Carvalho (described by the congregation as "neat and accurate") in Rachel Wischnitzer, *United States*, p. 22.

32. N[atanael] L[evin], "The Jewish Congregation of Charleston," *Occident* 1, no. 10 (January 1844): 493–494.

33. Wolf and Whiteman, *Jews of Philadelphia*, p. 119.

34. See the 1954 reconstruction designs by architect Alfred Bendiner, reproduced in Wischnitzer, *United States*, p. 30.

35. Shearith Israel minutes, October 13, 1817, New York, N.Y., Papers of Congregation Shearith Israel, microfilm collection no. 1, American Jewish Archives, Cincinnati, Ohio (hereafter cited as AJA).

36. Pool and Pool, *Old Faith*, p. 50.

37. Michael A. Meyer, *Response to Modernity: A History of the Reform Movement in Judaism* (New York: Oxford University Press, 1988), pp. 54–55.

38. Pool and Pool, *Old Faith*, p. 50. In Philadelphia's 1825 synagogue, there was space for 192 men and 164 women (equal to 46 percent). Wischnitzer, *United States*, p. 33.

39. Gotthold Salomon, one of the temple's preachers, in a collection of sermons given at the temple, published in 1820, observed: "His house of God must become for the Israelite that which once the holy temple in Jerusalem was for him." Quoted in Meyer, *Response to Modernity*, p. 405 n. 120.

40. For more on the Hamburg Temple, see Meyer, *Response to Modernity*, pp. 55–59.

41. The first suggestion of a Reform Jewish ideology in America arose in Charleston, South Carolina, in 1824. See Charles Reznikoff and Uriah Z. Engleman, *The Jews of Charleston* (Philadelphia: Jewish Publication Society, 1950); Robert Liberles, "Conflict over Reforms: The Case of Congregation Beth Elohim, Charleston, South Carolina," in Wertheimer, *American Synagogue*, pp. 274–296; Lou H. Silberman, *American Impact: Judaism in the United States in the Early Nineteenth Century* (Syracuse: Syracuse University, 1964).

42. Quoted in A. B. Levy, *The 200-Year-Old New Synagogue, 1760–1960* (London: New Synagogue, 1960?), p. 17.

43. The 1825 Philadelphia building had fixed blocks of seats set in a semicircle, rather than the customary parallel rows of often movable benches; in addition, its *bimah* was placed along the west wall, across from the ark. Wischnitzer, *United States*, pp. 30–31.

44. Nancy Halverson Schless argues for the direct influence of the Bevis Marks Synagogue on the design of Newport's Touro Synagogue, yet she does not note the difference between Bevis Marks's latticed gallery and Newport's open gallery. Schless, "Peter Harrison."

45. Isaac Leeser, "Consecration of the Synagogue at Baltimore," *Occident* 3, no. 8 (November 1845): 364; "Consecration of Lloyd Street Synagogue," *Baltimore American and Commercial Advertiser,* September 15, 1860, p. 1.

46. Wilbur H. Hunter Jr., "Lloyd St. Synagogue 3rd Oldest in the U. S.," *Baltimore Jewish Times,* May 24, 1963, p. 3.

47. Pool and Pool, *Old Faith,* p. 46. The congregation had good reason not to offend the unmarried Rachel Pinto, a member of a prominent congregational family. When she died in 1815 at the age of ninety-one, she left a "large charitable bequest to the Congregation and its societies." N. Taylor Phillips, "Family History of the Reverend David Mendez Machado," *PAJHS* 2 (1894): 49.

48. See Meyer, *Response to Modernity,* p. 108 n. 168. See also Samuel Echt, *Die Geschichte der Juden in Danzig* (Leer-Ostfriesland: Rautenberg, 1972), pp. 45, 49. On this point Krinsky, (*Synagogues of Europe,* p. 28) cites Cecil Roth (*The Great Synagogue, London, 1690–1940* [London: E. Goldston, 1950]), who cites Gamaliel Ben Pedahzur [pseud.], *The Book of Religion, Ceremonies, and Prayers; of the Jews, as Practised in their Synagogues and Families on all Occasions: On their Sabbath and other Holy-Days Throughout the Year* (London, 1738). This last work, which was meant as an informative, though critical, portrait of Jewish customs, reported that "none of their Women go to Prayers at the Synagogue till they are married; excepting on the Holyday of *Simchas Tora* . . . and of *Purim*" (p. 78).

49. Pool and Pool, *Old Faith,* p. 46.

50. Minutes of Parnassim and Adjuntas, July 16, 1786, reprinted in "Minute Book of the Congregation Shearith Israel, New York," *PAJHS* 21 (1913): 154.

51. Pool and Pool, *Old Faith,* p. 272.

52. Pool and Pool, *Old Faith,* pp. 270–271. Holly Snyder identifies Miss Hays and Miss Mears as cousins; Snyder, "Queens of the Household."

53. Abraham E. Israel to Zalegman Phillips, April 11, 1825, in Joseph L. Blau and Salo W. Baron, eds., *The Jews of the United States, 1790–1840: A Documentary History,* vol. 2 (Philadelphia: Jewish Publication Society, 1963), pp. 522–523. Tension over seat assignments for women was also recorded in Savannah, where in 1793 Cushman Polock withheld his synagogue contributions until "this Adjuncta will . . . restore [Mrs. Polock] to her seat which is her right." Quoted in Saul Jacob Rubin, *Third to None: The Saga of Savannah Jewry, 1733–1983* (Savannah: Congregation Mickve Israel, 1983), pp. 52–53.

54. Rebecca Gratz to Benjamin Gratz, February 27, 1825, in *Letters of Rebecca*

Gratz, ed. David Philipson (Philadelphia: Jewish Publication Society, 1929), p. 76.

55. For more on decorum among women in the synagogue, see Chapter 3.

56. *El Libro de los Acuerdos, Being the Records and Accounts of the Spanish and Portuguese Synagogue of London from 1663 to 1681,* trans. Lionel D. Barnett (Oxford: Oxford University Press, 1931), p. 4.

57. Grinstein, *New York,* p. 471.

58. Grinstein, *New York,* p. 64. Shearith Israel minutes, September 4, 1844 record an application for a seat from Mrs. Rachel Rehine. Shearith Israel Seatholders and Contributors Book, 1861–1902, microfilm collection no. 1-f, AJA, documents seat payments in 1861 from Miss Brandon, ($14), Mrs. Grace Cohen ($5), and Esther Cardoza ($3), for example. These records also indicate that some women contributed regular offerings to the congregation.

59. A Mikveh Israel document from October 20, 1824, records, "It is Hereby Certified that Rachel Etting is entitled to the possession of the Seat No. Eighteen——up stairs in the Hebrew Synagogue of the *K. K. Mickve Israel* [written in Hebrew] in the city of Philadelphia to be held during her natural life." Reprinted in Steven Alan Fox, "A History of Congregation Mikveh Israel, Philadelphia, 1824–40, As Reflected in the Minutes of the Board of Managers" unpublished paper, 1980, small collections no. 9623, AJA.

60. Rodeph Shalom minutes, August 3, 1849, Philadelphia, Pa., Papers of Congregation Rodeph Shalom, collection no. 517, AJA. See also Bene Israel vestry minutes, May 29, 1836; August 7, 1859; Cincinnati, Ohio, Papers of Congregation Bene Israel, collection no. 24, AJA; Bene Yeshurun minutes, August 11, 1850, Cincinnati, Ohio, Papers of Congregation Bene Yeshurun, collection no. 62, AJA.

61. For example, see Constitution, 1870, Sherith Israel Congregation, San Francisco, Calif., p. 14, sections 9, 10 on sons and daughters, Klau Library, Hebrew Union College–Jewish Institute of Religion, Cincinnati, Ohio.

62. Bene Yeshurun minutes, March 25, 1849; see also Bene Yeshurun minutes, August 28, 1855.

63. Baltimore Hebrew Congregation minutes, January 25 and February 1, 1852, Baltimore, Md., Papers of Baltimore Hebrew Congregation, collection no. 369, AJA.

64. The experience of those who remained nonaffiliated is difficult to document. As for the relative frequency of unmarried individuals, the family of Rebecca Gratz (1781–1869) may provide an illuminating case. Of her nine brothers and sisters, four in addition to herself remained unmarried. Two out of five sisters did not marry, and three out of five sons did not marry. Of her parents' thirty-one grandchildren, twelve never married. Dianne Ashton, *Rebecca Gratz: Women and Judaism in Antebellum America* (Detroit: Wayne State University Press, 1997), p. 41.

65. Beth Shalome records, Richmond, Va., Papers of Congregation Beth Ahabah–Beth Shalome, collection no. 298, box 1, file 10, AJA. An 1834 list of congregants at Beth Shalome includes Miss Emma and Miss Wilhemina Marx; Mrs. Myers; Mrs. Solomon Jacobs; Miss Catherine and Miss Slowey Hays; Miss Ella, Miss Rebecca, and Miss Rachel Myers; and Miss Catherine, Miss Julia, and Miss Harriet Myers. List reprinted in Herbert T. Ezekiel and Gaston Lichtenstein, *The History of the Jews of Richmond from 1769 to 1917* (Richmond, Va.: H. T. Ezekiel, 1917), p. 242.

66. Grinstein, *New York,* p. 350; Rodeph Shalom minutes, December 15, 1850.

67. Bene Yeshurun minutes, January 1, 1860; March 25, 1860.

68. Rodeph Shalom minutes, September 1, 1849.

69. It is interesting to note that until 1997 Bene Israel's Rockdale Temple in Cincinnati still listed the number of widows who had acceded to membership in its annual report. This accounting was a vestige, even in a Reform synagogue that has long counted its members according to family units, of the awkward categories of the synagogue community. See "By-Laws of Congregation Bene Israel, Cincinnati, Ohio," March 27, 1938, Article XI, Section 5: "The widow of a member, in good standing at the time of his decease, shall be admitted to membership without petition or ballot." SC box, B-91, 46, Klau Library, Hebrew Union College-Jewish Institute of Religion, Cincinnati, Ohio. The 1997 update of the congregation's bylaws, the "Amended Code of Regulations of Kehal Kodesh Bene Israel," removed this provision.

70. Bene Yeshurun minutes, September, 17, 1843.

71. Bene Yeshurun minutes, October 3, 1842.

72. Bene Israel vestry minutes, May 12, 1844.

73. See Hasia R. Diner, *A Time for Gathering: The Second Migration, 1820–1880* (Baltimore: Johns Hopkins University Press, 1992), pp. 92–105; or Grinstein, *New York,* pp. 103–114, 131–162.

74. Pool and Pool, *Old Faith,* p. 118; Wolf and Whiteman, *Jews of Philadelphia,* p. 120; Israel Goldstein, *A Century of Judaism in New York: B'nai Jeshurun, 1825–1925, New York's Oldest Ashkenazic Congregation* (New York: Congregation B'nai Jeshurun, 1930), p. 61.

75. Lori D. Ginzberg, *Women and the Work of Benevolence: Morality, Politics, and Class in the Nineteenth-Century United States* (New Haven: Yale University Press, 1990), p. 37.

76. Wolf and Whiteman, *Jews of Philadelphia,* pp. 171, 465 n. 101. For more on the Female Association, see Ashton, *Rebecca Gratz,* pp. 61–63.

77. Wolf and Whiteman, *Jews of Philadelphia,* pp. 272–273. A later example of the impact of Jewish participation in nonsectarian women's organizations was in Chicago, where participation in the Chicago Woman's Club by a few Jewish women like Hannah Solomon helped to educate the group of women who became instrumental in creating the National Council of Jewish Women.

78. *Occident* 1, no. 9 (December 1843): 451.
79. Jacob Rader Marcus, *The American Jewish Woman: A Documentary History* (New York: KTAV Publishing, 1981), p. 89.
80. Mrs. Rebecca Phillips, widow of Jonas Levy, served in 1820 as first directress, Rebecca Gratz as secretary, and Rebecca's married sister, Richea Hays, as one of the managers. It is unclear whether Miss Hannah Levy, a manager in 1820 and one of the two ladies who first put forth the call for the new organization, was the same Miss Levy who participated in the Female Association. Henry Samuel Morais, *The Jews of Philadelphia: Their History from the Earliest Settlements to the Present Time* (Philadelphia: Levytype, 1894), pp. 150–151.
81. Wolf and Whiteman, *Jews of Philadelphia*, pp. 277, 465 n. 100; Ashton, *Rebecca Gratz*, p. 101.
82. Pool and Pool, *Old Faith*, p. 362.
83. See, for instance, two important studies of Jewish women's benevolence in Philadelphia: Ashton, *Rebecca Gratz*, pp. 22–23; and Evelyn Bodeck, "'Making Do': Jewish Women and Philanthropy," in Murray Friedman, ed., *Jewish Life in Philadelphia, 1830–1940* (Philadelphia: ISHI Publications, 1983), pp. 144, 162. In her article, "'Souls Have No Sex': Philadelphia Jewish Women and the American Challenge," Dianne Ashton argues, as will be suggested here, that the work of Philadelphia activist Jewish women "provided models for other Jewish women in other cities;" in Murray Friedman, ed., *When Philadelphia Was the Capital of Jewish America* (Philadelphia: Balch Institute Press, 1993), p. 36.
84. Jacob Rader Marcus, *The American Jewish Woman, 1654–1980* (New York: KTAV Publishing, 1981), p. 52; Ashton, *Rebecca Gratz*, pp. 152–153.
85. Anne M. Boylan, *Sunday School: The Formation of an American Institution, 1790–1880* (New Haven: Yale University Press, 1988), pp. 11, 61.
86. Quoted in Solomon Solis-Cohen, "History of the Sunday Schools," in *Proceedings of the Commemorative Celebration of the Fiftieth Anniversary of the Founding of Hebrew Sunday Schools in America* (Philadelphia: Hebrew Sunday School Society, 1888), p. 17.
87. *Occident* 4, no. 8 (November 1846): 390.
88. Matilda H. Cohen, "Secretary's Report," Fiftieth Anniversary Meeting of the Female Hebrew Benevolent Society, November 3, 1869, Charles J. and Mary M. Cohen Collection, manuscript 3, Center for Judaic Studies, University of Pennsylvania. Henry Samuel Morais, *The Jews of Philadelphia*, pp. 150–151. Dianne Ashton points out that the story of Gratz's refusal of a marriage proposal by a Christian suitor because of her commitment to Judaism, which many claimed was the inspiration for the character of Rebecca in Sir Walter Scott's *Ivanhoe*, helped to make Gratz's unmarried, and thus potentially undesirable life experience, into a worthy and exemplary model for other acculturated American Jewish women. Ashton, *Rebecca Gratz*, pp. 239–256.

89. For more on the achievements of these women, see Ashton, "Souls Have No Sex," and Morais, *Jews of Philadelphia.*
90. Jacob R. Marcus, *United States Jewry,* vol. 1 (Detroit: Wayne State University Press), p. 330; Grinstein, *New York,* pp. 152–154; Pool and Pool, *Old Faith,* p. 366; *Occident* 2, no. 9 (December 1844): 446; 7, no. 8 (November 1849): 418; 5, no. 9 (December 1847): 461; Hasia Diner, "German Immigrant Period," in Paula E. Hyman and Deborah Dash Moore, eds., *Jewish Women in America: An Historical Encyclopedia* (New York: Routledge, 1997), pp. 505–506; Ezekiel and Lichtenstein, *Jews of Richmond,* p. 231.
91. See, for example, "The Israelites of Boston," *Asmonean* 9, no. 18 (February 17, 1854): 141.
92. Maria Baader, "Inventing Bourgeois Judaism: Jewish Culture, Gender, and Religion in Germany, 1800–1870" (Ph.D. dissertation, Columbia University, forthcoming). Maria Baader, "Jewish Women in Germany Between Community and Domesticity," (paper presented at the annual meeting of the Association of Jewish Studies, Boston, Mass., December 21, 1998).
93. Correspondents to the Female Hebrew Benevolent Society in Norfolk, Virginia, for example, addressed the group as the "Norfolk Israelitish Frauen Verein." Female Hebrew Benevolent Society minutes, A. Falk to Mrs. A. Reis, May 18, 1868, box 2, Papers of Ohef Sholom Temple, collection no. 548, AJA.
94. Rebecca Gratz to Miriam Cohen, June 20, 1842, box 1, folder 2, Rebecca Gratz Papers, manuscript collection no. 236, AJA.
95. Grace Aguilar to Miriam Cohen, November 11, 1842; February 3, 1843; box 1, folder 8, Miriam Gratz (Moses) Cohen Collection, collection no. 2639, Southern Historical Collection, University of North Carolina at Chapel Hill.
96. *Occident* 3, no. 7 (October 1845): 357–358. Rubin, *Third to None,* pp. 101–102.
97. *Occident* 4, no. 1 (April 1846): 57.
98. Morais, *Jews of Philadelphia,* p. 135.
99. Bene Israel trustee minutes, April 18, 1847; October 20, 1850; November 3, 1864. Bene Yeshurun minutes, May 28, 1851; September 19, 1852; May 19, 1855; January 9, 1859; September 23, 1860; September 28, 1862.
100. Simon Cohen, *Shaaray Tefila: A History of Its Hundred Years, 1845–1945* (New York: Greenberg, 1945), p. 9.
101. *Occident* 12, no. 5 (August 1854): 258–259.
102. Bertram Wallace Korn, *The Early Jews of New Orleans* (Waltham, Mass.: American Jewish Historical Society, 1969), p. 256. For a copy of the will itself, see Max J. Kohler, "Judah Touro, Merchant and Philanthropist," *PAJHS* 13 (1905): 104–111.
103. Although the will specifies a bequest to "the Ladies' Benevolent Society," and does not specify that this is a Jewish group, its appearance in the will in the middle of other organizations that are clearly identified as Jewish sug-

gests that this too was a Jewish group and not a nondenominational or general society.

104. Korn, *New Orleans*, p. 255.

105. Kohler, "Judah Touro," p. 108.

106. See *Encyclopedia Judaica*, 1972 ed., s.v. "Mikveh."

107. Grinstein, *New York*, p. 35.

108. "Historical Sketch by Naphtali Phillips," *PAJHS* 21 (1913): 194.

109. Wolf and Whiteman, *Jews of Philadelphia*, p. 118. They note that Jonas Phillips's reference to a *mikveh* is the first mention that can be found regarding a ritual bath in Philadelphia.

110. The petition is reprinted in Jacob R. Marcus, *American Jewry: Documents, Eighteenth Century* (Cincinnati: Hebrew Union College Press, 1959), pp. 135–136. Marcus attributes the petition to Josephson; Wolf and Whiteman cite both Josephson and Joseph Carpeles.

111. Wolf and Whiteman, *Jews of Philadelphia*, p. 141.

112. Ibid.

113. This description is included in a narrative that, though quite respectful of the Jewish religion, is in essence a Christian conversion narrative. Mrs. Cohen went on to recount her unease in neglecting her religion of birth, her extreme discomfiture at the circumcisions of her two infant sons, her own inevitable reembrace of Christianity, and the deathbed conversion of her young son Henry. The narrative of her immersion is one of a number of descriptions of Jewish ceremonial and domestic rituals that she suggested might "instruct" or "amuse" her readers. Jewish authors anxious to impress readers with the grandeur and sublimity of Jewish practice were less likely to focus on the institution of the *mikveh*, which was perhaps too disturbingly connected with bodily processes and primitive rites and taboos. Her account provides a rare glimpse of an early-nineteenth-century American *mikveh*. Mrs. S. J. Cohen, *Henry Luria; or, the Little Jewish Convert* (New York, 1860), pp. 63, 64.

114. "The Earliest Extant Minute Book of the Spanish and Portuguese Congregation Shearith Israel in New York, 1728–1861," *PAJHS* 21 (1913): 81. When Shearith Israel moved to its next location on Crosby Street in 1833, a *mikveh* was not built along with their new facilities, in part, presumably, because there were other *mikveh* facilities available in New York.

115. "New Jewish Synagogue," *American and Commercial Daily Advertiser*, September 25, 1845, p. 2.

116. Samuel Bruel, "The Israelitish Institutions of Cincinnati," *Israelite* 1, no. 4 (August 4, 1854): 26; Bene Israel Vestry records, October 31, 1841; James G. Heller, *As Yesterday When It Is Past: A History of the Isaac M. Wise Temple K. K. B'nai Yeshurun, 1842–1942* (Cincinnati: Isaac M. Wise Temple, 1942), pp. 26–27.

117. Bene Israel trustee minutes, November 1, 1846; April 7, 1847; July 18,

1847; July 25, 1847; January 30, 1848. On May 7, 1848, it was reported that *mikveh* expenses ran to $2,300.

118. Stuart E. Rosenberg, *The Jewish Community in Rochester, 1843–1925* (New York: American Jewish Historical Society, 1954), p. 28.

119. Grinstein, *New York,* p. 298, p. 573 n. 29.

120. *Occident* 17, no. 5 (April 28, 1859): 29. Leeser notes of such faithful followers, "It were indeed to be wished that their numbers might increase manifold; but this is best promoted by furnishing the means to enable people to become strict conformists as has been done in this case." See also *Occident* 15, no. 6 (September 1857): 308 (Anshe Maariv in Chicago); 14, no. 10 (January 1857): 503 (Rochester, N.Y.); 9, no. 7 (November 1851): 373 (Syracuse, N.Y.).

121. *Occident* 17, no. 7 (May 12, 1859): 42.

122. Bene Israel trustee minutes, October 25, 1857; November 9, 1857; April 18, 1858.

123. "Mikvah Synagogue," advertisement, *Asmonean* 8, no. 12 (July 8, 1853): 95.

124. "*Mikvah* [in Hebrew] To the Ladies of New York," advertisement, *Asmonean* 7, no. 7 (December 3, 1852): 80.

125. Mrs. H. Moses et. al. to Parnas and Members of K. K. Bene Israel, June 5, 5613 [1853], Papers of Congregation Bene Israel, AJA.

3. The Quest for Respectability: Mixed Choirs and Family Pews

1. *Israelite,* June 15, 1855; November 6, 1857; March 26, 1858; April 2, 1858; April 16, 1858.

2. *Israelite,* October 12, 1855; January 11, 1856; November 21, 1856; October 23, 1857; April 16, 1858.

3. M. Myers, "Correspondence to the Israelite," *Israelite* 2, no. 29 (January 25, 1856): 237.

4. *Occident* 13, no. 9 (December 1855): 467.

5. Contained in a description of the constitution and bylaws of the newly chartered congregation "K.[hilath] Anshe Mayrive Chicago," *Asmonean* 12, no. 3 (May 4, 1855): 20. For the centrality of the quest for respectability in the creation of the Reform movement, see Leon Jick, *The Americanization of the Synagogue* (Hanover, N.H.: University Press of New England). For the emphasis on respectability and an American style in more traditional synagogues, see Jeffrey S. Gurock, "The Orthodox Synagogue," and Marsha L. Rozenblit, "Choosing a Synagogue: The Social Composition of Two German Congregations in Nineteenth-Century Baltimore," in Jack Wertheimer, ed., *The American Synagogue: A Sanctuary Transformed* (Cambridge: Cambridge University Press, 1987), pp. 37–84, 327–362.

6. For the emergence of "refinement" as a value in American society, see Rich-

ard L. Bushman, *The Refinement of America: Persons, Houses, Cities* (New York: Knopf, 1992).

7. Bene Yeshurun minutes, February 27, 1848, Cincinnati, Ohio, Papers of Congregation Bene Yeshurun collection no. 62, AJA.

8. Quoted in Edwin Wolf 2nd and Maxwell Whiteman, *The History of the Jews of Philadelphia from Colonial Times to the Age of Jackson* (Philadelphia: Jewish Publication Society, 1957), p. 121.

9. Jerome W. Grollman, "The Emergence of Reform Judaism in the United States" (rabbinical thesis, Hebrew Union College, 1948), p. 41.

10. "Bye Laws of the Congregation of *Shearith Israel,*" reprinted in Daniel J. Elazar, Jonathan D. Sarna, and Rela G. Monson, eds., *A Double Bond: The Constitutional Documents of American Jewry* (Lanham, Md.: University Press of America, 1992), p. 110.

11. Bene Israel trustees minutes, May 7, 1848, Cincinnati, Ohio, Papers of Congregation Bene Israel, collection no. 24, AJA.

12. Jick, *Americanization of the Synagogue,* p. 54.

13. Anshe Chesed minutes, March 3, 1846, and April 24, 1847, quoted in Hyman B. Grinstein, *The Rise of the Jewish Community of New York, 1654–1860* (Philadelphia: Jewish Publication Society, 1945), p. 276. Provisions such as these were commonplace. An 1839 resolution in Easton, Pennsylvania, instructed that "all prayers shall be quietly and devoutly uttered." Any that were to "be spoken and sung aloud shall be spoken or sung only by the precentor." Joshua Trachtenberg, *Consider the Years: The Story of the Jewish Community of Easton, 1752–1942* (Easton, Pa.: Centennial Committee of Congregation B'rith Shalom, 1942), pp. 120, 136.

14. See Saul J. Berman, "Kol 'Isha," in Leo Landman, ed., *Rabbi Joseph H. Lookstein Memorial Volume* (New York: KTAV Publishing, 1980), pp. 45–66.

15. Grinstein, *New York,* p. 278.

16. One Jewish attendant at an 1847 synagogue consecration in New York concluded his account of the festivities with these words: "Thus finished one of the most interesting ceremonies that have ever taken place on this continent." A. Abraham, "Consecration of the New Synagogue," *Occident* 5, no. 5 (August 1847): 228.

17. For the development of consecration services in New York, see Grinstein, *New York,* pp. 174–179. Joseph Jonas continued his description of the Cincinnati consecration, "We therefore selected the clergy and the families of those gentlemen who so liberally had given donations towards the building." Jacob R. Marcus, ed., *Memoirs of American Jews, 1775–1865,* vol. 1 (Philadelphia: Jewish Publication Society, 1955), p. 211.

18. Grinstein, *New York,* p. 175; I. Harold Scharfman, *The First Rabbi: Origins of Conflict between Orthodox and Reform; Jewish Polemic Warfare in pre–Civil War America, a Biographical History* (n.p.: Joseph Simon, 1988), p. 375. Referring to the presence of mixed choirs at the synagogue dedica-

tions of Shearith Israel in 1818 and Shaaray Tefila in 1847, Grinstein observes, "Undoubtedly these ... orthodox synagogues reasoned that a consecration was a special occasion which did not require the strictness demanded of a regular service." Grinstein, *New York,* p. 281.

19. S. M. Isaacs, "The Corner Stone," *Occident,* 4, no. 5 (August 1846): 235; H. S., "Laying the Corner Stone of the Synagogue Shaaray Tefilla," *Occident* 4:5 (August 1846): 228.

20. Grinstein, *New York,* p. 281; Simon Cohen notes, "The arrangements of the synagogue at Wooster Street conformed to all the requirements of Orthodox Jewish worship." *Shaaray Tefila: A History of Its Hundred Years, 1845–1945* (New York: Greenberg, 1945), p. 11.

21. Cohen, *Shaaray Tefila,* p. 11; Grinstein, *New York,* pp. 281–282; and Scharfman, *First Rabbi,* p. 375.

22. Reprinted in Marcus, *Memoirs,* pp. 211–212.

23. Bene Israel trustee minutes, August 1, 1852.

24. Bene Israel trustee minutes, August 29, 1852.

25. Grinstein, *New York,* p. 278.

26. Myer Stern, *The Rise and Progress of Reform Judaism, Embracing a History made from the Official Records of Temple Emanu-El of New York, with a Description of Salem Field Cemetery* (New York, 1895), p. 28; Scharfman, *First Rabbi,* p. 375.

27. Grinstein, *New York,* pp. 279, 281.

28. Quoted in Grinstein, *New York,* p. 281.

29. Bene Israel trustee minutes, May 9, 1848.

30. Bene Israel trustee minutes, February 12, 1848; Bene Yeshurun minutes, February 27, 1848.

31. Isaac M. Wise, *Reminiscences,* 2nd ed., trans. and ed. David Philipson (1901; New York: Central Synagogue of New York, 1945), pp. 53–54; "The Choir," *Israelite,* 1, no. 5 (August 11, 1854): 38.

32. [Isaac M. Wise], "Does the Canon Law permit Ladies to sing in the Synagogue?" *Israelite* 2, no. 5 (August 10, 1855): 36; no. 6 (August 17, 1855): 44–45.

33. S. Jacobs, letter to the editor, *Israelite* 2, no. 15 (October 19, 1855): 117; no. 16 (October 26, 1855): 132–133; the two-part article was also reprinted as "Ladies' Singing in the Synagogue," in the *Occident* 13, no. 9 (December 1855): 445–448; no. 10 (January 1856): 492–496.

34. Isidor Kalish, "Justification of Women's Singing in the Synagogue, cont'd," *Israelite* 2, no. 46 (April 11, 1856). "Rev. Mr. Jacobs calls my *kal v'chomer* (*minor* and *major*) a quaint style. Does he, an orthodox Jew, not know that this quaint style, as he denominates it, is delivered to us in the ... thirteen logical rules by which the law is explained? Does he not know that *asam din cal v'chomer m'atzmo;* every man can make deduction through such a way of thinking?" (p. 325).

35. Isidor Kalish, "Supplement," *Israelite* 2, no. 18 (November 9, 1855): 149.

See also Isidor Kalish, "Justification of Women's Singing in the Synagogue," *Israelite* 2, no. 24 (February 29, 1856): 276; Kalish, "Justification, cont.," 325–326.

36. Kalish, "Justification, cont.," 326.

37. On the Cleveland conference, see Michael A. Meyer, *Response to Modernity: A History of the Reform Movement in Judaism* (New York: Oxford University Press, 1988), pp. 243–245. Leeser's account of the proceedings appear in *Occident*, 13, no. 7 (October 1855): 407–414. Wise's recollections of the conference appear in *Reminiscences*, pp. 312–321. Under attack from radical Reformers over claims made for the Talmud's authority, Wise noted, "I was compelled to write and publish in the *Israelite* several articles, however unwillingly [defending the 'morality of the Talmud and orthodoxy'] . . . Kalisch wrote likewise" (p. 321).

38. S. Bruel, "The Challenge Answered," *Israelite* 2, no. 11 (September 21, 1855): 83.

39. For more on this controversy and the founding of Anshe Emeth, see Wise, *Reminiscences*, pp. 155–174. See also the following biographies of Wise: James G. Heller, *Isaac M. Wise: His Life, Work, and Thought* (New York: Union of American Hebrew Congregations, 1965); Sefton D. Temkin, *Isaac Mayer Wise: Shaping American Judaism* (New York: Oxford University Press, 1992), pp. 68–72; and Max B. May, *Isaac Mayer Wise, the Founder of American Judaism: A Biography* (New York: G. P. Putnam, 1916), pp. 99–125.

40. Temkin, *Isaac Mayer Wise*, p. 77; Wise, *Reminiscences*, pp. 210, 212.

41. "Three Reforms in the Synagogue," *American Israelite*, September 1, 1876, p. 4; Jonathan D. Sarna, "The Debate over Mixed Seating in the American Synagogue," in Wertheimer, *American Synagogue*, pp. 363–394.

42. *Occident* 9, no. 9 (December 1851): 477. See also Sarna, "Mixed Seating," p. 368.

43. Sarna, "Mixed Seating," p. 368.

44. Wise, *Reminiscences*, pp. 112, 116–118.

45. S., "The Temple—Twelfth Street," *Asmonean* 9, no. 25 (April 7, 1854): 196–197.

46. E. B., "On Jewish Reform," *Asmonean* 13, no. 2 (October 26, 1855): 14. There is similarly no mention of mixed seating in Talmud Americus, "Another Visit to the Temple in New York," *Israelite* 2, no. 2 (July 20, 1855): 15.

47. H[enry] A. Henry, "The Ritual and its Emendators," *Asmonean* 13, no. 10 (December 21, 1855): 76. On Henry A. Henry's career, see Jay Henry Moses, "Henry A. Henry: The Life and Work of an American Rabbi, 1849–1869" (rabbinical thesis, Hebrew Union College–Jewish Institute of Religion, Cincinnati, 1997).

48. D. Merzbacher, "Women-rights in the Synagogue, or Ladies and Gentlemen on equal footing in the Place of Worship," *Asmonean* 13, no. 12 (January

4, 1856): 93. Although the author of the article is identified as "Dr. D. Merzbacher," presumably the author is Reverend Leo Merzbacher of Temple Emanu-El, who died soon after this article was published.

4. The Trouble with Jewish Women

1. "The Hebrew and German Benevolent Societies," *Jewish Messenger* 4, no. 19 (December 24, 1858): 147.

2. John F. Kasson, *Rudeness and Civility: Manners in Nineteenth-Century Urban America* (New York: Hill and Wang, 1990), pp. 128–129; Stuart M. Blumin, *The Emergence of the Middle Class: Social Experience in the American City, 1760–1900* (Cambridge: Cambridge University Press, 1989), pp. 183–184; and Nancy F. Cott, *The Bonds of Womanhood: "Woman's Sphere" in New England, 1780–1835* (New Haven: Yale University Press, 1977), pp. 128–129.

3. Quotation from C. A. Ogden, *Into the Light; or, The Jewess* (Boston, 1868), p. 7.

4. Hyman B. Grinstein, *The Rise of the Jewish Community of New York, 1654–1860* (Philadelphia: Jewish Publication Society, 1945), p. 276. B'nai Yeshurun minutes, February 27, 1848, Cincinnati, Ohio; Papers of Congregation Bene Yeshurun collection no. 62, AJA. See also "Constitution and By-laws" for Congregation B'nai Scholom, Huntsville, Ala. (undated): "The forgoing rules apply equally as well to the ladies as the gentlemen;" Klau Library, Hebrew Union College–Jewish Institute of Religion, Cincinnati, Ohio.

5. Joshua Trachtenberg, *Consider the Years: The Story of the Jewish Community of Easton, 1752–1942* (Easton, Pa.: Centennial Committee of Congregation B'rith Shalom, 1942), p. 135.

6. Baltimore Hebrew Congregation minutes, October 10, 1852, Baltimore, Md., Papers of Baltimore Hebrew Congregation, collection no. 369, AJA.

7. Bene Israel trustee minutes, January 28, 1849, Cincinnati, Ohio, Papers of Congregation Bene Israel, collection no. 24, AJA.

8. Keneseth Israel minutes, October 3, 1852, Philadelphia, Pa., originals and translations in possession of Congregation Keneseth Israel.

9. Quoted in I. Harold Scharfman, *The First Rabbi: Origins of Conflict between Orthodox and Reform; Jewish Polemic Warfare in pre–Civil War America, a Biographical History* (n.p.: Joseph Simon, 1988), pp. 190–191. After his contentious employment by the Baltimore Hebrew Congregation, Rice resigned in 1849 to run a dry goods store.

10. S. M. Isaacs, "The Synagogue as it was, as it is, as it should be," *Occident* 3, no. 2 (May 1845): 90.

11. Scharfman, *First Rabbi*, p. 191.

12. "The New Synagogue," *Asmonean* 2, no. 5 (May 24, 1850): 58.

13. "Consecration of the New Synagogue, Shaaray Tefilla, New York,"

Occident 5, no. 5 (August 1847): 218; D. Merzbacher, "Women-rights in the Synagogue, or Ladies and Gentlemen on equal footing in the Place of Worship," *Asmonean* 13, no. 12 (January 4, 1856): 93. Leeser called Shaaray Tefila "by far the finest Synagogue in America" but observed, "the style of building is so new to us, and so little idea had we of the interior arrangements, that we have not as yet been able to make up our mind, whether to approve it for a Synagogue or not."

14. "Greene Street Synagogue," *Asmonean* 4, no. 24 (October 3, 1851): 214.
15. Tiered galleries also appeared in many of the grand synagogues built by the Jewish communities of many large European cities during the 1850s and 1860s. See Carol Herselle Krinsky, *Synagogues of Europe: Architecture, History, Meaning* (Cambridge: MIT Press, 1985), pictures of Oranienburgerstrasse in Berlin, 1866, p. 269; Dohany Street in Budapest, 1859, p. 158; Hannover, 1870, p. 312. In the United States, Orthodox synagogues adopted tiers, even as Reform synagogues began to introduce family pews.
16. "Lara," writing in the *Asmonean* in 1856, had declared a desire to avoid just this situation by maintaining the separation of the sexes. Lara, "Women in the Synagogue," *Asmonean* 13, no. 14 (January 18, 1856): 109.
17. Une Enfante Terrible, "Correspondence," *Jewish Messenger* 7, no. 18 (May 11, 1860): 140.
18. An Observer, "Correspondence," *Jewish Messenger* 7, no. 19 (May 18, 1860): 148.
19. I. S. H. "Orthodoxy vs. Reform," *Asmonean* 11, no. 20 (March 2, 1855): 157.
20. Ibid.
21. A Sephardimist, "The Antiquated Form of Synagogue Worship," *Asmonean* 11, no. 18 (February 16, 1855): 141.
22. Ibid, emphasis in original.
23. "Correspondence," *Asmonean* 13, no. 12 (January 4, 1856): 93.
24. Zepho, "Prayer," *Asmonean* 5, no. 23 (March 26, 1852): 230.
25. Ibid.
26. S. M. I[saacs], "The Synagogue," *Jewish Messenger* 2, no. 9 (October 23, 1857): 68.
27. Rational Worship, "Orthodox Jewish Worship," *Asmonean* 10, no. 21 (September 22, 1854): 180. An 1860 observer asked, "How is it that when a stranger visits a synagogue, on a rainy Saturday (or frequently even on a pleasant day) he notices a number of woefully empty benches and among those present anything but the semblance of devotion?" Judaeus, "A Few Thoughts on Synagogue Worship," *Jewish Messenger* 7, no. 23 (June 15, 1860): 181.
28. "The Synagogue," *Israelite* 3, no. 8 (August 20, 1856): 60.
29. S. M. I[saacs], "The Synagogue," *Jewish Messenger* 3, no. 1 (January 1, 1858): 4.

30. "Now we say it with shame, nevertheless boldly, there are Israelites, both male and female, who seldom or never come in time, who seem to think it a species of sin to be present when prayers commence." Isaac Leeser, "Synagogue Reforms," *Occident* 6, no. 3 (June 1848): 112.

31. Ibid., 112–114.

32. Jacob Ezekiel to Isaac Leeser, September 4, 1852, Isaac Leeser Papers, microfilm no. 200, AJA.

33. Karen Halttunen, *Confidence Men and Painted Women: A Study of Middle-Class Culture in America, 1830–1870* (New Haven: Yale University Press, 1982), p. xiv.

34. An Israelite, "Judaism in America: As It Is—As It Should Be," *Asmonean* 12, no. 2 (April 27, 1855): 13.

35. S. M. I[saacs], "The Synagogue," *Jewish Messenger* 3, no. 1 (January 1, 1858): 4; "Our Spiritual Condition," *Jewish Messenger* 7, no. 3 (January 20, 1860): 20.

36. See, for example, reprint from *Cleveland Herald* (January 4, 1856) in *The Temple, 1850–1950* (Cleveland: The Temple, 1950), p. 17; excerpt from *Milwaukee Sentinel,* quoted in Louis J. Swichkow and Lloyd P. Gartner, *The History of the Jews of Milwaukee* (Philadelphia: Jewish Publication Society, 1963), pp. 39–40; "K. K. 'Emanuel,' San Francisco," *Asmonean* 10, no. 26 (October 13, 1854): 204; excerpt from *Boston Traveler* (September 1854), quoted in Arthur Mann, ed., *Growth and Achievement: Temple Israel, 1854–1954* (Cambridge, Mass.: Board of Trustees of Temple Adath Israel, 1954), p. 27; and excerpt from *Intelligencer,* reprinted in "St. Louis," *Asmonean* 12, no. 2 (April 27, 1855): 13. A report from the *Chicago Tribune* ("An hour with the Children of Israel," reprinted in *Asmonean* 12, no. 19 [August 24, 1855]: 150) mentions the "neat and tasteful building" and also injects a romantic element into the description: "We were politely shown to a seat . . . and were left to our own meditations . . . Around us were the descendants of God's own peculiar people . . . The ancestors of the men we now saw had stood before Mount Sinai when it smoked and trembled with the presence of the Lord."

37. David de Sola Pool and Tamar de Sola Pool, *An Old Faith in a New World: Portrait of Shearith Israel, 1654–1954* (New York: Columbia University Press, 1955), p. 459.

38. Reprinted in Lee M. Friedman, "Mrs. Child's Visit to a New York Synagogue in 1841," *PAJHS* 38 (1948–1949): 173–184.

39. Ibid., 177–178.

40. Ibid., 181.

41. Ibid., 176–177.

42. American Sunday-School Union, *The Jew at Home and Abroad* (Philadelphia, 1845), p. 138.

43. Ibid., pp. 63, 65. Although the text of *The Jew at Home and Abroad* emphasizes the barriers that defined women's galleries, the illustrations of

synagogue interiors in the book depict women in clear view occupying open galleries. Different illustrations appear in different copies of the book; the two illustrations that I have seen seem to show American congregations. Wischnitzer identifies one of them as Mikveh Israel in Philadelphia (see p. 53 in this volume). *Home and Abroad,* p. 68; Rachel Wischnitzer, *Synagogue Architecture in the United States: History and Interpretation* (Philadelphia: Jewish Publication Society), p. 28.

44. Herman Baer, *Ceremonies of Modern Judaism* (Nashville, 1856).

45. Ibid., p. 35.

46. Ibid., pp. 54, 58.

47. Aunt Hattie [Harriette Newell Woods Baker], *Lost but Found; or, the Jewish Home* (Boston, 1867), p. 157; Ogden, *Into the Light,* p. 7.

48. Simon Tuska, *The Stranger in the Synagogue* (Rochester, 1854). For more on Tuska and his family see Abraham J. Karp, "Simon Tuska's *The Stranger in the Synagogue,*" *University of Rochester Library Bulletin* 14, no. 1 (1958): 1–11; Stuart E. Rosenberg, *The Jewish Community in Rochester, 1843–1925* (New York: American Jewish Historical Society, 1954), pp. 22–24, 34, 37.

49. Tuska, *Stranger in the Synagogue,* p. 46.

50. Ibid., p. 7.

51. Ibid., pp. 47–48.

52. "Present State of the Jewish People in Learning and Culture," *North American Review* 83 (1856): 371.

53. A. Abraham, "Consecration of the New Synagogue," *Occident* 5, no. 5 (August 1847): 224.

54. Joseph Jonas to Leeser, February 29, 1852; Joseph Abraham to Leeser, July 27, 1859; Leeser Papers.

55. S[amuel] Bruel, "The Challenge Answered," cont., *Israelite* 2, no. 13 (October 5, 1855): 102–103.

56. [Isaac M. Wise], "Does the Canon Law permit Ladies to sing in the Synagogue?" *Israelite* 2, no. 5 (August 10, 1855): 36. In response to Bruel, Wise commented, "We abstained studiously from making any remarks to the argument of our friend S. Bruel, not only on account of respect to the old gentleman, but also because we consider it unnecessary to do so. The Talmudist knows himself how much merit there is in the argument of our friend." "The Challenge Answered," *Israelite* 2, no. 14 (October 12, 1855): 110.

57. H[enry] A. Henry, "The Ritual and its Emendators," *Asmonean* 13, no. 10, (December 21, 1855): 76.

58. S. Jacobs, "Ladies' Singing in the Synagogue," *Occident* 13, no. 10 (January 1856): 496.

59. B., "Women's Rights in Collision with the Prayers," *Occident* 15, no. 4 (July 1857): 175–179.

60. Barbara Welter, "The Cult of True Womanhood, 1820–1860," *American Quarterly* 18 (Summer 1966): 151–174.

61. Lara, "Women in the Synagogue."
62. Lilienthal's eventful early career included stints as a reforming rabbi in Russia and as chief rabbi for the German synagogues in New York City. For more on Lilienthal's career in Russia, see Michael Stanislawski, *Tsar Nicholas I and the Jews: The Transformation of Jewish Society in Russia, 1825–1855* (Philadelphia: Jewish Publication Society of America, 1983), pp. 69–96.
63. [Max] Lilienthal, "Letters on Reform Addressed to the Rev. I. Leeser, Letter IV," *Israelite* 3, no. 25 (December 26, 1856): 197.
64. Ibid.
65. I. Leeser "Reverend Dr. Lilienthal on Reform," *Occident* 14, no. 11 (February 1857): 536.

5. Women in the Reforming Synagogue: Resistance and Transformation

1. "Rochester," *Occident*, 13, no. 8 (November 1855): 417.
2. Ibid., 13, no. 9 (December 1855): 467.
3. "Radical Reform in Cleveland," *Occident* 19, no. 2 (May 1861): 88.
4. Quoted in Samuel M. Silver, "One Hundred Years of Religious Progress," in *The Euclid Avenue Temple: Congregation Anshe Chesed* (Cleveland, 1946), p. 11.
5. On the Cleveland conference, see Michael A. Meyer, *Response to Modernity: A History of the Reform Movement in Judaism* (New York: Oxford University Press, 1988), pp. 243–244. Apart from Isidor Kalish, at that time the progressive rabbi of Tifereth Israel, the Jews of Cleveland apparently took little interest in the conference. See Isaac M. Wise, *Reminiscences,* 2nd ed., trans. and ed., David Philipson (1901; New York: Central Ave. Synagogue, 1945), p. 312.
6. After discussion, this formulation was altered to describe someone of "liberal principles, who shall not overreach the Laws of Moses." Tifereth Israel minutes, November 13, 1859, Cleveland Ohio, Papers of Congregation Tifereth Israel, collection no. 504, AJA.
7. Tifereth Israel minutes, November 20, 1859.
8. Tifereth Israel minutes, November 30, 1859; April 9, 1860.
9. Lloyd P. Gartner, *History of the Jews of Cleveland* (Cleveland: Western Reserve Historical Society, 1978), p. 39.
10. Tifereth Israel minutes, January 6, 1861.
11. Tifereth Israel minutes, January 27, 1861; April 9, 1861.
12. Unless otherwise noted, all quotations from Peixotto come from B. F. Peixotto to Isaac Leeser, November 16, 1859, Isaac Leeser Papers, microfilm no. 200, AJA.
13. In 1864 Peixotto was reaccepted as a member of Tifereth Israel. Tifereth Israel minutes, April 24, 1864.
14. Peixotto to Leeser, April 12, 1861, Leeser Papers.

15. For more on Peixotto's later career see Lloyd P. Gartner, "Roumania, America, and World Jewry: Consul Peixotto in Bucharest," *American Jewish Historical Quarterly* 58 (1968): 25–117.

16. Tifereth Israel minutes, April 9, 1861.

17. Tifereth Israel minutes, April 14, 1861. The influence of the belief in the sanctity and primacy of the family unit, which was an important argument in favor of family pews, was echoed by the introduction some months later of family plots into Tifereth Israel's cemetery. The general custom in early American Jewish burial grounds was to inter bodies on a sequential basis. Burial benefits came with congregational membership (for children, this right was conferred by virtue of the their fathers' membership, for married women, by their husbands'). The introduction of family plots, which would be paid for in advance, reflected an emphasis on family, the emerging idea of the cemetery as a private garden spot in American culture, and the realization that the sale of family plots would add to synagogue coffers. Tifereth Israel minutes, September 29, 1861.

18. Joseph Abraham to Leeser, January 27, 1859, Leeser Papers.

19. Abraham to Leeser, July 11, 1859. On the contest between traditionalists and reformers for religious authority in Cincinnati, see Karla Goldman, "In Search of an American Judaism: Rivalry and Reform in the Growth of Two Cincinnati Synagogues," in Jeffrey S. Gurock and Marc Lee Raphael, eds., *An Inventory of Promises: Essays on American Jewish History in Honor of Moses Rischin* (Brooklyn: Carlson Publishing, 1995), pp. 137–150.

20. Abraham to Leeser, February 28, 1860.

21. Abraham to Leeser, July 11, 1859.

22. Abraham to Leeser, July 11, 1859.

23. Abraham did not understand the German in which the rabbi addressed his congregation.

24. "New Haven," *Occident* 15, no. 4 (July 1865): 200.

25. Jonathan Sarna identifies "family togetherness, women's equality, conformity to local norms, a modern, progressive image, and saving the youth" as decisive issues for supporters of the change, and "abandonment of tradition, violation of Jewish law, assimilation, Christianization, and promiscuity" as central to opponents. Jonathan D. Sarna, "The Debate over Mixed Seating in the American Synagogue," in Jack Wertheimer, ed., *The American Synagogue: A Sanctuary Transformed* (Cambridge: Cambridge University Press, 1987), p. 378.

26. Louis Klein, "Reforms to be Proposed at the Next Conference," *Israelite* 3, no. 6 (August 15, 1856): 44.

27. "Reform, II," *Jewish Messenger* 1, no. 13 (June 19, 1857): 104.

28. *Reform Congregation Keneseth Israel: Its First 100 Years, 1847–1947* (Philadelphia: Drake Press, 1950), p. 11. For galleried synagogues see *Jewish Messenger* 2, no. 6 (September 11, 1857): 46 (Philadelphia, Beth-El Emeth); 3, no. 11 (May 21, 1858): 85 (Mobile, AL); 1, no. 9 (April

24, 1857): 73 (New Orleans); August 5, 1859 (Mishkan Israel, New Haven).

29. David Einhorn, "Predigt, vom Herausgeber dieser Blätter gehalten im Tempel der Har-Sinai-Gemeinde," *Sinai* 3, no. 1 (February 1858): 824; Einhorn, "Über Familiensitze in den Synagogen," *Sinai* 6, no. 7 (August 1861): 205–207.

30. Sarna, "Mixed Seating," p. 371.

31. Bernard Felsenthal, *The Beginnings of the Chicago Sinai Congregation* (Chicago, 1898), pp. 22, 26, 28.

32. Isaac Leeser, "Union of Israelites, No. III," *Occident* 21, no. 8 (November 1863): 346.

33. Manuscript of address reprinted in Ethel Rosenberg and David Rosenberg, *To 120 Years! A Social History of the Indianapolis Hebrew Congregation, 1856–1976* (Indianapolis: Indianapolis Hebrew Congregation, 1979), p. 27.

34. *Israelite* 10, no. 12 (September 18, 1862): 92.

35. The two published histories of Congregation B'nai Yeshurun, one authored by Isaac M. Wise and Max B. May and the second by a rabbinical successor to Wise, do not mention the institution of family pews at B'nai Yeshurun at all, nor does James Heller's biography of Wise, although these works do list other significant reforms. Presumably, their authors did not want to reveal that the congregation of a rabbi famous for first introducing mixed seating was slow to enact the innovation. See *The History of the K. K. Bene Yeshurun, of Cincinnati, Ohio* (Cincinnati, 1892); James G. Heller, *As Yesterday When It Is Past: A History of the Isaac M. Wise Temple, K. K. B'nai Yeshurun, 1842–1942* ([Cincinnati]: Isaac M. Wise Temple, 1942); and James G. Heller, *Isaac M. Wise: His Life, Work, and Thought* (New York: Union of American Hebrew Congregations, 1965).

36. Bene Israel minutes, April 8, 1863, Cincinnati, Ohio, Papers of Congregation Bene Israel, collection no. 24, AJA.

37. Sherith Israel minutes, October 30, 1869, San Francisco, Calif. Papers of Congregation Sherith Israel, microfilm no. 2443, AJA.

38. Jerome W. Grollman, "The Emergence of Reform Judaism in the United States" (rabbinical thesis, Hebrew Union College, 1948), pp. 94–95.

39. Ibid., pp. 17, 18.

40. Bene Israel minutes, October 29, 1884. See also Bene Israel minutes, October 17, 1880; October 30, 1881; October 22, 1882; November 21, 1886; and October 12, 1890.

41. Israel Goldstein, *A Century of Judaism in New York: B'nai Jeshurun, 1825–1925, New York's Oldest Ashkenazic Congregation* (New York: Congregation B'nai Jeshurun, 1930), p. 153. At Shaaray Tefila the innovation came two years after the death of S. M. Isaacs, who had served as rabbi since the congregation's inception. One correspondent to the *American Hebrew* observed, "We all regret that the name of the late S. M. Isaacs should have

to be coupled with a synagogue which has so violently swerved from the beaten path of orthodoxy, but we must in all justice remember that the storm must have been brewing even in his time . . . Indeed, I know members of that congregation who at least ten years ago expressed the belief—shall I say hope—'Reform would come' after Mr. Isaacs' departure and stating that the architectural plans of the magnificent building were prepared with eventual location of organ, pews, etc., in the same." Experientia Docet, "The Forty-Fourth Street Synagogue," *American Hebrew* 4, no. 3 (September 3, 1880): 32. The 1880 innovations were introduced over the objections of F. De Sola Mendes, the congregation's new rabbi: "The cause of Reform has been adopted by my congregation against my advice." *American Hebrew* 3, no. 13 (August 13, 1880): 145. At Rosh Hashanah services that year, De Sola Mendes "characterized the changes mentioned as extraneous and needless, and expressed sincere grief at their adoption . . . and in eloquent tones he implored the mothers present to follow the example of Hagar and Hannah of old, and by their influence secure this much desired increase of religious feeling, then these changes would turn from sorrows into blessings, and he would become a defender of them." "Rosh-Hashanah," *American Hebrew* 4, no. 4 (September 10, 1880): 44.

42. Rodeph Shalom minutes, July 7, 1867, Philadelphia, Pa., Papers of Congregation Rodeph Shalom, collection no. 517, AJA.

43. Rodeph Shalom minutes, August 21, 1870.

44. Rodeph Shalom minutes, August 28, 1870.

45. Moshe Davis, *The Emergence of Conservative Judaism* (Philadelphia: Jewish Publication Society, 1965), pp. 143–145; Adolf Guttmacher, *A History of the Baltimore Hebrew Congregation [Nidhe Yisrael], 1830–1905* (Baltimore: Lord Baltimore Press, 1905), p. 45.

46. See Sarna, "Mixed Seating," pp. 372–378.

47. "A Hopeful Sign," *Jewish Reformer* 1, no. 17 (April 23, 1886): 9.

48. Talmud Americus, "Another Visit to the Temple in New York," *Israelite* 2, no. 2 (July 20, 1855): 15.

49. "A Neglected Duty," *Jewish Reformer* 1, no. 9 (February 26, 1886): 1.

50. Tifereth Israel minutes, August 11, 1861; Sherith Israel minutes, October 29, 1878.

51. Maria Baader observes a similar pattern in contemporaneous German synagogues; "Jewish Women in Germany between Community and Domesticity," (paper delivered at the annual meeting of the Association of Jewish Studies, Boston, Mass., December 21, 1998).

52. See Chapter 2.

53. "Complimentary Present to the Rev. Dr. Lilienthal," *Israelite* 2, no. 15 (October 15, 1855): 115.

54. "The Ladies of K. K. Benai Yeshurun, Cincinnati, Ohio," *Israelite* 1, no. 5 (August 11, 1854): 39.

55. Abraham to Leeser, undated, Leeser Papers.
56. Goldman, "American Judaism," p. 149.
57. Patricia R. Hill, *The World Their Household: The American Woman's Foreign Mission Movement and Cultural Transformation, 1870–1920* (Ann Arbor: University of Michigan Press, 1985), pp. 2–3; Peggy Pascoe, *Relations of Rescue: The Search for Female Moral Authority in the American West, 1874–1939* (New York: Oxford University Press, 1990), pp. 4–6; Anne Firor Scott, *Natural Allies: Women's Associations in American History* (Urbana: University of Illinois Press, 1992), pp. 85–110.
58. Scott, *Natural Allies*, p. 77.
59. Ibid., p. 85.
60. See Jonathan D. Sarna, "The American Jewish Response to Nineteenth-Century Christian Missions," *Journal of American History* 68 (June 1981): 35–51. See also Hannah Solomon, "Report," *Papers of the National Council of Jewish Women read at the Second Triennial of the National Council of Women of the United States held in Washington, D.C., February 19–March 2, 1895* (no publication information); "We hope also to enter the missionary field. Our work will be among the poor and ignorant of our own faith. We will not attempt to make inferior in quality Jews out of inferior in quality Christians . . . nor will we attempt to proselyte among any of the historic faiths, feeling quite skeptical as to the sort we should get, judging from inference in our own case. We do not wish to be understood as underestimating the magnificent work done for humanity by those heroes, the Christian missionaries, among the savages and barbarians. Yet it is a sad statement that two hundred thousand dollars should be spent annually in converting Jews, for such converts are neither loss nor gain to any faith, and I make not a single exception" (p. 10).
61. In later years, the *Jewish Exponent,* noting the growing agitation and the expression of support among many Christian ministers for prohibition, objected to the temperance movement as a threat to the "barrier which has been erected between Church and State . . . We protest against this invasion by the Church upon the prerogatives of the State . . . We very seriously question the propriety of any denomination taking an official stand upon this question. We believe it to be . . . subversive of what has hitherto been one of the safeguards of our nation." "The Church and Prohibition," *Jewish Exponent,* March 1, 1889, p. 4.
62. Nancy G. Garner, "'A Prayerful Public Protest': The Significance of Gender in the Kansas Woman's Crusade of 1874," *Kansas History* 20 (Winter 1997–1998): 220.
63. "Constitution des Unabhängigen Ordens Treuer Schwestern" from 1864 is found in the papers of the United Order of True Sisters, donated to the American Jewish Archives in August 1999, collection no. 638. I thank Cornelia Wilhelm for sharing this document with me. Wilhelm's research into the United Order of True Sisters should teach us much more about the

scope of mid-nineteenth-century Jewish women's organizational involvement.

64. Evelyn Bodeck, "'Making Do': Jewish Women in Philanthropy," in Murray Friedman, ed., *Jewish Life in Philadelphia, 1830–1940* (Philadelphia: ISHI Publications, 1983), pp. 151, 158; *Occident* 24, no. 3 (June 1866): 143. Jewish women also contributed to the war effort in other ways, like Philadelphia's Ladies' Hebrew Relief Sewing Society, which produced "a large quantity of lint and bandages manufactured for the sick and wounded." In Cincinnati, local Jewish women made undergarments for military patients and for the destitute wives and children of soldiers. *Israelite* (February 28, 1862): 276, cited by Stanley Brav, "The Jewish Woman, 1861–1865," *American Jewish Archives* 17 (1965): 53–55.

65. Scott, *Natural Allies*, pp. 61–62.

66. "First Annual Report to the Directors of the United Hebrew Relief Association of Chicago" (Chicago, 1860), pp. 3, 6.

67. *Jewish Messenger* 5, no. 6 (February 11, 1859): 43.

68. "Fürsorge in Bezug auf israelitischen Frauen," *Die Deborah* 7, no. 14 (October 4, 1861): 56; "Cincinnati," *Die Deborah* 13, no. 51 (June 26, 1868): 203.

69. Henry Samuel Morais, *The Jews of Philadelphia: Their History from the Earliest Settlements to the Present Time* (Philadelphia: Levytype, 1894), pp. 114, 135, 143.

70. Evelyn Bodeck, "'Making Do,'" pp. 148–151.

71. Jewish Foster Home and Orphan Asylum, Board of Managers minutes, October 28, 1874; May 5, 1875; Papers of the Jewish Foster Home and Orphan Asylum, Association for Jewish Children Records, collection no. 5, series 1, Philadelphia Jewish Archives Center.

72. David de Sola Pool and Tamar de Sola Pool, *An Old Faith in a New World: Portrait of Shearith Israel, 1654–1954* (New York: Columbia University Press, 1955), pp. 154, 363.

73. "Verein zur Gründung eines Asyls für Wittwen und Waisen," *Die Deborah* 8, no. 43 (May 1, 1863): 170.

74. Ibid.; "Ueber die Wittwen- und Waisen-Gesellschaft," *Die Deborah* 9, no. 18 (September 11, 1863): 74.

75. "Orphan Asylum of District No. 2, I. O. B. B., at Cleveland, Ohio" (New York, 1868), pp. 16, 18; "First Annual Report of the Board of Trustees of the Orphan Asylum, District No. 2, I. O. B. B. at Cleveland, Ohio" (Cincinnati, 1869) pp. 8, 10, 23–24, 28–29, 36–38.

76. "First Annual Report of the Board of Trustees of the Orphan Asylum," p. 3; "Third Annual Report of the Board of Trustees of the Orphan Asylum, Districts Nos. 2 and 6, I. O. B. B., at Cleveland, Ohio" (Cincinnati, 1871), pp. 4, 20; "Fourth Annual Report of the Board of Trustees of the Orphan Asylum, Districts Nos. 2 and 6, I. O. B. B., at Cleveland, Ohio" (Cincinnati, 1872), pp. 8, 11.

77. Congregation Beth El Frauenverein Minute Book, 1863–1888, July 12, 1863, Detroit, Michigan, box X-32, AJA; "Report of the President," The Ladies Society for the Support of Hebrew Wives and Orphans Minute Book, 1888–1907, October 31, 1888, Detroit, Michigan, box 3, folder 1, Papers of Temple Beth El, collection no. 527, AJA.

78. "Report of the President," Detroit Ladies Society for the Support of Hebrew Wives and Orphans Minute Book, October 31, 1888.

79. Ibid.

80. Hebrew Ladies Aid Association Minute Book, 1865–1940, January 6, 1869; December 7, 1870; Natchez, Mississippi, box X-358, Temple B'nai Israel Records, AJA.

81. Baton Rouge Ladies Hebrew Association Minute Book, 1871–1923, Baton Rouge, La. box 1, folder 3, collection no. 384, AJA.

82. Jacob Rader Marcus, *The American Jewish Woman: A Documentary History* (New York: KTAV Publishing, 1981), p. 212.

83. Natchez Hebrew Ladies Aid Association Minute Book, March 22, 1865; September 20, 1868; November 4, 1868; January 6, 1869; June 9, 1869; August 31, 1870; December 7, 1870; January 24, 1872; January 16, 1878.

84. Baton Rouge Ladies Hebrew Association Minute Book, January 29, 1871; September 23, 1872; December 22, 1872; June 28, 1874; October 18, 1874; September 17, 1876; March 22, 1877.

85. Baton Rouge Ladies Hebrew Association Minute Book, June 21, 1878; April 13, 1879; November 24, 1879; January 29, 1882; March, 1885; June 20, 1885; July 28, 1885; July 6, 1885; June 2, 1887.

86. Norfolk Female Hebrew Benevolent Society Minute Book, 1869–1907, May 7, 1869; May 13, 1869; November 11, 1869; December 1, 1878; December 3, 1878; Norfolk, Va., Papers of Ohef Sholom Temple, box 2, collection no. 548, AJA. Ohef Sholom minutes, December 1, 1878; December 8, 1878; Norfolk, Va., Papers of Ohef Sholom Temple.

87. Norfolk Female Hebrew Benevolent Society minutes, October 5, 1873; October 1, 1876; December 2, 1877; January 4, 1880; January 8, 1882.

88. "Unterstützung für hülfsbedürftige Studenten von den Damen Cincinnati's," *Die Deborah* 27, no. 20 (November 17, 1876): 4; Ladies' Educational Aid Societies, "Rolls of Honor," box X-206, AJA; "The Roll of Honor," *Israelite*, January 5, 1877, p. 4.

89. Beth Israel minutes, March 21, 1875; April 11, 1875; April 15, 1875; Portland, Oreg., Papers of Congregation Beth Israel, collection no. 554, AJA; William Toll, *The Making of an Ethnic Middle Class: Portland Jewry over Four Generations* (Albany: State University of New York Press, 1982), p. 48.

90. Tifereth Israel minutes, June 1, 1871; May 30, 1872; June 3, 1877; July 31, 1879; May 29, 1883; March 5, 1889.

91. Tifereth Israel minutes, June 3, 1877.

92. "School Director's Report," Sherith Israel minutes, October 15, 1871.

6. Kaufmann Kohler and the Ideal Jewish Woman

1. On Felix Adler, see Benny Kraut, *From Reform Judaism to Ethical Culture: The Religious Evolution of Felix Adler* (Cincinnati: Hebrew Union College Press, 1979).

2. Kaufmann Kohler, "Woman's Influence on Judaism" (address delivered before the Cincinnati Section of the National Council of Jewish Women, 1906), reprinted in *Hebrew Union College Addresses* (Cincinnati: Ark Publishing, 1916), p. 294.

3. Kaufmann Kohler, untitled Pittsburgh Conference paper, in *Proceedings of the Pittsburgh Rabbinical Conference* (1885) reprinted in Walter Jacob, ed., *The Changing World of Reform Judaism: The Pittsburgh Platform in Retrospect* (Pittsburgh: Rodef Shalom Congregation, 1985), p. 96.

4. Michael A. Meyer, *Response to Modernity: A History of the Reform Movement in Judaism* (New York: Oxford University Press 1988), p. 271. For other treatments of Kohler see Samuel S. Cohon, "Kaufmann Kohler the Reformer," *Mordecai M. Kaplan Jubilee Volume* (New York: Jewish Theological Seminary of America, 1953), pp. 137–155; Ellen Messer, "Franz Boas and Kaufmann Kohler: Anthropology and Reform Judaism," *Jewish Social Studies* 48 (1986): 127–140; Adolph S. Oko, "Kaufmann Kohler," *Menorah Journal* 12 (1926): 513–521; Oko, *Studies in Jewish Literature*, Kohler Festschrift (Berlin, 1913), pp. 1–38; and Yaakov Ariel, "Kaufmann Kohler and His Attitude Towards Zionism: A Reexamination," *American Jewish Archives* 43, no. 2 (Fall–Winter 1991): 207–223. The present chapter is adapted from Karla Goldman, "The Ambivalence of Reform Judaism: Kaufmann Kohler and the Ideal Jewish Woman," *American Jewish History* 79, no. 4 (Summer 1990): 477–499.

5. Kohler, "Das Reform-Judenthum und die Würdigung des Weibes," *Jewish Reformer*, February 5, 1886, p. 12.

6. Kohler, "Is the Talmud the Life-Regulator of American Orthodoxy?" *Jewish Reformer*, February 5, 1886, p. 8.

7. Kohler, "Das Frauenherz oder das Miriambrünnlein im Lager Israels," *Jewish Times* 2, no. 51 (February 17, 1871): 812.

8. Kohler, "Woman's Influence," 1906, p. 274.

9. Ibid., p. 279.

10. Kohler, "Frauenherz," 12.

11. Ibid.

12. Kohler, "Woman's Influence on Judaism," *American Hebrew* 66, no. 9 (January 5, 1900): 304.

13. Kohler, "Esther or the Jewish Woman," *Temple Beth-El Sunday Lectures* 16 (February 26, 1888): 2.

14. Kohler, "Woman's Influence," 1906, p. 295.

15. Kohler, "Der Beruf des Weibes," *Jewish Times* 7, no. 12 (May 21, 1875): 188–190.

16. Kohler, "The Ideal Jewish Womanhood," sermon, 1898, box 6, folder 1, Kaufmann Kohler Papers, collection no. 29, AJA.

17. Kohler, "Frauenherz," 12. Paula Hyman, citing this reading of Kohler as one example, has identified a general pattern in which the responsibility for the Jewish education of children was transferred almost exclusively to women and in which women were held responsible for the inability of the Jewish home to resist assimilation, Paula E. Hyman, *Gender and Assimilation: The Roles and Representation of Women* (Seattle: University of Washington Press, 1995), pp. 29, 44–49.

18. Kohler, Pittsburgh Conference paper, p. 92.

19. Kohler, "Frauenherz," 12.

20. Kohler, "American Judaism and Its Wants," *Jewish Times* 7, no. 11 (May 14, 1875): 163.

21. Kohler, "A United Israel," lecture, 1898, in *A Living Faith: Selected Sermons and Addresses from the Literary Remains of Dr. Kaufmann Kohler,* ed. Samuel S. Cohon (Cincinnati: Hebrew Union College Press, 1948) p. 11.

22. Kohler, "Esther or the Jewish Woman," pp. 7–8.

23. Isaac M. Wise's German language newspaper, *Die Deborah,* was intended for a female audience. The German sections of many Jewish newspapers were often directed at women, as was demonstrated when the "German Part" of Kohler's paper, the *Jewish Reformer,* was renamed the "Jewish Family Page." See *Jewish Reformer,* May 7, 1886, p. 11.

24. Board of American Israelites and the Union of American Hebrew Congregations, *Statistics of the Jews of the United States* (Philadelphia, 1880), p. 57. See also Leon A. Jick, *The Americanization of the Synagogue, 1820–1870* (Hanover, N.H.: University Press of New England, 1976) p. 190; Jick, "The Reform Synagogue," in Jack Wertheimer, ed., *The American Synagogue: A Sanctuary Transformed* (Cambridge: Cambridge University Press, 1987), pp. 88–89.

25. Kohler, "Würdigung des Weibes," p. 13.

26. Kohler, Pittsburgh Conference paper, p. 99.

27. Kohler, "Backwards or Forwards," pamphlet ([New York], 1885), p. 8.

28. Ibid., pp. 12, 4.

29. Ibid., pp. 11, 16.

30. Ibid., p. 28.

31. Ibid., p. 11.

32. Ibid., pp. 28–29; Kohler, "Woman's Influence," 1906, p. 295.

33. Kohler, Pittsburgh Conference paper, p. 104. In *Response to Modernity,* (see note 4 of this chapter) Michael Meyer points to the pressures of conservatism, represented by Kohut, and of de-Judaization, represented by Felix Adler's Ethical Culture movement, as the forces that pushed Kohler to seek an authoritative and positive statement of Reform Judaism like that expressed in the Pittsburgh Platform. For more on the Pittsburgh Platform see

Jacob, *Changing World,* which includes a reprint of the 1885 *Proceedings;* Sefton D. Temkin, "The Pittsburgh Platform: A Centenary Assessment," *Journal of Reform Judaism* (Fall 1985): 1–12; and Jonathan D. Sarna, "New Light on the Pittsburgh Platform of 1885," *American Jewish History* 76 (1986–1987): 358–368.

34. Kohler, Pittsburgh Conference paper, p. 92.
35. Ibid., pp. 93–94, 105.
36. Ibid., p. 96.
37. Ibid., pp. 96, 102.
38. Ibid., p. 102.
39. Kohler, "Woman's Influence," 1906, p. 294.
40. Kohler, "Frauenherz," 811–812.
41. Kohler, "Esther or the Jewish Woman," p. 3.
42. Ibid.
43. Kohler, "Esther or the Woman in the Synagogue," *American Hebrew,* March 23, 1900, p. 604.
44. Kohler, "Esther or the Jewish Woman," p. 3.
45. Kohler, "Der Beruf des Weibes," 188.
46. Kohler, "The Spiritual Forces of Judaism," *Central Conference of American Rabbis Yearbook* 5 (1894), p. 142.
47. Kohler, "Ideal Jewish Womanhood." In a similarly titled 1899 sermon, Kohler noted that "the best part of both Sabbath and religion is offered by woman." "The Jewish Ideal of Womanhood," 1899, box 6, folder 2, Kohler Papers.
48. Kohler, "Movement to the Abandonment of the Mosaic Sabbath: No Violation of the Jewish Laws in the Alteration" (published in *Inter-Ocean,* August 22, 1873, p. 4), in Kohler Papers, box 6, folder 2.
49. Kohler, "The Origin of the Sabbath," lecture, November 19, 1876, p. 19, box 6, folder 7, Kohler Papers.
50. Kohler, "Are Sunday Lectures a Treason to Judaism?" *Temple Beth-El Sunday Lectures* 12 (January, 8, 1888): 7.
51. Ibid., 9.
52. Ibid., 7–8; Kohler, "Origin of the Sabbath," p. 19.
53. Kohler, "The Need of a Living Force," *Temple Beth-El Sunday Lectures* 26 (October 14, 1888): 7.
54. Kohler, "Jew and Gentile," *Temple Beth-El Sunday Lectures,* 23 (April 15, 1888): 7.
55. Kohler, "Rocks Ahead," *Reform Advocate* 2, no. 13 (November 14, 1891): 215.
56. Kohler, "The Sabbath Day of the Jew" (published in *Menorah* 2 [1891]), typescript copy, pp. 8–11, box 6, folder 10, Kohler Papers.
57. Kohler, "The Principles and Ideals of the Jew," n.d., p. 2, box 6, folder 8, Kohler Papers.
58. Kohler, "Beruf des Weibes," 189.

59. Kohler, "Sabbath Day of the Jew," pp. 6–7; Kohler, "Sukkoth Sermon," n.d., p. 2, box 6, folder 10, Kohler Papers.
60. Kohler, "A Revaluation of Reform Judaism," *Central Conference of American Rabbis Yearbook* 34 (1924), pp. 228–229.
61. Kohler, "Sabbath Observance and Sunday Lectures," December 27, 1879, p. 8, box 6, folder 10, Kohler Papers.
62. Kohler, "Revaluation of Reform Judaism," p. 228.
63. Ibid., p. 229.
64. Kohler, "Is Reform Judaism Destructive or Constructive?" *Central Conference of American Rabbis Yearbook* 3 (1892), p. 111.
65. Kohler, "Rocks Ahead," 214; Kohler, "Jewish Ideal of Womanhood," p. 3.
66. Kohler, "Revaluation of Reform Judaism," p. 228. Kohler expressed this sentiment throughout his career; see, for example, Pittsburgh Conference paper, p. 102; and "Jewish Ideal of Womanhood."

7. Beyond the Gallery: American Jewish Women in the 1890s

1. Alan Silverstein shows that at the four Reform congregations he studied, congregants were overwhelmingly of central and western European origin. For instance, of 266 members of Philadelphia's Keneseth Israel congregation found in the 1900 census, "123 were German born . . . 88 were the American-born children of German parents and 9 were American-born offspring of 1 German-born parent and 1 American parent." In addition, there were 10 members from Austria, 2 from Hungary, and 33 who were third-generation American. The parents of most of the rest were from western or northern Europe. In all, Silverstein identifies only 4 members with any trace of eastern European or Russian background, and all four were married to women from central European families. Alan Silverstein, *Alternatives to Assimilation: The Response of Reform Judaism to American Culture, 1840–1930* (Hanover, N.H.: University Press of New England, 1994), pp. 76–77.
2. Moshe Davis, *The Emergence of Conservative Judaism* (Philadelphia: Jewish Publication Society, 1965), pp. 143–145.
3. Jeffrey S. Gurock, "The Orthodox Synagogue," in Jack Wertheimer, ed., *The American Synagogue: A Sanctuary Transformed* (Cambridge: Cambridge University Press, 1987), p. 43.
4. Isaac M. Wise, "Opening Address," *Central Conference of American Rabbis Yearbook* 5 (1897), p. xii.
5. For descriptions of modernized and cushioned congregational worship see, for instance, "Organ, Choir, Temples, Family Pews," *Jewish Times*, 2, no. 52 (February 24, 1871): 822; and "Synagogue Indications," *Jewish Exponent*, April 27, 1888, p. 6; or "New York Detractors," *Jewish Exponent*, December 9, 1887, p. 11.
6. Joseph Stolz, "Inauguration Address," *Reform Advocate* 10, no. 21 (January 11, 1896): 809.

7. Patricia R. Hill, *The World Their Household: The American Woman's Foreign Mission Movement and Cultural Tranformation, 1870–1920* (Ann Arbor: University of Michigan Press, 1985); Peggy Pascoe, *Relations of Rescue: The Search for Female Moral Authority in the American West, 1874–1939* (New York: Oxford University Press, 1990); Anne Firor Scott, *Natural Allies: Women's Associations in American History* (Urbana: University of Illinois Press, 1992); and Ruth Bordin, *Women and Temperance: The Quest for Power and Liberty, 1873–1900* (Philadelphia: Temple University Press, 1984).

8. William T. Noll, "Women as Clergy and Laity in the Nineteenth-Century Methodist Protestant Church," *Methodist History* 15, no. 2 (1977): 114–116; Rosemary Skinner Keller, "Creating a Sphere for Women in the Church: How Consequential an Accommodation?" *Methodist History* 18, no. 2 (1980): 85; Lois A. Boyd and R. Douglas Brackenridge, *Presbyterian Women in America: Two Centuries of a Quest for Status* (Westport, Conn.: Greenwood Press, 1983), pp. 107–117; Frederick A. Norwood, "Expanding Horizons: Women in the Methodist Movement," in Richard L. Greaves, ed., *Triumph over Silence: Women in Protestant History* (Westport, Conn.: Greenwood Press, 1985), pp. 151–172.

9. [Rosa Sonneschein], "Editorial," *American Jewess* 3, no. 2 (August 1896): 605–606.

10. Rebekah Kohut, in *Papers of the Jewish Women's Conference, Chicago, 1893,* (Philadelphia, 1894), pp. 191–192. In mentioning "Mrs. J. B. Lowell," Kohut is probably referring to Josephine Shaw Lowell, who founded the New York Charity Organization Society in 1882. See Lori D. Ginzberg, *Women and the Work of Benevolence: Morality, Politics, and Class in the Nineteenth-Century United States* (New Haven: Yale University Press, 1990), p. 196.

11. "Editorial," *American Jewess* 3, no. 2 (August 1896): 606–607.

12. Flora Schwab, discussion, in *Proceedings of the First Convention of the National Council of Jewish Women, New York, 1896* (Philadelphia, 1897), p. 115.

13. *Jewish Exponent,* November 9, 1888, p. 4. Observers also recognized that, even in the face of mounting need, the existing societies were not always prepared to rise to the challenge. Thus, the *Exponent*'s editors praised the work of the Hebrew Ladies' Sewing Society of Baltimore but observed, "The number of Ladies in attendance at the Monday afternoon sewing circle is now very small, and with the advent of a rigorous winter even this will be decreased." *Jewish Exponent,* November 30, 1888, p. 4.

14. "The Sisterhoods of Personal Service and the United Hebrew Charities," *American Hebrew* 45, no. 1 (November 7, 1890): 5.

15. *Societies of Personal Service of New York City Connected with Jewish Congregations* (New York, 1893), pp. 8–11. Felicia Herman has studied the history of the New York Sisterhoods of Personal Service in some detail; "From

Priestess to Hostess: The Sisterhoods of Personal Service, 1887–1936," (paper delivered at the conference "Consultation on the Religious Lives of American Jewish Women," Temple University, March 22, 1998).

16. "Sisterhoods of Personal Service," *American Hebrew* 46, no. 5 (March 6, 1891): 91; "The Sisterhoods of Personal Service and the United Hebrew Charities," *American Hebrew,* 45:1 (November 7, 1890): 5.

17. Aaron Ignatius Abell, *The Urban Impact on American Protestantism, 1865—1900* (Cambridge: Harvard University Press, 1943), pp. 219–222.

18. Ibid., pp. 195–204.

19. Ibid., p. 204.

20. "Sisterhoods of Personal Service," *American Hebrew* 46, no. 5 (March 6, 1891): 91.

21. Ibid.

22. *Societies of Personal Service of New York.* See also Jenna Weissman Joselit, "The Special Sphere of the Middle-Class American Jewish Woman: The Synagogue Sisterhood, 1890–1940," in Wertheimer, *American Synagogue,* pp. 206–230. Joselit discusses the Rodeph Shalom Sisterhood of Personal Service, which was founded in 1891, as well as two twentieth-century synagogue sisterhoods.

23. Mrs. M. H. Moses, speech reprinted in Myer Stern, *The Rise and Progress of Reform Judaism, Embracing a History Made from the Official Records of Temple Emanu-El of New York* (New York, 1895), p. 141.

24. *American Hebrew,* 46, no. 5 (March 6, 1891): 81.

25. It also served to further the movement. In Buffalo, Rabbi I. Aaron convened the ladies of his congregation in May 1891 to propose their organization into "an order analogous to 'The King's Daughters' in Christian Churches, which as published in the columns of THE AMERICAN HEBREW, has been done in a Jewish congregation in Baltimore." In "Sisters of Zion," *American Hebrew* 46, no. 13 (May 1, 1891): 251.

26. "Sisterhoods of Personal Service," *American Hebrew* 46, no. 10 (April 10, 1891): 191.

27. "Sisterhoods of Personal Service," *American Hebrew* 46, no. 8 (March 27, 1891): 151.

28. *Reform Advocate* 1, no. 6 (March 27, 1891): 89.

29. "A Neglected Duty," *Jewish Reformer* 1, no. 20 (May 14, 1886): 8.

30. Quoted in David Kaufman, *Shul with a Pool: The "Synagogue-Center" in American Jewish History* (Hanover, N.H.: University Press of New England, 1999), p. 13.

31. [Adolph] Moses, quoted in "Authentic Report of the Proceedings of the Rabbinical Conference Held at Pittsburg," reprinted in Walter Jacob, ed., *The Changing World of Reform Judaism: The Pittsburgh Platform in Retrospect* (Pittsburgh: Congregation Rodeph Shalom, 1985), p. 115.

32. *American Hebrew* 37, no. 1 (November 9, 1888): 2, quoted in Kaufman, *Shul with a Pool,* pp. 13–14.

33. "Reformer," letter from Syracuse, *Jewish Reformer* (February 26, 1886): 5.

34. Kaufmann Kohler, untitled Pittsburgh Conference paper, reprinted in Jacob, *Changing World of Reform Judaism*, p. 92.

35. H[enry] Pereira Mendes, "The Sphere of Congregational Work" (New York, 1885), pp. 8, 19.

36. [Isaac M. Wise], "Woman in the Synagogue," *American Israelite*, September 8, 1876, p. 4.

37. "Woman Suffrage," *Jewish Times* 3, no. 4 (March 17, 1871): 50.

38. "The American Jewess," *Jewish Messenger* 51, no. 13 (August 5, 1881): 5.

39. The *Exponent*'s editors seemed to be referring to an expansion of the elective franchise within congregations or to efforts to encourage young men to become members; they are not talking about an expansion of synagogue activities. Rabbi Joseph Krauskopf initiated the "Society of Knowledge Seekers," a literary society connected to Temple Keneseth Israel, in October 1887, the first such extrasynagogal organization in Philadelphia, where the *Exponent* was published. See Kaufman, *Shul with a Pool,* p. 24.

40. "Congregational Activity," *Jewish Exponent*, April 29, 1887, p. 6.

41. Ibid.

42. Henry Berkowitz, "How to Organize a Hebrew Sabbath-School," pamphlet (Cincinnati, 1889).

43. For more on the development of the Reform temple as synagogue-center, see David Kaufman, *Shul with a Pool,* pp. 10–50. Disputing the notion that the origins of the twentieth-century synagogue-center can be traced to Mordecai Kaplan, Kaufman notes that a self-conscious "movement" to transform the Reform temple into a synagogue-center did not emerge until after 1900.

44. Quoted in Frank Adler, *Roots in a Moving Stream: The Centennial History of Congregation B'nai Jehudah of Kansas City, 1870–1970* (Kansas City: The Temple, Congregation B'nai Jehudah, 1972), p. 85.

45. "The Popularization of the Synagogue," *Jewish Exponent*, November 2, 1888, p. 1.

46. Ibid.

47. Adler, *Roots in a Moving Stream,* pp. 85–86. At first the acronym stood for Literary, Lecture, and Library Committee; Aid Committee; Congregational Cooperation Committee; and Educational Committee. For more on Berkowitz and the L.A.C.E. Society, see Kaufman, *Shul with a Pool,* pp. 25–31.

48. *Year Book of Reform Congregation Keneseth Israel,* no. 1 (Philadelphia, 1889).

49. Ibid., no. 2 (1890–1891): 13; no. 5 (1893–1894): 11; no. 6 (1894–1895): 6. See also Kaufman, *Shul with a Pool,* p. 24.

50. See Kaufman, *Shul with a Pool,* p. 35, for the numerous congregations that built new synagogues soon after the arrival of American-born HUC-trained rabbis.

51. Kaufman, *Shul with a Pool,* pp. 20–22, 34.

52. "Shearith Israel, the Congregational Activities," *American Hebrew* 61, no. 3 (May 21, 1897): 75.

53. Ibid., 75–78.

54. E. G. Hirsch, "Signs of the Times," *Reform Advocate* 11, no. 12 (May 9, 1896): 239.

55. "Sisterhoods of Personal Service," *American Hebrew* 47, no. 4 (May 29, 1891): 95.

56. I. Aaron, "Daughters of the Star," *American Hebrew* 47, no. 3 (May 22, 1891): 74.

57. "First Annual Convention of the Daughters of Israel," *American Hebrew* 47, no. 3 (May 22, 1891): 74–75.

58. "Sisterhoods of Personal Service," *American Hebrew* 47, no. 1 (May 8, 1891): 11.

59. Hannah G. Solomon, "The Council of Jewish Women: Its Work and Possibilities," *Reform Advocate* 13, no. 2 (February 27, 1897): 26.

60. For more on the organization of the Jewish Women's Congress and the early years of the NCJW, see Faith Rogow, *Gone to Another Meeting: The National Council of Jewish Women, 1893–1993.* (Tuscaloosa, Ala.: University of Alabama Press, 1993), esp. pp. 9–35.

61. "Jewish Women's Congress," *Reform Advocate* 5, no. 11 (April 29, 1893): 209–210.

62. "Domestic News," *Reform Advocate* 5, no. 14 (May 20, 1893): 273.

63. "Women's Work in Judaism," *Jewish Exponent,* reprinted in *Reform Advocate* 13, no. 4 (March 13, 1897): 60. Sadie American, secretary of the national organization, explained: "As a National body it was necessary our plan should be broad enough to hold those of the most varied feeling and endowments . . . and that it should be of that fluid character which will adapt itself to all needs . . . This seeming lack of definiteness has been one of our main obstacles . . . [but] it is our strength . . . [W]e have entered the field of life free to develop as we grow, determined to do with our might whatever work before us lies." American, "National Council of Jewish Women: First Annual Report of the Recording Secretary," *Reform Advocate* 9, no. 21 (July 13, 1895): 333.

64. Critics denounced the women of the NCJW for mistaking their proper sphere: "When she leaves the home to 'convene,' she misses her aim and neglects her duty . . . If they are burning with a thirst for knowledge of Jewish literature and history, let them study it at home daily and not make a periodically spasmodic pretense . . . [T]he whole scheme is a fad and an 'ad' and a piece of personal vanity and puffing." Israel H. Peres, "The Council of Jewish Women," *Reform Advocate* 12, no. 20 (January 2, 1897): 325. Emil G. Hirsch, who actually served as mentor to the Chicago women who founded the NCJW, also expressed skepticism about the movement's purposes: "We had our misgivings when we noticed how the council of Jewish women arranged lectures by its members on subjects like 'The development of reli-

gious ideas among Semitic nations,' which only two or three rabbis of this country are capable of discussing. The worst feature of the thing is, that these women who have turned 'philologists' and 'philosophers' and 'theologians' over night rush into print and bring ridicule on the council." Hirsch, *Reform Advocate* 12, no. 4 (September 12, 1896): 56.

65. Hirsch, "Signs of the Times," 239.

66. Schwab discussion, in *First Convention,* p. 115.

67. Sophie C. Axman and Hannah Solomon, discussion, in *First Convention,* pp. 118, 184.

68. Laura Jacobson, discussion, in *First Convention,* p. 120.

69. Julia Richman, "Religious School Work—Report," in *First Convention,* p. 205.

70. Ellen M. Henrotin, discussion, in *First Convention,* p. 28.

71. The vice president for the Colorado section of the NCJW reported of her attendance at the State Federation of Women's Clubs: "I must say, of all the reports of the women's clubs none was listened to with more interest than ours, they were so interested in our work . . . We stand very well in the club world of Colorado." "Report of the Vice-President for Colorado," in *First Convention,* pp. 64–65.

72. Schwab, discussion, in *First Convention,* p. 117.

73. Mrs. Henry Solomon, "Council of Jewish Women," *Reform Advocate* 17, no. 4 (March 11, 1899): 107–108.

74. Rebekah Kohut, *My Portion (An Autobiography)* (New York: T. Seltzer, 1925), pp. 192–205.

75. Hannah G. Solomon and Sadie American, "National Council of Jewish Women," *Reform Advocate* 10, no. 22 (January 18, 1896): 831.

76. This was the case in Atlanta, where the NCJW section, founded in 1895, served immigrant families and organized study classes, but also assumed responsibility for temple activities at the Hebrew Benevolent Congregation. See Steven Hertzberg, *Strangers within the Gate City: The Jews of Atlanta, 1845–1915* (Philadelphia: Jewish Publication Society, 1978), p. 119; Janice O. Rothschild, *As But a Day: The First Hundred Years, 1868–1967* (Atlanta: Hebrew Benevolent Congregation, 1967), p. 54.

77. Tifereth Israel minutes, July 30, 1887, Cleveland, Ohio, Papers of Congregation Tifereth Israel, collection no. 504, AJA.

78. Adolf Guttmacher, *A History of the Baltimore Hebrew Congregation [Nidhe Yisrael], 1830–1905* (Baltimore, 1905), pp. 61–62.

79. Adair W. Herman, "Sisterhood of Har Sinai Temple," in C. A. Rubenstein, *History of Har Sinai Congregation of the City of Baltimore* (Baltimore: Kohn and Pollock, 1918), p. 75. The carpets were purchased for $1,800 (p. 76).

80. Quoted in Rothschild, *As But a Day,* p. 55.

81. Tifereth Israel minutes, September 24, 1894; November 5, 1894; October 14, 1895.

82. Marjorie Hornbein, *Temple Emanuel of Denver: A Centennial History* (Denver: Congregation Emanuel, 1974), pp. 53, 85. At the Baltimore Hebrew Congregation, according to Guttmacher, "Mr. David Wiesenfeld, who was the Superintendent of the Sabbath School, called a meeting of the teachers of the school July 6th 1890 for the purpose of forming an auxiliary among the ladies of the Congregation." Guttmacher, *Baltimore Hebrew Congregation*, p. 61. In Nashville a Temple Ladies' Auxiliary was created at the urging of Rabbi Lewinthal in 1891. Fedora Small Frank, *Beginnings on Market Street: Nashville and Her Jewry, 1861–1901* (Nashville: Frank, 1976), p. 21.

83. "Bellaire, O.," *American Hebrew* 59, no. 12 (July 24, 1896): 317.

84. "Syracuse Letter," *American Hebrew* 58, no. 13 (January 31, 1896): 369.

85. "Woman's Temple Association," in *First Annual of The Temple, Cleveland, Ohio, 1898 (5659)* (Cleveland, 1899), p. 44.

86. Tifereth Israel minutes, March 2, 1897.

87. "Woman's Temple Association," pp. 44–47.

88. "The Auxiliary Society of Congregation Rodeph Shalom," in *Annual of the Congregation Rodeph Shalom, 1894–1895* (Philadelphia, 1894), pp. 16–17.

89. *Annual of the Congregation Rodeph Shalom, 1897–1898* (Philadelphia, 1898), pp. 6–7.

90. "National Council of Jewish Women," *American Hebrew,* 59, no. 2 (May 15, 1896): 37. The committee in Chicago reported, "As regards the placing of women upon the Sabbath school boards I would say that several of our most important congregations have not responded, but we feel convinced that ere long they will see the wisdom of such a decision and act accordingly." Rosalie Solzberger, "Report of the Sabbath School Committee," reprinted in "Council of Jewish Women," *Reform Advocate* 13, no. 12 (May 8, 1897): 196.

91. *First Annual of the Temple*, p. 35.

92. "The following congregations have already chosen women for [appointment to their respective Sunday school boards]: Beth Israel, Adath Jeshurun, Rodef Shalom and Mickve Israel." "National Council of Jewish Women," *American Hebrew* 58, no. 26 (May 1, 1896): 748.

93. Bene Israel trustee minutes, October 25, 1903; November 2, 1906; Cincinnati, Ohio, Papers of Congregation Bene Israel, collection no. 24, AJA.

94. Board of Trustees to Stella S. Rosenberg, November 2, 1906, Bene Israel Letterpress Book, box 1, folder 2, Bene Israel Papers, AJA. For one all-male list of officers, see *Annual of Temple Oheb Shalom, 1896–1897 (5657)* (Baltimore, 1896), pp. 3–4; the list does include the officers of the Ladies' Auxiliary Society.

95. M. A. Marks, "President's Message," Tifereth Israel minutes, October 14, 1895.

96. Trustee minutes, Congregation Tifereth Israel, September 2, 1895.

97. Tifereth Israel minutes, October 19, 1896.

98. In addition to sources listed in note 8, see Carolyn De Swarte Gifford, ed., *The Debate in the Methodist Episcopal Church over Laity Rights for Women,* Women in American Protestant Religion, (1800–1930), no. 3 (New York: Garland, 1987); Carolyn De Swarte Gifford, ed., *The Defense of Women's Rights to Ordination in the Methodist Episcopal Church,* Women in American Protestant Religion, 1800–1930, no. 4 (New York: Garland, 1987).

99. See Barbara Brown Zikmund, "The Struggle for the Right to Preach," in Rosemary Radford Ruether and Rosemary Skinner Keller, eds., *Women and Religion in America,* vol. 1, *The Nineteenth Century,* (San Francisco: Harper and Row, 1981), pp. 193–241; Virginia Lieson Brereton and Christa Ressmeyer Klein, "American Women in Ministry: A History of Protestant Beginning Points," in Rosemary Ruether and Eleanor McLaughlin, eds., *Women of Spirit* (New York: Simon and Schuster, 1979), pp. 301–332; Evelyn Brooks Higginbotham, *Righteous Discontent: The Women's Movement in the Black Baptist Church, 1880–1920* (Cambridge: Harvard University Press, 1993).

100. [Wise], "Woman in the Synagogue," 4.

101. "How to Benefit Judaism," *American Israelite,* reprinted in *Boston Hebrew Observer,* September 11, 1885.

102. Reprinted in "The Jewess and the Synagogue," *Jewish Messenger* 51, no. 13 (May 13, 1882): 5.

103. "The American Jewess," *Jewish Messenger,* August 5, 1881, p. 4.

104. "The Jewish Minister's Association," *Jewish Reformer* 1, no. 19 (May 7, 1886): 3–4.

105. "Congregation Mickve Israel," September 1, 1884 (5644), Philadelphia, Pa., Papers of K. K. Mickve Israel, Resolutions, Appeals, and Decisions of the Board of Managers, 1848–1885, small collection no. 9631, AJA; "Seat-Holders (both male and female) are eligible to membership after holding seats in the Synagogue for one year." My thanks to Ruth Alpers for locating this document.

106. M. Landsberg, "Position of Woman among the Jews," *Reform Advocate* 6, no. 15 (November 25, 1893): 238.

107. *American Jewess* 1, no. 3 (June 1895): 153; "Editor's Desk," *American Jewess* 2, no. 1 (October 1895): 63.

108. I. S. Moses, "Ideal Religion," *Reform Advocate* 8, no. 12 (November 11, 1894): 186. Max Landsberg wrote, "Only if this last step has been taken, when our women will be enabled to contribute their full share to our religious activity, shall we have some prospect of removing that baneful indifferentism of which there is so much just complaint everywhere." Landsberg, "Position of Woman," 238.

109. "The American Jewess," *Jewish Messenger,* August 5, 1881, p. 4.

110. On Ray Frank, see Reva Clar and William M. Kramer, "The Girl Rabbi of the Golden West: The Adventurous Life of Ray Frank in Nevada, California, and the Northwest," *Western States Jewish History* 18, no. 2 (1986): 99–111; no. 3 (1986): 223–36; no. 4 (1986): 336–51.
111. [Emil G.] H[irsch], "Woman in the Pulpit," *Reform Advocate* 6, no. 13 (November 11, 1893): 201.
112. "Domestic News," *American Hebrew* 22, no. 6 (March 20, 1885): 93.
113. "Richmond, Va," *American Hebrew* 59, no. 7 (June 19, 1896): 185.
114. On the role of girls in confirmation services, see, for instance, "Shebuoth. Confirmation Services," *American Hebrew* 3, no. 1 (May 21, 1880): 9.
115. Mary M. Cohen, "A Problem for Purim," *Jewish Exponent*, March 15, 1889, p. 1.
116. Landsberg, "Position of Woman," 238.
117. "Woman in the Synagogue," *Reform Advocate* 13, no. 1 (February 20, 1897): 7.

Epilogue: Twentieth-Century Resonances

1. Mary McCune has argued that although male Zionist leaders envisioned Zionism as a movement for "manly men," American Zionist women, working chiefly through Hadassah, "refused to remain simply passive onlookers or supportive assistants . . . Hadassah provided a forum by which middle-class, and to some degree working-class, Jewish women in the United States could express their Zionist consciousness concretely." Mary McCune, "Social Workers in the *Muskeljudentum:* 'Hadassah Ladies,' 'Manly Men,' and the Significance of Gender in the American Zionist Movement, 1912–1928," *American Jewish History* 86, no. 2 (June 1998): 136–137.
2. It may be noted that my mother is left out of this generational story. In part, her omission reflects the changing shape of public identities available to Jewish women in the second half of the twentieth century. Although my mother has both a strong Jewish identity and a strong public identity, those aspects of her life have remained separate. She has never participated actively in Jewish women's organizations, nor in women's organizations generally. Rather, as a scholar of Chinese history she has pursued a public role in which both gender and religion appear to be extraneous. The field of Chinese studies in postwar America, although dominated by men like most academic disciplines, was, as an emerging field, relatively open to women's participation. Combining her professional identity with the role more typical of her generation as the mother of four children, my mother felt little need and had little time to devote herself to the Jewish associational life that had been so important to her mother. Her experience prefigured a general mass movement of middle-class women in later decades who found public identities in vocational roles that were not specifically related to their identities as Jews or as women.

3. David Kaufman refers to the larger, more Americanized immigrant synagogue as the "community synagogue," as opposed to the smaller conventicle setting, known as a *landsmanshaft* shul, *hevre, anshe,* or *shtibl.* Kaufman, *Shul with a Pool: The "Synagogue-Center" in American Jewish History* (Hanover, N.H.: University Press of New England, 1999), p. 168.

4. Kaufman, *Shul with a Pool,* pp. 183–184, 186–190.

5. See Jonathan D. Sarna, trans. and ed., *People Walk on Their Heads: Moses Weinberger's Jews and Judaism in New York* (New York: Holmes and Meier, 1982), pp. 13–14, 98–105; Jeffrey S. Gurock, "The Orthodox Synagogue," in Jack Wertheimer, ed., *The American Synagogue: A Sanctuary Transformed,* (Cambridge: Cambridge University Press, 1987), pp. 49–50; Mark Slobin, *Chosen Voices: The Story of the American Cantorate* (Urbana: University of Illinois Press, 1989), pp. 52–60; and Kaufman, *Shul with a Pool,* pp. 176–177.

6. Jeffrey S. Gurock, *When Harlem Was Jewish, 1870–1930* (New York: Columbia University Press, 1979), pp. 117–118; Kaufman, *Shul with a Pool,* pp. 191–192.

7. Jenna Weissman Joselit, *New York's Jewish Jews: The Orthodox Community in the Interwar Years* (Bloomington: Indiana University Press, 1990), p. xi.

8. Ibid.; see especially the chapter "The Jewish Priestess and Ritual: The Sacred Life of American Orthodox Women," pp. 97–122.

9. Ibid., p. xii.

10. Kaufman, *Shul with a Pool,* p. 265.

11. Deborah Dash Moore, "A Synagogue Center Grows in Brooklyn," in Wertheimer, *American Synagogue,* p. 302; Mel Scult, *Judaism Faces the Twentieth Century: A Biography of Mordecai M. Kaplan* (Detroit: Wayne State University Press, 1993), p. 161. Ewa Morawska reports that when the members of Congregation Rodef Sholom of Johnstown, Pennsylvania, began to adopt a Conservative stance in the 1930s after hiring a graduate of the Jewish Theological Seminary, women and men would sit together for Friday night services, but women returned to the balcony on Saturday morning and for High Holidays. Ewa Morawska, *Insecure Prosperity: Small-Town Jews in Industrial America, 1890–1914* (Princeton: Princeton University Press, 1996), pp. 149–150.

12. Marshall Sklare, *Conservative Judaism: An American Religious Movement* (Glencoe, Ill.: Free Press, 1955), p. 88.

13. Jenna Weissman Joselit, "The Special Sphere of the Middle-Class American Jewish Woman: The Synagogue Sisterhood, 1890–1940," in Wertheimer, *American Synagogue,* p. 213.

14. *Proceedings of the National Federation of Temple Sisterhoods,* (1915), p. 13.

15. Bene Yeshurun minutes, December 1, 1912; January 26, 1913; February 23, 1913; March 30, 1913; November 2, 1913; and November 12, 1913;

Cincinnati, Ohio, Papers of Congregation Bene Yeshurun, collection no. 62, AJA. Karla Goldman, "The Public Religious Lives of Cincinnati's Jewish Women" (paper delivered at the conference "Consultation on the Religious Lives of American Jewish Women," Temple University, March 22, 1998).

16. *Fifteenth Annual of the Temple, Cleveland, 1912–1913* (Cleveland, 1913), pp. 42–48; *Sixteenth Annual of the Temple, Cleveland, 1913–1914* (Cleveland, 1914), pp. 46–47.

17. *Congregation Rodeph Shalom Annual,* 1913–1914, no. 21 (Philadelphia, 1914), pp. 30–31; *Congregation Rodeph Shalom Annual,* 1914–1915, no. 22 (Philadelphia, 1915), pp. 13–14.

18. Shuly Rubin Schwartz, "Women's League for Conservative Judaism," in Paula E. Hyman and Deborah Dash Moore, eds., *Jewish Women in America: An Historical Encyclopedia,* vol. 2 (New York: Routledge, 1997), pp. 1493–1497; Joselit, "Synagogue Sisterhood," p. 213.

19. See, for example, Beth S. Wenger, "Jewish Women of the Club: The Changing Public Role of Atlanta's Jewish Women, 1870–1930," *American Jewish History* 76, no. 3 (March 1987): 324–325.

20. Pamela S. Nadell and Rita J. Simon, "Ladies of the Sisterhood: Women in the American Reform Synagogue, 1900–1930," in Maurie Sacks, ed., *Active Voices: Women in Jewish Culture* (Urbana: University of Illinois Press, 1995), p. 67; Schwartz, "Women's League," pp. 1493–1494; Joselit, *New York's Jewish Jews,* pp. 107–109; and Joselit, "Synagogue Sisterhood," p. 216.

21. Nadell and Simon date the Sisterhood Sabbath to the early 1920s. "Ladies of the Sisterhood," p. 68.

22. Faith Rogow, *Gone to Another Meeting: The National Council of Jewish Women, 1893–1993* (Tuscaloosa: University of Alabama Press, 1993), pp. 116–117, 133; see also Ellen Sue Levi Elwell, "The Founding and Early Programs of the National Council of Jewish Women: Study and Practice as Jewish Women's Religious Experience," (Ph.D. dissertation, Indiana University, 1982).

23. Rebekah Kohut, *My Portion (An Autobiography)* (New York: T. Seltzer, 1925), pp. 265–284.

24. Deborah Dash Moore, "Hadassah," in Hyman and Moore, *Jewish Women in America,* pp. 571, 576–577.

25. McCune, "Social Workers," 156–158.

26. See, for instance, Evelyn Bodeck, "Jewish Women and Philanthropy," in Murray Friedman, ed., *Jewish Life in Philadelphia, 1830–1940* (Philadelphia: ISHI Publications, 1983), p. 151. Efforts to create a charitable federation in Toronto in 1916 were typical: "The Ladies' Montefiore, although they participated, were not enthusiastic about a new system. The East European women's societies were also reluctant to submerge themselves in a colossus which would be inimical to their independent identities and would demand an annual report of activities, income and expenditure . . . Then, to

add insult to injury, the board approved a constitution which excluded women, despite their having been the backbone of Jewish philanthropy in Toronto since the 1860s. After a protest by Ida Siegel, who was also active in the women's suffrage movement, they agreed to admit one female." Stephen A. Speisman, *The Jews of Toronto: A History to 1937* (Toronto: McClelland and Stewart, 1979), pp. 262–263.

27. Felicia Herman, "A Priestess to Herself and Others: Sisterhoods of Personal Service, 1887–1930s" (paper delivered at the conference "Consultation on the Religious Lives of American Jewish Women," Temple University, March 22, 1998); Joselit, *New York's Jewish Jews,* p. 106; Joselit, "Synagogue Sisterhood," pp. 210–212.

28. This discussion omits consideration of the very public and influential roles that Jewish women took in twentieth-century labor activism and radical politics. Although it is important to understand the public lives of women like Emma Goldman, Rose Schneiderman, Clara Lemlich, and others in terms of their Jewish backgrounds, they created their public identities in worlds beyond the organized Jewish community. See Annelise Orleck, *Common Sense and a Little Fire: Women and Working-Class Politics in the United States, 1900–1905* (Chapel Hill: University of North Carolina Press, 1995); Joyce Antler, *The Journey Home: Jewish Women and the American Century* (New York: Free Press, 1997), pp. 73–97.

29. See, for example, Beth S. Wenger, "Jewish Women of the Club," 327; Jonathan D. Sarna and Karla Goldman, "From Synagogue-Community to Citadel of Reform: The History of K. K. Bene Israel (Rockdale Temple) in Cincinnati, Ohio," in James P. Wind and James W. Lewis, eds., *American Congregations,* vol. 1, *Portraits of Twelve Religious Communities* (Chicago: University of Chicago Press, 1994), p. 188.

30. See Ellen M. Umansky, "Women's Journey toward Rabbinic Ordination," in Gary Zola, ed., *Women Rabbis: Exploration and Celebration* (Cincinnati: HUC-JIR Rabbinic Alumni Association Press, 1996), pp. 27–41; Pamela S. Nadell, *Women Who Would Be Rabbis: A History of Women's Ordination, 1889–1985* (Boston: Beacon Press, 1998), pp. 62–72; and *Central Conference of American Rabbis Yearbook* 32 (1922), pp. 156–177.

31. Nadell, *Women Who Would Be Rabbis.*

32. For an introduction to the ways in which the complexity of 1950s gender realities transcended simplistic TV sitcom images, see Joanne Meyerowitz, ed., *Not June Cleaver: Women and Gender in Postwar America, 1945–1960* (Philadelphia: Temple University Press, 1994).

33. Nadell, *Women Who Would Be Rabbis,* pp. 120–125.

34. Nadell, *Women Who Would Be Rabbis,* pp. 152–157.

35. A 1992 decision by leaders of the Conservative movement to categorically deny admission of "avowed homosexuals to our rabbinical or cantorial schools" has remained a source of tension. See "Activists Renew Fight for

Gay Ordination," *Jewish Week,* April 9, 1999; "Gay Rights Riling Seminary—Orthodoxy As Well," *Forward,* April 2, 1999. In the Reform movement, which has endorsed the ordination of gay and lesbian students, controversy has focused upon the question of whether rabbis should officiate at gay marriages or commitment ceremonies. Challenges like this one have brought forth both tension and creativity. The CCAR Responsa Committee's report on the Jewish legal questions at stake in this issue and the appropriate liberal Jewish response notes that disagreeing members of the committee found "little ground for common persuasive discourse. Argument, in other words, has come to an end." The majority of committee members decided that, in spite of all the ways that Reform Judaism had redefined traditional understandings of *qiddushin,* the legal contract that defines Jewish marriage, "the historic definition of that term, its legal content, and the notions of *qedushah* [defined by the committee as sanctity] which lie at its foundations rule out its application to anything but heterosexual Jewish marriage." Theologian Rachel Adler, however, suggests that Jews should be able to celebrate a committed union without relying upon the legalistic contract of *qiddushin,* which she sees as a way in which men acquire women as sexual property. Adler posits a new ritual that would ground Jewish marriage between men and men, women and women, or men and women in a mutual partnership, while creating a new ceremony that still resonates with Jewish tradition. "On Homosexual Marriage," *CCAR Journal* 45 (Winter 1998): 7, 24. Rachel Adler, *Engendering Judaism: An Inclusive Theology and Ethics* (Philadelphia: Jewish Publication Society, 1998).

36. See, for instance, Adler, *Engendering Judaism;* Judith Plaskow, *Standing Again at Sinai: Judaism from a Feminist Perspective* (San Francisco: Harper and Row, 1990); Havurat Siddur Project, *Birkat Shalom* (Somerville, Mass.: Havurat Shalom Siddur Project, 1991); and Marcia Falk, *Book of Blessings* (San Francisco: HarperCollins, 1996).

Index